Also by Edward Jay Epstein

The Rise and Fall of Diamonds
Inquest: The Warren Commission and the Establishment of Truth
Counterplot: Garrison vs. the U.S.
Agency of Fear
Cartel (a novel)
Legend: The Secret World of Lee Harvey Oswald
Between Fact and Fiction
News from Nowhere: Television & the News

DECEPTION

*The Invisible War Between
the KGB and the CIA*

EDWARD JAY EPSTEIN

SIMON AND SCHUSTER

NEW YORK   LONDON   TORONTO   SYDNEY   TOKYO

Simon and Schuster
Simon & Schuster Building
Rockefeller Center
1230 Avenue of the Americas
New York, New York 10020

SIMON AND SCHUSTER and colophon are registered trademarks
of Simon & Schuster Inc.

Designed by Irving Perkins Associates
Manufactured in the United States of America

1   3   5   7   9   10   8   6   4   2

Library of Congress Cataloging in Publication Data

Epstein, Edward Jay.
Deception : the invisible war between the KGB and the CIA / Edward
Jay Epstein.

p.   cm.
Bibliography: p.
Includes index.
1. United States. Central Intelligence Agency.   2. Soviet Union.
Komitet gosudarstvennoĭ bezopasnosti.   I. Title.
JK468.I6E67 1989   89-4075
327.1′2′06073—dc19   CIP
ISBN 0-671-41543-3

For my mother

"Deception is a state of mind
—and the mind of the state."

—James Jesus Angleton

CONTENTS

Contents

EPILOGUE
Angleton's Questions   *280*

PART ONE

The State of Mind

CHAPTER ONE

Through the Looking Glass

On May 14, 1987, some of the most powerful men in Washington, including senators, ambassadors, cabinet officers, generals, and two former directors of Central Intelligence, jammed into a small Congregational Church in Arlington, Virginia, to pay their last respects to James Jesus Angleton. They stared at a wreath of giant purple orchids while the poet Reed Whittemore read passages from "Gerontion." The orchids had been sent by Angleton's former comrades in the OSS, the organization where forty-four years earlier he had begun his career as a spy; the poem, written by his friend T. S. Eliot, described the "wilderness of mirrors," which had come to represent for him the war of deception between the CIA and the KGB. The memorial service for the poet-spy was over in less than forty minutes.

It was eleven years earlier that I had met James Jesus Angleton. At that time, in 1976, I knew nothing about his secret world of deception. Nor had I even heard of concepts such as "disinformation," "dangles," "false flags," "penetrations," or "control," which were central elements in it. I had come to see him about Yuri Nosenko, a KGB officer who had defected to the United States two months after the assassination of President John F. Kennedy.

I had just begun a book on Lee Harvey Oswald, the alleged

assassin. Although Oswald had been investigated by the Warren Commission, the FBI, and other intelligence services, there was still a missing piece in the jigsaw puzzle—the nearly two years that he spent in the Soviet Union before he returned to the United States in 1962 and proceeded to Dallas. What had happened to Oswald during this period? Had he had any connection with Soviet intelligence? Had the KGB sponsored his return to the United States? Had he been given any mission?

When the editors of *Reader's Digest* proposed the idea of this book to me in 1976, they also offered to arrange for me to interview a source who was in a position to furnish definitive answers to all these questions—Nosenko. Nosenko, as an officer of the Second Chief Directorate of the KGB, which is responsible for Soviet counterespionage, reported he had been assigned to Oswald's case in Moscow in 1959. And then, in December 1963, after the assassination, he reported he had also reviewed Oswald's entire KGB file before he defected to the CIA.

I began my interviews with Nosenko in January 1976. After I had questioned him for six hours, I found his answers not only imprecise and evasive but troubling. Several of the assertions he made about the KGB's treatment of Oswald were clearly inconsistent with other facts established by the Warren Commission. He categorically insisted, for example, that the KGB had never contacted Oswald during his stay in the Soviet Union. But there was considerable evidence, including intercepted letters and the reports of U.S. Embassy officials concerning offers Oswald had made to turn over to the Soviets secret U.S. data of "special interest," which made Nosenko's version difficult to swallow.

After the interview was over, I discussed these inconsistencies with Donald Jameson, the CIA contact that *Reader's Digest* had provided for my dealings with Nosenko. Jamie, as he preferred to be called, was in a wheelchair, having lost the use of his legs in some way that he could not openly discuss. He explained that he was a close friend of Nosenko's, and he was sure any problems stemmed from Nosenko's faltering command of the English language. "Nosenko is utterly reliable on the subject of Oswald. He had full access to KGB records," he assured me, as he wheeled himself off.

My concern was not entirely alleviated, however. I had lunch later that week with a Soviet diplomat in Washington, Igor Agou, to facilitate getting a visa for going to Moscow and Minsk. I explained to Agou that I wanted to interview some of the Russian citizens who had been acquaintances of Oswald's. Agou shook his head, saying, "Just between us . . . there is no need for you to go to Russia. The best source on Oswald's visit there is in America . . . Yuri Nosenko." I found it curious that the Soviet Embassy would recommend that I see a Soviet traitor—indeed, the same traitor the CIA had also recommended to me.

Disquieted further by this coincidence, I went back to see Jameson. I pressed him as to why the Warren Commission had not used Nosenko as a witness if he was so reliable. After all, there was no secret that he had defected: the KGB must have known that he had access to the Oswald file. Calling him would not have compromised any secret intelligence.

Jamie then told me, for the first time, that initially there had been some "minor problem" with Nosenko. "It took a year or so to clear up the confusion over his defection—all minor details, of course."

When I asked about the nature of the "details," Jamie said that it was "too sensitive" to be discussed. He closed the issue by saying, "In any case, it is not relevant to your book. Don't worry about it."

But I did. Moreover, I found that the CIA and FBI officers I had been put in contact with flatly refused to talk about Nosenko. The only remaining alternative was to find an ex-officer of the CIA who would have been involved in the case of this defector. Earlier that year, a number of CIA executives had been publicly fired after Seymour Hersh published in *The New York Times* an exposé of the CIA's illicit activities. The most prominent of these men was the chief of the counterintelligence staff—

James Jesus Angleton. His name rang a bell since his staff had served in 1964 as liaison between the CIA and the Warren Commission, which suggested he might be able to explain why Nosenko was never used by the Commission as a witness.

Making contact with Angleton was not difficult: he was listed in the Virginia telephone directory. When I told him I had interviewed Nosenko, he said, "I wouldn't have thought they would be letting him out so soon—but I would be very interested in what he says." I had no idea who "they" were or what "letting him out" meant, but I invited him to dinner to hear more about Nosenko. He suggested the restaurant in the Madison Hotel in Washington which he said would be convenient because it had "a secure garage."

I did some research on him before the meeting; although his name appeared in the clip file, the Who's Who entry was intriguingly brief. James Jesus Angleton was born on December 9, 1917, in Boise, Idaho. His father James Hugh Angleton, a cavalry officer in the Idaho National Guard, had met, and carried away, his mother on General John J. Pershing's celebrated punitive raid into Mexico. She was Carmen Jesus Moreno, a seventeen-year-old Mexican beauty (which accounted for his middle name). When Angleton was fifteen, his father, becoming the European representative for the National Cash Register Company, moved him to Milan. After a year in Italy he was sent to school at Malvern, an elite public school in Worcestershire, England. Then, in 1937, with war tensions building in Europe, he went on to Yale. There, together with Reed Whittemore, he founded *Furioso*, a quarterly devoted to original poetry, and persuaded such leading poets as Ezra Pound, Archibald MacLeish, e. e. cummings, and T. S. Eliot to contribute. After he graduated in 1941, he went on to Harvard Law School; but he never got his law degree. Instead, he volunteered for the OSS—America's first centralized intelligence service (nicknamed "Oh-So-Social" because it drew its recruits from Ivy League colleges). His father was already in the OSS.

Angleton was almost immediately assigned to the counterintelligence unit, called appropriately X-2, and ended the war in Rome. When the CIA was formed in 1947, he joined it. He then virtually disappeared from public view—until he was fired in 1974.

He arrived at the hotel in a black homburg, looking like someone that Central Casting might have chosen for the part of a counterintelligence chief. Even though he was over six feet tall, he shuffled down the corridor with a stoop that made him seem shorter—and older. He was ghostly thin, with deepset eyes accentuated by arched eyebrows. He had an enigmatic smile, and a finely sculptured face which, I later learned, had been proposed half-facetiously as an appropriate logo for the CIA.

He lit a long Virginia Slims cigarette as we sat down at the table—and coughed. He explained that he suffered from both emphysema and an ulcer, but that didn't stop him from chain-smoking or drinking. A quarter of a century in counterintelligence had evidently exacted some toll.

I had no idea at this first meeting that the defector I wanted to speak to Angleton about had helped bring about his downfall. Or that Nosenko had been the center of a bitter battle within the CIA that had been buried, along with a half-dozen careers, but not settled. I merely wanted to know at this point whether there was any reason to doubt Nosenko's account of Oswald's activities in Russia. I began by asking Angleton what his position was in the CIA in January 1964 when Nosenko defected.

"I was chief of the counterintelligence staff—that's now part of the public record, thanks to Seymour Hersh and *The New York Times*," he said with a tinge of real bitterness. "But for twenty years, what I did was so secret that not even my wife knew what my job was."

"Did it concern defectors?" I asked.

"We had the responsibility, at least then, of establishing the bona fides of intelligence defectors." He explained that "bona fides" was a term of art the CIA used when it accepted that a defector, or other intelligence source, had permanently left the service of a foreign power and was no longer under its control. A bona fide defector was, in other words, deemed an authentic source.

"But are there false defectors?" The alternative was that the person in question was a false defector—only pretending to switch sides while remaining under the control of another intelligence service.

Angleton answered quietly, "Truth is always complicated when it comes to defectors." He added, with a trace of a smile, "There are defectors whose bona fides cannot be established."

"Was there any problem with Nosenko's bona fides?" I pressed.

"I can't discuss specific cases," he said with a shrug. With that, he abruptly cut off the conversation about Nosenko and effortlessly moved on to a subject of which I had no understanding at all: orchids.

"There are over ten thousand identified species of orchids, divided into tribes," I heard him say. He finished off a second bottle of premier cru Chablis as he began describing orchid tribes, growing at different levels of the jungle, with such exotic names as *Dendrobium, Phalaenopsis, Cattleya, Cymbidium, Brassia,* and *Odontoglossum.* While half-listening to this esoterica, I tried, without success, to get him back to the subject at hand: Was the Soviet defector on whom I was about to base a book some kind of fraud?

Angleton simply waved off these interruptions like bothersome flies. When he got up to leave, he said, "You might do well looking at some of these orchids . . . if you want to see how deception works in the real world."

The next week I met Angleton again—this time in the steamy main greenhouse of Kensington Orchids in Maryland. He talked, as we walked through the greenhouse, as if he were conducting a lecture tour.

"With most species of orchids, it is not the fittest but the most deceptive ones that survive." The problem is that most orchids are too dispersed through the jungle for the wind to carry pollen to them; they depend on insects or birds for this crucial service. But since they do not provide any food or other nutrients for these carriers, orchids have to trick them into perpetuating their species.

Angleton seemed to take particular delight in elaborately describing these modes of deception. "They can play on greed, lust, or fear." He pointed to a tubelike column surrounded by five-inch-long spidery-looking petals that belonged, according to its label, to the *Epidendrum* tribe. "This orchid deceives mosquitoes." He described the deception, level by level. First, the orchid emits a fragrance that simulates the nectar the mosquito feeds on. Then the mosquito, following the scent, is lured from the flower petals into the narrow tube. Here it runs into the orchid's pollen pod, gets jammed in the eye, and is blinded. Finally, leaving the orchid, the blinded mosquito flies on until it passes another orchid of the *Epidendrum* tribe and gets a whiff of the same false nectar odor. Again, it pushes its way into the orchid's narrow tunnel, only this time it deposits the pollen that has stuck to its eye.

"Other orchids use what is called pseudo-copulation," Angleton continued, "to trigger the sexual instincts of an insect." He described how the Tricerus orchid has on its flower a three-dimensional replica of the underside of a female fly. It even bristles with the hairs—and odors—of a fly. When the male fly sees this replica, he lands on it and attempts to have sex with it. In doing so, he comes in contact with the pollen pod, which attaches itself to his underside. Eventually, he flies off. If he then passes another Tricerus orchid, he repeats the frustrating process, and delivers the pollen.

Angleton then directed my attention to an amazing orchid

that had on its flower a picture of a bee's head. He explained that when a wasp sees this image, it assumes its mortal enemy is just below it, and instinctively attacks. The wasp's stinger plunges through the picture of the bee petal into the pollen pod, which sticks to it. By repeating this "pseudo-attack" when it passes another such orchid, it pollinates it.

Angleton said these deceptions depended on "a process of provocation." The victims are duped because they are keyed to respond to certain information in nature. Insects do not have the ability to discriminate between what is real and what is mimicked.

The orchid house was an odd sort of education. But it was clear that he was not talking just about orchids, or insects. They were a metaphor for a world in which he saw deception as a norm rather than an aberration. It was a world in which intelligence services could be provoked, seduced, lured into false trails, blinded, and turned into unwitting agents—through the same failure to discriminate between real and simulated information.

Angleton finally got to Nosenko as we lingered in the greenhouse. "Why do you think Nosenko, after all these years of silence, decided to tell his story to you—now?"

I explained that, as best I knew, he had just walked into the Washington office of *Reader's Digest* and befriended an editor there. He then suggested he would be willing to discuss Oswald, and the editor contacted me. I hesitated, seeing that Angleton, with his cocked smile, looked skeptical.

"I know that a journalist might not want to look a gift horse in the mouth," he continued, "but did you assume he walked in on a whim?"

I had no immediate answer. The idea that a Soviet defector would selflessly provide an author with material of great public interest seemed far less implausible to me at the time. Instead, I asked defensively whether he believed Nosenko did not contact the *Digest* of his own free will.

"I'm only suggesting you make some inquiries about his motive." He added, with conspicuous understatement, "I don't know what Nosenko's status is, but some defectors have contractual obligations to the Agency that might prevent them from just walking into the office of a magazine and volunteering an interview." His point was evident.

When I returned to Washington, I began asking about the *Digest*'s connection with Nosenko. I found, as Angleton indirectly suggested, that Nosenko indeed was under contract to the CIA. The contract, which I later located a copy of, prohibited discussion of any aspect of the intelligence relationship except with an "authorized government representative or such other persons as he may specifically approve." Nosenko therefore presumably had CIA approval to make his contact with the *Digest* editor—and provide information to me. Such approved information was called a brief.

Jamie Jameson, the "mutual friend" who arranged for my meeting with Nosenko, turned out to be a CIA consultant. Although nominally detached from the CIA itself, Jameson had the job of bringing Soviet bloc defectors like Nosenko together with journalists so that they could deliver their authorized briefs. It was a way of getting stories into magazines, newspapers, and books. I subsequently learned that this CIA program of surreptitiously planting news stories even involved writing entire books and publishing them under defectors' names. *The Penkovsky Papers*, a best seller published by Doubleday in 1966, was the most successful of these "operations." One defector, a former Czech general, told me that the CIA handed him a completed "autobiographical" manuscript to be published under his name; when he asked for the right to make changes, it was taken away from him and the identical manuscript was later published under the name of another Czech defector.

This program of surreptitious authorship had disturbing implications. It meant that much of the material in the public record on the history of the spy war that came from first-hand witnesses—i.e., defectors—had been authorized and selected, if not written, by an interested party: the CIA.

Angleton showed little surprise when I told him at our next meeting at the Madison that Nosenko had been sent to me. He had known that, of course, from the start. I reasoned, perhaps overly defensively, that the fact that Nosenko's story was authorized by the CIA, and possibly censored by his CIA briefing officer, did not necessarily mean it was untrue.

"Right," Angleton agreed. He paused, as if to weigh what else he could tell me, and in the interval ordered a large snifter of Armagnac brandy from the waiter. Then he continued, "What that means is that the Agency has now decided to go public with Yuri Nosenko. I would expect that his autobiography is already in the works." (As it turned out, he was right. Jameson had already mentioned the book to a *Digest* editor.)

"Why shouldn't his story be made public?" After a month of looking at orchids, I decided that the time had come to force an answer. "What was wrong with his information?"

He explained in a quiet but precise voice: "Up until the time I left the Agency, all reports based on what Nosenko said carried a label I had insisted on. That label specified 'From a source whose bona fides have not been established.' "

It seemed incredible to me that Nosenko, who had defected in 1964, still was not considered a bona fide defector ten years later. "Are you saying that Nosenko was a false defector?"

"I am stating a fact: As of December 31, 1974, my staff was unable to certify Nosenko's bona fides, and by agreement with the Director, all information provided by him was so labeled." He finished his Armagnac, then added, with what appeared to be some strain in his voice, "This policy has obviously changed."

It was becoming increasingly evident that the issue of Nosenko's label was just the tip of the iceberg. What still remained submerged was the real dispute that had led to the abrupt departure of Angleton and his staff. "Did the problem proceed from what Nosenko said about Oswald?" I continued.

He looked at his watch, signaling it was time for him to leave. "It was much more than Oswald . . . All I can say for now is that the problem concerned defining the basic concept of Soviet deception."

Since I planned to continue my interview with Nosenko—if the CIA permitted him to meet with me again—I asked Angleton what sort of questions might get at this concept. He excused himself at that point and returned from the cloakroom with his coat on. Just as I assumed the interview was over, he motioned me to pick up a pencil and, without further hesitation, he rattled off thirteen questions for Nosenko.*

Angleton's questions contained specific Soviet names, relationships, and KGB departments, all of which were completely unfamiliar to me. Nor did the questions seem relevant to the issue of Oswald, at least at the time. (Only years later, rereading Angleton's questions in my notebook, would I realize that they obliquely contained in them Angleton's theory of the Kennedy assassination.)

When I finished writing down the thirteen questions, I asked him to explain how they related to Nosenko. Was Nosenko not who he said he was? Had he misinformed the Warren Commission about Oswald? Did Angleton believe he might still be under KGB control—after more than a decade? Could the CIA, with all its resources, be duped by a single man?

Angleton answered this spate of questions by asking one of his own. "Do you know about the Trust?"

I looked blankly at him. I had never heard of the Trust before.

"If you want to understand Soviet deception, you have to go back to the Trust. It is the prototype." He added, as he walked to his parked Mercedes, "Talk to the Rock. He knows more about the Trust than anyone else outside of Russia."

*See Appendix A.

CHAPTER TWO

The Trust

The Rock was Raymond Rocca, a tall, bearded man in his early sixties who looked more like a professor than an intelligence officer. Angleton had told me that he had been his Chief of Research for over a quarter of century. He had first met "the Rock" when they were in the same counterintelligence unit in the OSS in Italy during World War II. Angleton, impressed by Rocca's monklike devotion to filtering through voluminous archival records, kept him, as he put it, "by his side" for the rest of his career in intelligence. In the CIA, Angleton gave Rocca the Herculean task of keeping the "serials," which were the fragmentary bits of unresolved intelligence, initially scrawled on 3 by 5 cards, which Angleton tried to fit into different jigsaw puzzles. "The problem was that we never could be sure which puzzle which piece belonged to," Angleton explained. When the day of reckoning came in December 1974 and Angleton was fired, the Rock left with him.

Rocca lived in a trim suburban house in Falls Church, Virginia—not far from Angleton's home in Arlington. When I arrived there, I couldn't help noticing two giant *Cattleya* orchids which, like his mentor, he took great pride in breeding. He explained that he was just recovering from a serious heart operation and was too weak to go out, but would be glad to answer my questions. I presumed, without ever asking him, that Angleton had called him on my behalf.

"The Trust," he explained, as he lit his pipe, "was the basic deception operation the Soviet state was built on." The story, which he had pieced together over twenty years, went back a half century.

It began, as far as Western intelligence services were concerned, in late August 1921. At that time, a high-ranking Soviet official named Aleksandr Yakushev, on his way to attend an international trade conference in Norway, slipped away from his delegation in Estonia, then an independent republic, and sought out an anti-Soviet exile he had known before the Revolution. He said that he, and other Soviet officials, had come to the conclusion that the Communist experiment in Russia had totally failed. The Soviet economy was on the verge of collapse, farmers were not delivering crops, and the army was on the point of mutiny. Lenin's Bolshevik government would fall of its own weight in a matter of months.

This news greatly excited the exile. He asked about Yakushev's plans: Would he defect?

Yakushev told him that there was no need to defect. He planned instead, with a close circle of other officials and technocrats, to seize power when the Bolsheviks faltered. Because they had recruited other disillusioned officials in the secret police, army, and key ministries, he and his co-conspirators had little to fear from the Bolsheviks. Though still underground, his group had become the equivalent of a de facto government.

After Yakushev left, the anti-Soviet exile immediately reported this astounding information to other exile groups which, in turn, passed it to British, French, and other intelligence services that were supporting their anti-Soviet activities. Yakushev's assertion that the Russian economy was failing seemed eminently plausible and fit in with assessments made by Western observers in Russia. His claim that the Bolsheviks were in disarray also dovetailed with conventional wisdom in the West. Earlier that year, Lenin had appeared to reverse communism by instituting his New Economic Policy, which legitimized free enterprise, private farms, banking, and foreign industrial concessions in Russia. There was even an underground dissident press springing up in Soviet cities. The issue was whether the Yakushev conspiracy was as far-reaching as he claimed—or whether he had exaggerated its power.

In the months ahead, a half-dozen other Soviet officials, diplomats, and military officers, temporarily defecting from their missions, made contact with other anti-Soviet dissidents in Europe, and told similar stories about the disintegration of the Bolshevik regime. They also claimed to be part of the same conspiracy to overthrow the government, which called itself the Monarchist Union of Central Russia. Bit by bit, it also emerged from these temporary defectors that they used as a cover for their conspiratorial activities an office building in downtown Moscow called the Municipal Credit Association Building, and, in case they were overheard, the group was referred to as "the Trust."

When he reappeared in Berlin in 1922, Yakushev asked to be put in touch with other leaders of the anti-Soviet movement in Europe. He suggested that the Trust could be of great use to them. It could act as their "service organization" inside Russia, arranging through its network of collaborators to smuggle out their relatives, possessions, other dissidents, and whatever secret documents these exile groups needed. Within a year, this offer was relayed to all the principal dissident groups in Europe. Yakushev, the Trust's ambassador, then made it possible for anti-Soviet groups in Paris, Berlin, Vienna, and Helsinki to use the Trust's facilities in Russia.

Initially, some of these exiles remained skeptical of the Trust, despite the freedom of movement Yakushev and his co-conspirators seemed to have. They demanded proof it had the influence it claimed. To demonstrate its worth, the Trust smuggled the families of dissidents out of Russia. It also delivered arms and supplies to their partisans inside Russia and contracted to undertake sabotage and assassination missions for them in Moscow and Petrograd. It even furnished exile leaders with fake passports and visas, which allowed them to sneak back into Russia to participate in these clandestine missions. As they saw with their own eyes police stations blown up and escapes arranged from prisons, these exiled leaders came to accept the Trust.

Then, they began receiving from the Trust secret documents on the Soviet economy and military, which they turned over to Western intelligence services. They found that these documents were of great interest to the intelligence services of France, Germany, Great Britain, Austria, Sweden, and Finland, which also paid them handsomely for the information. In the triangular trade that developed, Soviet secrets went from the Trust to the Soviet dissidents to a half-dozen Western intelligence services.

By the mid-1920s, no fewer than eleven Western intelligence services had become almost completely dependent on the Trust for information about Russia. The Trust even arranged tours of the underground for émigré writers, in which they attended dissident meetings in Moscow and met with editors of dissident journals.

When fitted together, the pieces of intelligence gathered through the Trust reinforced the view that communism was over in Russia and that, whether by Yakushev's awaited coup or through a less dramatic accommodation, such as the New Economic Policy, the Soviet Union would abandon its revolutionary goals.

By the late 1920s, however, problems developed with the Trust. Exile leaders were suddenly kidnapped or vanished on their missions to Moscow. Top agents, such as Sydney Reilly and Boris Savinkov, brought back to Russia under the protection of the Trust, were arrested, given show trials, and executed. Secret documents proved to be unreliable—or false—the New Economic Policy faded away, and underground journals disappeared. The Soviet regime, instead of collapsing as predicted, turned out to have consolidated its power.

Finally, in 1929, a top Trust official called Edward Opperput defected to Finland. During his debriefings in Helsinki, he revealed that he had organized the Trust, not as a dissident but as a Soviet intelligence officer, taking his orders directly from Feliks Dzierzhinski, Lenin's intelligence chief. He admitted that Yakushev, as well as all his co-conspirators, had only feigned to be disloyal: they all had been his agents, under the control of the secret police. The Trust building, rather than being the cover for a subversive conspiracy, was the secret police headquarters for this seven-year sting. It fed out all the secret documents, briefed all the false defectors, published the dissident newspapers, made all the passport and travel arrangements, and even blew up Soviet buildings to make the deception more credible. Since the secret police was running the show, it could also guarantee the success of the smuggling, jail breaks, and assassinations. Opperput also told how Soviet intelligence used the money it received from Western intelligence services for the documents to finance spies in the West, forced labor camps in Siberia, and other activities. He provided so many specific details—including dates and times of contacts going all the way back to Yakushev's original meeting in Estonia—that there could be no remaining doubt that the Trust had been a brilliant creation of Soviet intelligence.

So ended the Trust. The exile leaders, now realizing they had been duped, were discredited—and demoralized. The Trust had sown massive distrust among dissidents. These revelations also left Western intelligence services in a state of confusion and disbelief. They had to explain to their foreign ministries how they had allowed themselves to be gulled and manipulated by the Soviets for eight years.

The final shock came when Opperput, after making all these revelations, quietly redefected to Moscow—and, under a different name, returned to work for Soviet intelligence. "He had been a dispatched defector," Rocca coolly concluded. Once he had accomplished his mission of blowing the secret of the Trust, he returned.

"But why," I interrupted, "would Soviet intelligence expose its own deception?"

"That was the final coup," he answered, with evident admiration for the ingenuity of his enemies. Since the deception had worn thin by 1929, and, with the abandonment of the New Economic Policy, no longer had a strategic objective, the Soviets decided to liquidate it in the most advantageous way. "The idea was to focus the attention of the West on this past fiasco, so as to distract it from the operations that replaced it."

Did this mean that there had been other Trusts? I asked.

Rocca now switched to a more conditional and hypothetical tone. "Soviet intelligence had demonstrated with the Trust a capacity for future deceptions." He spoke almost proudly of the Soviet adversary, as if he were discussing what a magician had proven he could do in earlier tricks. "It demonstrated it could control double agents, like Yakushev, in foreign countries and over extended periods of time." Yakushev was the classic "dangle" which, in the invisible intelligence war, is someone who, while loyally taking orders from his own intelligence service, feigns disloyalty to his country to attract the attention of the other side, like the bait on a fish hook. The dangle may even pretend to defect—in which case he is called a "dispatched agent." "Soviet intelligence also showed it could orchestrate events over the better part of a decade so as to turn these controlled agents into sources on which the West relied." This "orchestration" involved simulating evidence to make a fake underground credible— which meant staging assassinations, bombings, car chases, and jail breaks. It also involved creating "false flags"—organizations like the Trust and other dissident groups that purposely misidentified their true political affiliation to lure their enemies into a trap. The "false flag" could be designed by intelligence services to appeal to virtually any interest since the invisible war, by its very nature, afforded few reference points to check the authenticity of credentials.

Finally, and most important to Rocca, Soviet intelligence demonstrated that it could artfully use this network of double agents to feed out to the West secret reports, clues, and documents that provided a false picture of the Soviet Union. This "disinformation" was carefully calculated to dupe the West into believing the Communist revolution was moribund—and therefore no threat. It resulted in Britain, France, and other European nations extending trade credits, technological transfers, and diplomatic recognition to what they assumed would quickly evolve into a non-Communist Soviet Union. "They were of course deceived," Rocca said, tapping out his pipe. It was clear that the seminar on the Trust was coming to an end.

"But what about Nosenko?" I asked, still trying to understand how this half-century-old deception could connect to the Kennedy assassination. "Was he delivering some kind of disinformation message?"

"I thought you only wanted a historical perspective," Rocca shrugged. "I wasn't involved in operational cases like Nosenko." He would not discuss the matter further. If I wanted an answer, I had to go back to Angleton.

Angleton invited me to Tucson, Arizona, later that month. He suggested I might like to see "his desert."

I was surprised to find that Angleton lived in what amounted to a private park in downtown Tucson. From the porch of his ranch house, one couldn't see another house or sign of the city. He proudly showed me the furniture which he had himself designed and built; he had even commissioned the recording of the music on the stereo he had made. He evidently enjoyed designing his own world.

I told him that I had not been allowed to see Nosenko again. I had submitted Angleton's thirteen questions to him through the medium of Jamie Jameson, but had not received a reply.

"You never will," Angleton predicted confidently. "It is not part of his brief." We sat on his terrace. Looking into the darkness, he told me that had I arrived earlier, while it was still light, I could have seen the Superstition Mountains. He then proceeded to sketch out for me with his finger, peak by peak, the view I might have seen.

There were numerous fireflies blinking their lights in the distance. Calling my attention to them, he pointed out that the female firefly uses a sort of Morse code of flashes to signal males of their availability. He then added, lest I assume it was a chance observation, "Of course one can't be sure it's a firefly." He explained that the assassination beetle, which was the firefly's natural predator, had learned over time to replicate this code of flashes. "The firefly responds to this mating call, and instead of finding a mate . . . is devoured by a beetle." It was part of the war of disinformation.

This was a subject that Angleton had been grappling with for a quarter of a century, and which he wanted to discuss. "The essence of disinformation is provocation, not lying." The assassination beetle did not lie when it sent out its flashes of light— they were what they appeared to be—but it nevertheless provoked the firefly, keyed to responding to this signal, into flying into the fatal trap. Angleton saw this as neither moral nor immoral in itself. He pointed out that when a homeowner leaves his lights on in his absence to ward off burglars, he is not falsifying reality; he is trying to protect himself by provoking, through this signal, potential thieves into assuming that the house is occupied. "When disinformation becomes the art of the state, as in the case of the Trust," he continued, "nations use their intelligence services to paint, brush stroke by brush stroke, a picture that will provoke its adversaries to make the wrong judgments." This "state art" involved intelligence services in the job of giving away selected secrets to the enemy. He suggested, "In peacetime, disinformation might be the chief job of an intelligence service."

I asked whether planting defectors was part of this job. Was this how Nosenko fit in?

"What you must understand is that dangles, false defectors, false flags are only part of the problem." He abruptly came to the point: false defectors were only the outside men who transmitted the messages. "A deception is a complex organism . . . to sustain it, the deceiver needs feedback. He must enter the mind of the victim." He explained that for deception to succeed, intelligence services had not only to pass disinformation, which was "the easy part," but to determine if it was being accepted or rejected, and, if held in abeyance, what additional messages were required to make it more credible.

This latter task required what Angleton called a "penetration" of this adversary's intelligence service. Such a penetration was usually a mole, or an intelligence officer who had been recruited years before and maneuvered into a position where he had access to the "mind" of his intelligence service—the unit that evaluated foreign intelligence.

It now was becoming apparent why the Nosenko case was such a sensitive subject in the CIA. If he had been a pawn in a grand Soviet disinformation scheme, it would suggest that the KGB had also established one or more "inside men," or moles, in American intelligence who could feed back to the KGB the CIA's assessments of the case. The question of Nosenko thus involved far more than the credibility of his information about Lee Harvey Oswald.

The connection between deception and penetration proved to be of more than hypothetical interest to Angleton. It had caused him great pain early in his intelligence career. Over the course of the next two days, he told me of how he had been introduced into this special universe of deception by Kim Philby.

CHAPTER THREE

Kim and Jim

Jim met Kim on a rainy day in early October 1949 at Harvey's Seafood House in downtown Washington, only a few blocks from his office at the CIA. He had fleetingly known Philby during his counterintelligence training in London five years ago, and he barely recognized the haggard but still handsome man who was now reputed to be the West's top expert on anti-Soviet intelligence. Angleton had been extensively briefed at the CIA on him.

Harold Adrian Russell Philby had been born on New Year's Day, 1912, in Ambala, India. His father, Harry St. John Philby, a British administrator in India, called him Kim after the character in the book by Rudyard Kipling. Philby went to school at Westminster in London, where he was captain of the school, as his father had been. Then, at the age of seventeen, he went on to Trinity College, Cambridge, where he graduated with honors in 1933. He worked as a special correspondent for *The Times* in Spain during the Civil War, and then covered the British Expeditionary Force in France before it was evacuated from Dunkirk in 1940. In February 1941, he joined MI6, the British espionage service, where he was put in charge of counterintelligence for the Iberian Peninsula, evaluating the credibility of the reams of intelligence from German diplomats in Spain and Portugal. Here he had remarkable success exposing German ruses and double agents. When MI6 revived its anti-Soviet unit,

31

"Section IX," toward the end of the war, Philby was chosen to head its counterintelligence staff. Working against Soviet intelligence officers in Europe and Turkey, Philby demonstrated an almost unerring ability to spot phony approaches by Soviet diplomats and military officers. Over and over again he was proven right by the subsequent actions of the Soviets. In light of this string of triumphs, Philby became head of the anti-Soviet section.

As the Cold War heated up, he also was placed in charge of the effort to coordinate anti-Soviet activities with the United States and Canada. He would take over the duties as liaison between MI6, on the one hand, and the CIA, FBI, and Royal Canadian Mounted Police, on the other.

Angleton, who had himself only returned from Europe three months earlier, had also become a leading specialist in counterintelligence. As one of a small elite group of recruits from Yale, Harvard, and Princeton who were handpicked to learn the most arcane part of espionage, counterintelligence, he had risen rapidly through the ranks of X-2. By the end of the war, at the age of twenty-seven, he had become the youngest division chief in X-2. He was responsible for counterintelligence for all of Italy, and was singled out by William Donovan, the Director of the Office of Strategic Services (OSS) as its star counterintelligence officer. After the OSS was dissolved, Angleton remained in a holding unit called the Central Intelligence Group, which became, in July 1947, the core of the newly formed CIA. When Colonel Donald H. Galloway created a "Soviet Division" that November to recruit Communist diplomats as sources, and organized other espionage activities, Angleton became his special assistant. His job involved maintaining 3 by 5 cards in the registry on those diplomats who, because of their possible collaboration with the Nazis or other problems in their past, were potential candidates for recruitment. To do this job, he maintained close relations with top officers in French, Italian, and West German intelligence. He also served as station chief in Rome.

In May 1949, at the age of thirty-one, Angleton returned to Washington to take over, among other things, the liaison with other Allied intelligence services. Since the CIA still relied heavily on the British, French, Germans, and other "partners" to do much of the recruitments and covert actions in postwar Europe, these so-called liaisons were the very mechanism through which the CIA organized the secret war against Soviet Russia.

Angleton thus had much in common with his luncheon partner. They both had been educated in England, spent much of their life abroad, and had similar literary and epicurean tastes. They liked English poetry, French wine, German music, and discussing cabbages and kings. They both also shared a common interest in a field that few outsiders knew existed: anti-Soviet counterintelligence.

Angleton also knew from that morning's briefing that Philby's assignment to Washington was anything but routine. Philby was not just another British intelligence executive furloughed to America; he was, as MI6 had informed the CIA, next in line to head the British Secret Service. His mission was temporary but critical. It concerned what was to be the major, though secret, American initiative of that era.

With the Cold War reaching a glacial impasse after the Communist coup in Czechoslovakia in 1948, the U.S. government, with bipartisan support in Congress, had committed itself to rolling back Soviet influence in Eastern Europe. Yet it wanted to achieve this strategic objective by means short of war, which meant covert action. The mechanism for undertaking this secret offensive was the so-called Office of Policy Coordination, which was the CIA's paramilitary arm, staffed by former OSS and Army subversion experts, and headed by Frank Wisner. It was charged by the President with developing anti-Communist undergrounds in Communist countries in Eastern Europe. They would have their own guerrilla forces, saboteurs, and political front groups— all orchestrated and coordinated by the CIA. They would be used to disrupt communications, paralyze the economy, harass Soviet forces, provoke general strikes and, through this orchestrated dissidence, undermine Soviet control.

Britain, with its half-century experience in East European espionage and its control over émigré groups in exile, was to be America's silent partner in this ambitious undertaking. MI6 would furnish what agents and other intelligence assets it had still operating in Eastern Europe, and help coordinate their activities with those of the CIA. And it had thus provided its best and brightest—Kim Philby—to work directly with the American policy planners.

The centerpiece of the offensive was the underground in Poland, which was called WIN, the acronym in Polish for "Freedom and Independence." Earlier that year, its representatives had made contact with Polish émigrés in London; WIN claimed that it had wide support in Poland and could now mobilize thirty thousand guerrilla fighters. It had become, in this respect, the successor to the Polish Home Army that had bitterly fought the Germans to a standstill in 1944.

Although Wisner's Office of Policy Coordination was at first skeptical of these claims, WIN gradually provided concrete evidence of its ability to undertake guerrilla actions. It attacked police stations, blew up military installations, and even fought a pitched battle against Soviet tanks—the aftermath of which could be documented by photographs. Wisner insisted that all WIN needed was antitank weapons "to drive the Red Army out of Warsaw." Then WIN began smuggling out of Poland reports and documents revealing the Soviet order of battle and its military capabilities in Eastern Europe. This intelligence apparently came from WIN moles inside the Defense Ministry.

By the time Philby had arrived in Washington, the CIA's Office of Policy Coordination had begun parachuting arms and gold coins into WIN. It was also pressing British intelligence to get the Polish government-in-exile in London to fully support WIN as its inside arm in Poland, and to help put all its agents into direct contact with its operatives. Other dissident movements in the Ukraine, Georgia, Lithuania, Albania, and Hungary would be used to divert and distract Soviet attention from the main target: Poland. That, at least, was the plan at the time of the lunch at Harvey's.

Philby, after gossiping briefly about their old colleagues in London and his rough crossing of the Atlantic on the S.S. *Caronia* the week before, began complaining about his first order of business. He called it "vetting the old Nazis." He explained that he had been given, among his other duties, the dirty job of checking through the files and locating the group of German counterintelligence officers who had been secretly relocated in Canada.

These men were of great importance to the planned offensive in Eastern Europe because they had the only available pool of potential agents. They were Polish and other Eastern European citizens who had been secretly turned into informers during the German occupation. Many had betrayed their comrades in the resistance to save their own lives, and, under German aegis, elevated themselves in the Communist underground. Some had been exposed, and were presumably dead or in prison, but others, who had managed to conceal their deadly secret, had gone on to work for the Communist regimes in their countries. Since they now could be possibly coerced into cooperating—or else face the consequences of exposure—they could be reactivated as agents (so long as the Soviets did not also find out). These "assets" could then be employed to help WIN and other undergrounds stage an effective uprising. Philby was on his way to see the Royal Mounted Police, which would presumably put him in touch with, or at least furnish the records of, the cadre of Hitler's ex-intelligence officers in Canada.

Over the course of the next eighteen months, Angleton continued to lunch with Philby on a weekly basis—sometimes at Harvey's, sometimes at the Army and Navy Club. By this time, Philby had been appointed as the British representative to the

Special Policy Committee, which assessed the general progress of the covert action offensive in Eastern Europe, and its intelligence product, and he recounted the problems it was encountering—as if Angleton was not himself fully apprised of these developments. For his part, Angleton couldn't help being amused by Philby's waspish humor about naive Americans and his cynical view of world politics. At times, Philby got down to business by presenting questions about CIA activities of interest to MI6; and, as CIA liaison, it was Angleton's job to give him answers for his service (unless the information was specifically embargoed from the British). They also discussed the more general problem of intelligence: guarding against deception. It was a very friendly relationship.

Meanwhile, the CIA was building up the capacity of WIN to challenge Soviet power. The ex-German counterintelligence officers, many of whom had been vetted by Philby, provided a long list of their candidates with hidden pasts in Poland and other satellite countries, and many of them were duly recruited by the CIA and put in contact with WIN and other Balkan undergrounds. The Agency also parachuted in special clandestine radios for WIN to transmit messages back to CIA bases in Germany—and sophisticated explosives and timers for its sabotage targets. Field reports suggested that WIN controlled entire regions, and its "home army" was growing every day. With help from its British colleagues, the CIA marshaled virtually the entire Polish émigré movement abroad in support of WIN. In return, WIN sent back so much intelligence that the CIA had to set up a special unit to process it. These fragmentary bits of data, as they were fitted together and analyzed, strongly suggested that Stalin, who was in trouble in Russia, was rapidly losing his grip on the Soviet satellites.

In the late spring of 1951, however, the CIA was thrown into turmoil. The problem began when the Army Security Agency accidentally obtained part of a Soviet World War II code book, and found that the Soviets had reused the same ciphers, apparently having run short of code books. This unexpected break allowed Army codebreakers to decipher sporadic Soviet messages sent from Moscow to its embassy in Washington. They contained shocking evidence that U.S. secrets that had been given to the British had been passed on to Soviet intelligence. The leak emanated directly from the British Embassy—and had continued into the postwar years. In a series of tense meetings in the Shoreham Hotel, attended by representatives of the FBI, CIA, Army Security Agency, and the British security service, MI5, British officials admitted that a British diplomat who had served in Washington in 1945 was suspected of being a Soviet agent. His name was Donald Maclean, and he was scheduled to be interrogated.

Then, three weeks later, on May 25, 1951, Maclean disappeared from London. He turned up in Moscow a few days afterwards with another former British intelligence officer, Guy Burgess. Both Burgess and Maclean were Soviet spies. Further, Burgess had been living in Philby's house in Washington—at the time Philby was told of the investigation. After reanalyzing the Soviet messages, both the CIA and the FBI became convinced that there had to be someone else besides Maclean and Burgess, and that the third spy was none other than Kim Philby.

As the pieces fitted together, British intelligence also came to the conclusion that Philby had been the leak—although the evidence was circumstantial at best, and the cryptographic evidence could not be revealed. In August 1951, Philby was recalled to London, and after an inconclusive interrogation, he was secretly cashiered from MI6.

Angleton was temporarily stunned by this turn of events. If Philby was indeed a mole, what had happened during the past eighteen months? As CIA liaison, answering the wide range of queries put to him, Angleton had been Philby's source. The implications were shattering. At the very minimum, the Soviets would have been able to determine the CIA order of battle. They would now know who was who in the world of American intelligence, and they would have personality assessments of the strengths and vulnerabilities of the major players. They would also know a good deal about the CIA's most prized methods, and the procedures it used for analyzing and checking reports from its sources. And they would have learned about the inner workings of its liaison relations, which Angleton was in charge of, with the intelligence organization of Reinhard Gehlen, which had formerly served Hitler, French counterintelligence, and the Italian security service. He knew that many of these foreign connections, if made public, were potentially embarrassing. And, of course, Philby entirely compromised British intelligence, which had been America's mentor in the spy war.

Angleton was therefore not surprised by the problems that began to develop in the intelligence coming out of WIN. He had reason to suspect that WIN was another Trust. The facts it reported about Eastern Europe did not check out with intelligence obtained through aerial reconnaissance, communication intercepts, and other sources. Moreover, its claims of military victories became less and less plausible in light of other evidence. Émigré agents, put in contact with WIN, were also not heard from again; and their radio transmissions became increasingly suspect. Despite these disturbing difficulties, WIN began in 1952 escalating its requests for weapons, radios, money, and names of agents it could contact in Poland. It even asked the CIA to parachute an American general into Poland to lead the uprising.

At this point, Angleton intervened, although he had no authority to do so. He went directly to General Walter Bedell Smith, who was then the Director of Central Intelligence, and told him why, in his opinion, American officers should not be air-dropped into Poland.

He reasoned that if Philby was a Soviet agent, as all the evidence now indicated, WIN and the other clandestine undergrounds that were being supplied by the Office of Policy Coordination were probably being run by Soviet intelligence— rather than by dissidents. How could it be otherwise? Philby, after all, knew all about the agents for this offensive that had been supplied by ex-German counterintelligence officers—he, in fact, had vetted the files—and therefore it had to be assumed that the identities of these agents were also known to the Soviets by the time the CIA was approached to assist WIN and the other groups. Under these circumstances, the Soviets would only allow them to help WIN if it was under Soviet control.

Bedell Smith listened carefully to Angleton, who was, among other things, his trout-fishing partner. He then called in Frank Wisner, who was still the driving force behind the covert action offensive.

Wisner, even though he had been a rival of Angleton's, seemed genuinely shaken by this logic. He clung nevertheless to the hope that Philby had never conveyed the information to Soviet intelligence—which, after all, was a possibility, since British counterintelligence had not broken Philby. If so, Wisner argued, WIN should still be viewed as a legitimate resistance organization. He agreed, however, not to parachute in an American general.

But that December the question of WIN was definitively settled in a way that shocked even Angleton. In a move that was reminiscent of the purposeful blowing of the Trust twenty-three years earlier, the Polish government told the story of WIN in a two-hour radio broadcast. It explained that the real Polish Home Army had been eliminated by security forces in 1947. In its place had been substituted the fictitious WIN, staffed by Communist officers. So that there could be no doubt that WIN had been a deception from the outset, the broadcast gave a full accounting of all the monies and weapons that had been sent to WIN from the first contact on. Then it went on to mock the CIA for its misplaced trust in this sham organization. It turned out that Polish security forces had staged mock battles, leaving burnt-out tank hulls to be photographed, to give WIN credibility. They had also taken over and operated the clandestine radios that the CIA had supplied, and used the CIA's gold coins to finance the deception.

By early 1953, the CIA determined that its agents had been identified from the outset, and arrested or brought under control, as were other true Polish dissidents who were lured into the trap by this fake underground.

It gradually emerged that WIN was not the only such fraud. A half-dozen other supposedly anti-Soviet undergrounds turned out to be creatures of Soviet intelligence. Some of these groups, such as the guerrilla army in the Carpathian Mountains in the Ukraine, had been authentic resistance movements until they were penetrated and eliminated by Soviet security forces. Others, such as the Estonian resistance, had been created de novo to manipulate exiles abroad.

The "intelligence" that WIN spoon-fed the CIA turned out, on reexamination, to be disinformation, cleverly contrived to dovetail with that from the other undergrounds and, in two cases, from reports of false defectors. The purpose of the disinformation, as Angleton now mirror-read it, was to distract the United States from the real weaknesses in the Soviet system of control in Eastern Europe, and to focus its attention as well as its limited intelligence resources on fake weaknesses instead.

Wisner was shattered by the revelations about WIN. Clearly, his Office of Policy Coordination had been led disastrously astray by Soviet deception planners and, more important, neither he nor his staff was able to recognize the deception—until the Poles had publicly revealed it. Both Bedell Smith and his deputy Allen Welsh Dulles now saw that Wisner's covert actions had been totally manipulated by the Soviet Union.

Angleton was assigned the job of analyzing how Soviet intelligence succeeded in falsifying a reality so completely. What were the conditions under which one side could fabricate dissident groups and underground movements and sustain the illusion over nearly four years? He brought in Ray Rocca, at this point, to reconstruct the Trust—and the deceptions that followed.

When Dulles became Director of Central Intelligence in 1953, he turned to Angleton, whom he had known since the days of the OSS. Angleton, whose suspicions about WIN had proven to be right, was given "No Knock" privileges—he could enter Dulles's office any time, day or night, without prior appointment—and assigned the job of organizing a unit, directly under the control of the Director, which could guard against systematic Soviet deceptions such as WIN. The result was a new "counter-intelligence staff" established in January 1954. At one level, it was to be a liaison—the CIA's connection with a dozen other intelligence services including the FBI, the National Security Agency, the British Secret Service, French counterintelligence, and the Israeli Mossad. At another level, it was given the responsibility for keeping the CIA's central registry of foreign agents, and determining which of the double agents were "bona fide" sources. But its true function, which not even many high executives in the CIA were told about, was, as Angleton explained it, "to provide the highest form of counterintelligence: a picture of the enemy's thinking." Angleton became its chief. He had thus ascended to the commanding heights of the CIA, while Philby went on to Beirut as a journalist, and then, in 1963, facing further interrogation, defected to Moscow, where he published a book, *My Silent War*, finally admitting he had worked all along for Soviet intelligence.

Even as he told the story, Angleton seemed obsessed by the deception perpetrated by his one-time friend. When I asked him about Philby's book (in which he describes Angleton as "one of the thinnest men I ever met, and one of the biggest eaters"), Angleton replied: "Book? It was the final card played in the deception. Every word was written under the strict control of the KGB, as were those in the 'interviews' he gave journalists."

The idea of *My Silent War,* he explained, was to "further muddy the waters." In reconstructing Philby's career with the advantage of hindsight, Angleton found that many of his successes against first the Germans and then the Soviets proceeded from Philby's having available to him secret information unavailable to other British intelligence officers. The most likely explanation, given what his connections turned out to be, was that these successes had been provided by Soviet intelligence. In other words, the Soviets had sacrificed agents and sources, like pawns in a chess game, to advance Philby's rapid rise in British intelligence. If so, his promotion to the head of Section IX, the center of anti-Soviet espionage, and then his posting in Washington, involved far more than the work of one man; it was part of a Soviet design. He added: "If Philby could be moved into such positions by Soviet intelligence, so could other of their agents."

Angleton also questioned Philby's boast about betraying the Albanian anti-Communists who were infiltrated into Albania under the auspices of the CIA. Many of these dissidents were in fact captured but, as Angleton determined, their organization had been compromised, and penetrated by Soviet agents, well before Philby was briefed on the operation. "By taking credit for a betrayal for which he wasn't responsible, Philby again attempted to divert from his real job in Washington."

This crucial mission was "feedback." Philby had not given away WIN. It had been a creature of Soviet intelligence years before Philby came to Washington. What Philby provided was feedback about the CIA's reactions to it. Angleton explained that up until "the Philby incident," he had never realized how vital feedback was to sustaining a deception. Without their inside man, who reported back on how the CIA was reacting to the activities of their bogus undergrounds, Soviet deception planners could not have continually modified their messages to keep them credible. But with Philby in place, they could accurately determine whether or not the reports fed to the CIA were believed or not, and what additions or revisions would make them credible. They could also find out the preconceived picture that the CIA had of anti-Communist groups, and then fit their messages to it. "The point was not that these movements were betrayed," Angleton said, "it was that they were made credible to the CIA."

CHAPTER FOUR

The Nosenko Incubus

After nearly a year of research, I still had not resolved the mystery of Nosenko, and the editors of *Reader's Digest,* who were financing my research, were understandably concerned. I was spending far more time questioning the authenticity of the first-hand source they had provided than with the assassination case that was the subject of my book. But the *Digest's* editor-in-chief, Edward Thompson, to his credit was willing to proceed with the Nosenko investigation, even if it discredited another *Digest* book for which Nosenko provided information. Still, he wanted some reassurance from someone, other than Angleton, that it was not a wild-goose chase.

I suggested Richard M. Helms. Helms, who had been the director of the CIA's clandestine operations at the time of the Nosenko defection and then Director of the Central Intelligence Agency, had certainly been in a position to clear up the confusion. Thompson agreed. The only problem was that Helms was then Ambassador to Iran, and in Teheran.

I had been introduced to Helms three years earlier at a diplomatic reception at his residence in Teheran. At the time, I found him to be an elegant man with a quiet voice, who could come right to the point. Helms told me, moments after I met him, "I know you're a journalist but please don't ask me about the CIA." Toward the end of the evening, as I lingered in the doorway, he said, "Please feel free to either stay and have a brandy or leave—but don't ooze in the doorway." I remained for another hour, and listened to his shrewd analysis of the political situation in Iran.

Now I needed to discuss with him the subject he had previously embargoed, and I knew that it was one of the CIA's most sensitive cases—one that impinged directly on the Kennedy assassination. When I called him and told him that I needed to ask him about the Nosenko affair, I expected him to politely hang up. Instead, he suggested I come to Teheran.

Helms then cabled me: "Would be delighted to see you in Teheran but must confess my memory has become decidedly hazy on matters in which you are interested. I can give you leads to other individuals if that would be helpful, but I don't want to mislead you into thinking I am a treasure trove while in Teheran with no documents from the past." He also invited me to stay at the embassy residence.

It was a long flight, and, with resistance to the Shah's rule increasing every day, the embassy compound was surrounded by an army of Iranian troops. After a leisurely dinner in his residence with Helms and his wife Cynthia, we went to his study to talk about Nosenko.

I told him that I had interviewed Nosenko—and that it had apparently been arranged by the CIA. I explained the problems I had had with his story about Oswald.

Helms shook his head, visibly distressed that this case was resurfacing. He said that the CIA "had no business giving you Nosenko in this way." He assumed (correctly) that Nosenko had been given a carefully rehearsed brief by the CIA to pass on to me. This message-passing might, he feared, reopen "old wounds" within the intelligence community.

"Angleton's?" I asked. I told him about my conversations with Angleton, and the thirteen questions he had dictated to me. "He insists that Nosenko did not get his bona fides."

"It goes much deeper." There was pain in his voice as he

recalled the case. In June 1964, Helms said, "Nosenko's reliability was key to determining what the KGB had to do with Oswald." Attorney General Robert F. Kennedy knew this, as did Chief Justice Earl Warren, who was considering calling Nosenko as a witness before the Commission he headed on President Kennedy's assassination. This added tremendous urgency to the situation. Finally, Helms went to see the Chief Justice in his chambers. It was a private meeting with no notes taken. He warned Warren then that there were two schools of thought on Nosenko within the CIA. The first held that he was a legitimate defector and could be believed about Oswald; the second held that he was still a KGB agent, under instructions to misinform the Commission about Oswald. Until the matter was resolved, he advised the Chief Justice not to see Nosenko—or base any of his conclusions on his information. Warren nodded his assent.

The Warren Commission issued its report without referring to Nosenko, but that did not end the matter. Helms said, with a crack of real anguish in his voice, "It hung over the CIA like an incubus."

I thought over his simile a moment. An incubus, in folklore, is an evil spirit that descends on a woman while she is fast asleep and has sexual intercourse with her—without her being aware of the rape. Was he suggesting at some level that Nosenko had caught the CIA unaware?

"All I am saying is the case was a nightmare—a nightmare that still won't go away." He explained that just before I had called him, he had had a visit from a CIA officer named John Hart, who told him he was reinvestigating "the Nosenko affair." He wanted, twelve years after Nosenko's defection, to settle the case.

"What did you tell him?" I asked.

"Just what I'm going to tell you," he answered, with a smile. "I have no memory of the details of the case." He paused, watching my face drop. Then he said, more sympathetically, "You'll have to speak to the officers who actually handled it." He jotted down a number of names on a piece of paper. "See them. If you can make sense of what they say, it's more than we did."

At the top of Helms's list was Tennent Peter Bagley. It was a name I had not heard before.

Helms explained that Pete Bagley had been one of the most promising officers in the CIA, the "golden boy" of its all-important Soviet Bloc Division, which recruits spies. At the age of thirty, he had become deputy director of his division, and was being considered a candidate to be a future Director of Central Intelligence. "That was when he arranged Nosenko's defection from Switzerland." Bagley became Nosenko's case officer and chief interrogator.

I asked what had happened to Bagley.

"I understand he has retired from the Agency," Helms cryptically concluded. He wrote down an address for me in Brussels; he said Hart had given it to him.

When I returned to New York, I immediately sent a letter to Bagley explaining that Helms had suggested I speak to him about Nosenko. When he did not reply, I sent him a follow-up note, then a cable. Weeks went by, and the deadline for the book drew nearer. Finally, I phoned his home number. His wife answered, and told me courteously that he would not return the call or speak to me—ever.

I had given up on Bagley when I received a phone call from a stranger, which provided me with an unexpected bargaining chip. The stranger was William C. Sullivan, the former Assistant Director of the FBI, in charge of counterespionage investigations. He was a man imbued with hatred for J. Edgar Hoover, who had not only fired him in 1971 but humiliated him by locking him out of his office.

Sullivan explained on the phone that he had been told about my investigation by a *Digest* editor, and that he knew "some background on the Nosenko case" he believed I might find useful.

I met Sullivan, as he requested, at a coffee shop in a large and anonymous shopping mall in Boxboro, Massachusetts. I had no difficulty recognizing him.

As he walked toward the table with a distinct limp, I could see that he was a wreck of a man. Since leaving the FBI he had had two serious car accidents from which, he said, he had not fully recovered. He also had been given a "rough time" by the Church Committee in its grueling hearings on the FBI's domestic counterintelligence program, which he had headed. Here was another ruined career, I thought, as he bitterly told how Hoover had turned him into the FBI's "fall guy."

Sullivan traced his "problem with Hoover" back to an investigation he had conducted of possible Soviet manipulation of the FBI's counterespionage staff in the late 1960s. He explained that it had all begun in the winter of 1962 when two Soviet diplomats stationed at the United Nations in New York separately approached American diplomats. Both men were Soviet intelligence officers, working under diplomatic cover. Both said that they had been unable to fulfill their espionage missions and were therefore in grave potential trouble with their superiors in Soviet intelligence. Each then offered to betray their country in return for the eventual opportunity to defect to the United States.

When these approaches were brought to his attention, Sullivan suspected that they might be Soviet "dangles," who had made their contacts at the behest and under the control of the KGB. "It all seemed too pat, too contrived," he explained. Nevertheless, Hoover decided to accept their offer and use them as double agents, which meant that, while nominally continuing to spy for Soviet intelligence in the United States, they would secretly report all these activities to the FBI. The first of these volunteers was code-named "Fedora," the second "Top Hat."

Both Fedora and Top Hat then asked the FBI to help them answer the questionnaires supplied to them by Moscow—which meant that the FBI had to do their espionage for them in order to help them maintain their credibility in the eyes of their superiors. To "play out this game," as Sullivan put it, Hoover had to give each of them American sources who could provide them with classified military documents. These "notional agents," as they are called in the intelligence business, are fictitious sources who are in a plausible position to copy and pass on classified documents needed to fulfill the spies' questionnaires. The data were then cleared by a special interagency review board, which decided what secrets the United States could afford to give away to the KGB. At first, the data were "chicken feed," but gradually Fedora and Top Hat began pressing for increasingly sensitive data, claiming that any delay or false information would make Moscow suspicious of their performance.

The game was getting out of control, as far as Sullivan was concerned. Hoover was becoming dependent on the suspect intelligence these two Soviets were providing, and was even taking some of Fedora's tidbits directly to the President. Convinced that they were phony through the result of various surveillance techniques, Sullivan recommended that rather than furnishing them with more U.S. secrets, the contacts be terminated. Again, he was overruled. "Fedora and Top Hat went on for another five years misleading us," he said gruffly. "All because Hoover wouldn't admit he had been duped."

I listened with great interest as Sullivan described the curious relationship that had developed between the FBI office and the KGB in New York. The FBI, by making the convenient assumption that Fedora and Top Hat were ultimately working under its control, could take credit for having developed two major spies; the KGB, meanwhile, could get the FBI to do much of its illicit research for it, by merely forwarding the questions it wanted answered. This game of deception reminded me of the scene in Peter Ustinov's comedy *Romanoff and Juliet,* in which the Prime Minister of a small European nation tells the Soviet Ambassador that the United States knows about a secret operation. The Soviet Ambassador replies, "We know they know." The Prime Minister next tells the American Ambassador, "They know you know," and he retorts, "We know they know we know."

He then returns to the Soviet Ambassador, who explains, "We know they know we know they know." When the American hears that, counting the levels of deception on his fingers, he suddenly throws his hands up in shock, and shouts, "What? They know that . . ."

But I still did not see what connection there was between Fedora and Top Hat, who contacted the FBI in New York in 1962, and Yuri Nosenko, who had defected to the CIA in Geneva in 1964. Finally, I asked Sullivan, "How does Nosenko fit in?"

He shook his head as if I had missed the central point. "Don't you understand? They were part and parcel of the same thing. That's what got Hoover in an uproar." He explained that when Nosenko defected in Geneva, Fedora gave the FBI specific details about the reaction of the KGB that tended to corroborate, point by point, Nosenko's story. Sullivan reasoned that if Fedora was providing the FBI with information on behalf of the KGB, as he assumed was the case, then the KGB was deliberately attempting to make Nosenko seem credible. Since the KGB would have no interest in helping Nosenko if he was a traitor, Sullivan concluded that he was "another dangle."

When Sullivan informed Hoover about this development, and that the CIA had prepared a set of forty-four questions about Oswald aimed at exposing Nosenko, Hoover "blew his top." He ordered Sullivan not to pursue the Fedora issue any further, and, protesting directly to the Director of Central Intelligence that the FBI was the agency charged with investigating the Kennedy assassination, Hoover prevented Bagley from asking Nosenko these questions. Sullivan concluded, "As far as I know, the cover-up is still going on."

That was the last time I saw Sullivan. He was killed six months later when a hunter, apparently mistaking him for a deer, shot him in a wood near his home.

The Fedora story was exactly the revelation I needed to interest Bagley in seeing me. I therefore made one final effort to get his side of the story by sending him a specially prepared outline of the Nosenko chapter, prominently mentioning Fedora's role. I also enclosed a copy of the list of Bagley's forty-four unasked questions that I had got under the Freedom of Information Act after Sullivan told me of their existence. In the covering note, I informed him that I would be in Brussels the following month, and asked him to contact me at my hotel.

When I arrived in Brussels, I was relieved to see that Fedora—or the questionnaire—had apparently done the trick. There was a message from Bagley. He proposed meeting me the next day at the Waterloo battlefield outside of Brussels. He said he would be standing in front of the circular mural in the museum.

I had no trouble recognizing Bagley from Helms's description of him. He was a rugged, good-looking man in his early fifties. As we walked around the battlefield, he told me about his life.

He was born in 1925, one of three sons in a prominent family in North Carolina. His two elder brothers both were fleet admirals in the U.S. Navy, and his cousin had served as a press secretary to President Roosevelt.

After serving three years in the Marines during the war, he then graduated from Princeton University, and went on to get a Ph.D. in political science at the University of Geneva in Switzerland. In 1950, he joined the CIA. He was assigned to the Soviet Division, which, at the heart of the CIA's espionage activity, had the job of recruiting Soviet citizens as American spies. Here he became a top recruiter, leading a team of Soviet specialists to international conferences or wherever a potentially vulnerable Soviet diplomat could be approached. By 1962, he had been put in charge of the division's counterintelligence, and in 1965, he had become deputy director of the division. That was his high point. Even though he still looked in his prime, he had retired from the CIA five years earlier—at the age of forty-seven.

He showed an impressive grasp of Napoleon's order of battle, taking me from position to position, and explaining the futility of Napoleon's last stand. He then turned to me, and said with what appeared to be carefully calculated naiveté that he did not understand the Freedom of Information Act. The idea that secret documents could be released to an outsider was "inconceivable." He expressed indignation that the CIA would make available the questionnaire, especially since it identified him by name.

He told me he had read the Nosenko outline I had sent him. He then added abruptly, "You've got it wrong."

"In what way?" I asked, trying to open up the discussion.

"Unfortunately, I can't tell you anything more."

I then asked him why John Hart was reinvestigating the case. Why had he seen Helms? And why had he been to Brussels?

He glared at me for a moment, then acknowledged that Hart had been to see him, but added, "I threw him out of my room."

If this was all he had to tell me, I wondered why he met me at all. Trying again, I suggested that he might point out the error I had made.

"If I told you that, I'd have to tell you everything," he answered.

He then said matter-of-factly that he had made a reservation at the Villa Lorraine, a very expensive three-star restaurant outside of Brussels. He asked if I would like to join him. I again assumed he had more to tell me, and accepted.

At dinner, he apologized for not being able to correct my error. He explained: "Nosenko was not just another case. It was at the heart of everything that happened at the CIA for a decade."

He seemed still obsessed—and angered—by Nosenko. I asked if he would be interested in seeing other material on the case that had been released under the Freedom of Information Act.

He couldn't resist the offer. It had been, after all, his case. He suggested that we meet the following day in a medieval nunnery at Bruges, thirty miles west of Brussels, and asked me to bring the entire Nosenko file.

It was as quiet a place as one could find. As I wandered around the cloisters looking at the stonework, Bagley sat on a bench, efficiently speed-reading through the file. When he finished, he handed it back, and whispered, with a bit of melodrama: "I've made my decision." He tersely explained that from what he had seen, the case had "already been blown." He further believed that it had been "selectively" released to me in such a way that it might permanently "confuse the record." Since he realized I was going to publish the Nosenko story, he had a duty to make sure it didn't have "egregious errors" in it. As it would take some time to reconstruct the case, he suggested that I find a "discreet location" for our future meetings.

I rented a house in the village of Gassin in southern France. Bagley arrived a week later and stayed for six days. After making all these arrangements, I wanted to know what the error was that I had made.

He replied: "Where you went wrong was that you assumed that it was after Kennedy had been assassinated in November 1963 that Nosenko first contacted the CIA."

I rechecked my notes, mystified by his point. The date I had been given was January 23, 1964, nine weeks after the assassination. I had assumed that Nosenko had contacted the CIA because of what he knew about the assassin—Oswald. I answered defensively, "That is what I was told by Angleton."

He shot back, "Angleton omitted telling you that Nosenko was supposedly working for us before the assassination. He was our man in Moscow." He added, "I should know, I recruited him." That was the missing piece—or at least one of them.

Bagley's story began in Switzerland in the summer of 1962. Officially, he was the Second Secretary at the American Embassy in Berne; unofficially, he was a CIA case officer, working in the Soviet Russia Division. In it, he headed the recruitment team that went after REDTOPS. REDTOPS were Soviet diplomats, military attachés, intelligence officers, or other government officials who were traveling through or temporarily stationed in the West. Bagley's mission was to arrange for these REDTOPS to be approached by a so-called access agent, usually some diplomat with a plausible excuse to meet them. Once contact was established, he would then use other agents to induce or persuade them to steal secrets for the CIA when they returned to the Soviet Union. It was not an easy job.

On June 8, he got an urgent call from Geneva. A Soviet security officer named Yuri Ivanovich Nosenko, who was at the Disarmament Conference there, had passed a note to an American diplomat at the meeting. It said only that he wanted to be put in touch with a "representative" of the U.S. government, which meant CIA.

Bagley caught the next plane to Geneva. Working through the American diplomat, he passed a message back to Nosenko containing only a time and an address. The address was that of a "safe house" that the CIA maintained in Geneva for just such a contingency. It was a small apartment with a terrace in an inconspicuous block of flats that would be used only for Nosenko, and then abandoned.

As he waited for Nosenko to show up, Bagley was joined in the apartment by another case officer in the Soviet Division, George Kisvalter. Kisvalter, who was born in Russia, spoke perfect Russian. He had just flown in that afternoon from Washington to assist Bagley with the interrogation.

Nosenko arrived about an hour and a half late, claiming that he had to make sure he wasn't followed. He was a powerfully built man, about six feet tall, with a massive jaw. He acted very professionally, and, without any resistance, rattled off answers to the questions as if he were there for a job interview. He also seemed to know that it was being taped.

The first question was mandated by CIA regulations for all REDTOPS. Kisvalter asked Nosenko whether he knew of any imminent Soviet plans to launch a military attack.

Nosenko smiled, as if he was expecting the question, then shook his head.

He was next asked why he had contacted the CIA. Hostile intelligence services previously had sent "dangles" to the CIA, as the secret Central Intelligence Directive on Defectors warned, "to penetrate or convey false or deceptive information to U.S. Intelligence services."

Nosenko replied that his motive was economic. He had spent 900 Swiss francs (or about $200) of KGB funds on a drinking binge and needed to replace it. In return, he offered to furnish the CIA with a KGB manual on its techniques for following Western diplomats in Moscow. He said it would explain how the KGB had caught one of the CIA's top agents.

Bagley then asked Nosenko if he wanted to defect to the West. If he did, crash arrangements would have to be made to get him out of Geneva.

Nosenko again said no. He had no intention of defecting; he had a wife and children in Moscow to whom he planned to return. He only wanted 900 Swiss francs.

This was the answer Bagley hoped to hear. The object of the exercise was not to encourage REDTOPS to defect but to get them to spy for the CIA. He handed Nosenko the 900 francs. He explained to Nosenko, who had already shown an interest in money, that the CIA would pay him handsomely if he assisted them by supplying information. He would, for example, be given an additional $25,000 for every Soviet source in the West his information helped to expose. The money could be deposited in a Swiss account for whenever he eventually decided to defect. He would, moreover, be given assistance in getting his family out of Russia.

Nosenko betrayed no emotional reaction at this offer to commit treason. He shrugged and said he would consider it.

Bagley still didn't know with whom he was dealing. In response to his "flash" cable, CIA files had no information, or "traces," on Nosenko. The only Nosenko in them was Ivan Nosenko, the Soviet Minister of Shipbuilding and a member of the Central

Committee of the Communist Party, who had died six years earlier.

Nosenko explained that he was Ivan Nosenko's son. He had been born October 20, 1927, in Nikolaev, Russia, and, as the son of a minister, had attended the elite Frunze Military Academy. In 1953, after serving briefly in naval intelligence, he joined the KGB. He was assigned to its Second Chief Directorate, which had the primary responsibility for recruiting foreigners in Russia and mounting counterintelligence initiatives against the West. He worked in both its "American Department," which attempted to recruit U.S. Embassy employees in Moscow, and the "Tourist Department," which attempted to recruit American tourists in Russia. He had been given the Geneva duty to watch over the Soviet delegation purely as a perk.

Bagley immediately realized that Nosenko, if his story checked out, was an incredible catch. Not only was he the son of a hero of the Soviet Union—Khrushchev himself had been a guard of honor at Ivan Nosenko's funeral bier—but he was in a key section of a part of the KGB which the CIA knew virtually nothing about—the Second Chief Directorate. Until two years before, the CIA had not even known of its existence. No one had ever been recruited from this directorate before. If Nosenko now could be induced to go back to Moscow and work as an "agent in place," the CIA would have a mole in the heart of KGB counterintelligence.

As the debriefing proceeded, Nosenko provided a wealth of clues to identify Soviet agents in the United States and England. He also revealed how the KGB had planted microphones in the U.S. Embassy in Moscow. He then left two hours after he arrived, and, as Bagley watched, he vanished into the night.

Two days later, he returned for another session. This time he brought with him the promised documents on surveillance. They revealed that the KGB had a chemical substance to be sprayed on the shoes of American diplomats in Moscow so that they could be invisibly followed by surveillance teams with dogs. Nosenko then agreed to act as a mole for the CIA in Moscow (although he refused to allow the CIA to contact him, because it would be too dangerous).

On June 11, Bagley cabled the CIA in Washington: "Subject has conclusively proved his bona fides. He has provided info of importance and sensitivity. Willing to meet when abroad." The CIA responded by providing Nosenko with a cryptonym—AE FOXTROT. Bagley was authorized to provide AE FOXTROT with a secret writing kit, a password, and a means of communicating with the CIA. Four days later, Nosenko (or AE FOXTROT, as he was now known in the CIA) returned to Moscow.

Bagley flew to Washington the next week believing he had "hooked the biggest fish yet." When he arrived at CIA headquarters that Saturday, he was personally commended by his superior, David Murphy, the chief of the Soviet Division, who believed Nosenko's career in the KGB could be systematically advanced by the CIA by arranging a string of dramatic successes in his counterintelligence work. As his case officer, Bagley's career would also be advanced.

Bagley also had a message that Angleton wanted to see him. There had always been some tension between Angleton, who had no "operational" responsibilities for agents but second-guessed their value, and the division that actually ran and supported agents in the Soviet Union. It was not unlike the competition that goes on in a news magazine between reporters, who find sources, and fact checkers, who question their reliability. Although Angleton had no direct authority over him or the division, Bagley decided it would be "politically wise" to see the counterintelligence staff chief right away.

When he arrived at Angleton's office, Angleton handed him a file to read, which he said pointedly was too sensitive to leave his office. It concerned another REDTOP defector who had fled a Soviet Embassy in Helsinki in 1961—a defector Bagley called

"Mr. X." Angleton suggested he review it before making any further judgments about AE FOXTROT.

As he pored over it that June weekend, Bagley was astounded. Each point in Nosenko's story paralleled information given by this earlier defector. When the two stories were compared, it became clear that Nosenko was a "provocation," sent to Bagley in Geneva by the KGB to supply clues that would divert from and confuse the intelligence the CIA already had from the real defector. The CIA called the practice "painting false tracks." Bagley understood, even before Angleton told him, that he had been duped by Nosenko.

Angleton seemed far less concerned about this turn of events. He suggested that now the division knew it was dealing with a KGB "controlled source," it could use him to the CIA's advantage. He would be treated as a "mailbox," in which the CIA would deposit messages of its choosing for the KGB. As far as any information that came from AE FOXTROT (and presumably the KGB), it would be labeled disinformation.

Bagley returned to Switzerland crestfallen. The mole he had recruited turned out to be a Soviet plant. Whether or not he would reemerge was problematical.

Then, on November 22, 1963, President Kennedy was assassinated. Less than a week later, the CIA established that the alleged assassin, Lee Harvey Oswald, had attempted to contact Soviet intelligence in Moscow during his stay there. The question was asked of CIA procedure experts: If Oswald had made contact with the KGB during that period, what unit of Soviet intelligence would have handled his case? The answer that came back was the Second Chief Directorate's Tourist Department. By coincidence, it was the one unit in which the CIA had, on paper at least, an agent—AE FOXTROT.

Some six weeks later, Nosenko sent a cable to an innocuous-sounding address in Europe. It was the prearranged signal that he had been given by the CIA. He indicated he would be arriving in Geneva the following week, where he would again be acting as the security officer for the Soviet disarmament delegation. He wanted a meeting with "George," the name by which he knew Bagley.

Bagley, now stationed in Washington, had risen to a central position in the Soviet Division. He headed its counterintelligence operations (which had no connection with Angleton's counterintelligence staff), and he was slated to be the deputy chief of the whole division. He still remained the case officer of the mystery agent AE FOXTROT. As soon as Nosenko's signal was flashed to Washington, Bagley booked a flight to Geneva. He assumed the rendezvous with Nosenko would lead to a few tidbits of disinformation. He had no idea of what was in store for him.

On January 23, Nosenko sauntered into the safe house, taking few precautions about security. He greeted Bagley like an old friend. As he poured himself a drink, he casually told Bagley he had made a "decision." Instead of returning to Russia, he would defect to the United States.

Bagley was speechless. Even if he believed Nosenko were genuine, CIA policy would be to discourage defections and to persuade REDTOPS to return to the Soviet Union, where they could do some good as spies. Since he believed Nosenko was controlled by the KGB, such a defection would be ludicrous. But before Bagley could question this decision, Nosenko brought up another surprise—Lee Harvey Oswald. He reported that he had information about Oswald that could be crucial to the United States.

Bagley asked how he knew about Oswald.

Nosenko explained that he had been the KGB officer assigned to Oswald's case when he arrived in Moscow. He was consulted on Oswald after Oswald returned to the United States. Then, after the assassination, he had been asked to read through Oswald's entire KGB file and act for the KGB as a sort of inspector general in the case. He in fact "signed off" on the case for the KGB. This put him in a unique position: he could testify to the relationship between Oswald and the KGB.

Bagley was totally unprepared for this turn of events. He didn't believe Nosenko, but he had to forward his report to Washington. He knew that Nosenko's claims of being Oswald's case officer would set off "bells" in the CIA. The President might even have to be briefed on the case. But there was nothing Bagley could do but continue the interrogation session and hope that the label on the file would alert headquarters to the danger of disinformation.

He asked the key question: What interest did the KGB have in Oswald?

"It was decided Oswald was of no interest whatsoever, so the KGB recommended he go home to the United States," Nosenko answered.

Bagley listened keenly, as he tried to figure out Nosenko's game. It appeared the KGB wanted its man in Washington. But why? Changing the subject, he asked him why he now wanted to defect.

Nosenko had a ready answer. He said that he had come under suspicion and feared he would be arrested if he returned to Russia. He said he had just received a telegram ordering him to return to Moscow on February 4. He had less than a week. He needed help from the CIA.

When the transcript of this interrogation was cabled to CIA headquarters, Helms had no choice but to authorize a "crash" defection for Nosenko. If he had done otherwise, the CIA could be accused of suppressing potentially important evidence on the Kennedy assassination; he was too proficient a bureaucrat to fall into that trap. So Helms gave Bagley the "go" signal. He specified Nosenko was to be taken out of Switzerland "black," without revealing his identity to the Swiss, which meant that military attaché planes, not open to border inspection, would be used.

After a brief stop at the U.S. debriefing center in Frankfurt, Nosenko arrived in Washington on a military transport on February 11, 1964. He was ensconced in a CIA safe house outside of Washington. This was the easy part.

59

The issue was what to do with him. Bagley's investigators quickly discovered that communications interceptions done by the National Security Agency contradicted Nosenko's claim that he had received in Switzerland a recall cable from Moscow. Its analysis showed that no Moscow telegram sent to Geneva on the day in question had the correct number of characters. Moreover, CIA document experts determined that Nosenko could not have held the rank or position he claimed in the KGB and that the travel papers he had in his possession had been concocted to give his defection credibility. And, under interrogation, Nosenko admitted these "mistakes."

The idea that these might be innocent errors might have been entertained by Bagley—if it were not for Fedora. Bagley took the fact that other KGB agents were going to great lengths to corroborate Nosenko's story as a powerful indication that the KGB was orchestrating the entire defection from Moscow. His chief, David Murphy, agreed, after reviewing Nosenko's biography, that it was most probably a "legend."

Murphy believed, moreover, that the KGB might have instructed Nosenko to break away at his earliest opportunity and go to a Soviet Embassy. He could then denounce the CIA for attempting to kidnap him. He might even claim the CIA was attempting to suppress his Oswald story. On February 17, less than a week after Nosenko's arrival, Murphy wrote Helms: ". . . there is greater evidence now I believe for the view that this operation is designed for long-term goals of utmost importance to the Soviets. One of these is probably a massive propaganda assault on the CIA in which Subject, most probably as a 're-defected CIA agent,' will play a major . . . role." In addition, he expressed concern that Nosenko's mission also was the "penetration of our operational effort," which could be accomplished by Nosenko's learning CIA procedures, and the "protection of past or possibly existing sources," which he could do by confusing ongoing investigations with false clues. Because of all this damage that Nosenko could do, Murphy recommended that preparations should be made to imprison him to prevent him from redefecting. He noted that "the big problem is one of timing: How long can we keep subject, or his KGB controllers, ignorant of our awareness of this operation?" At some point, Nosenko would have to be confronted and broken through a process of "hostile interrogation."

Bagley knew that this inevitable confrontation was strongly opposed by Angleton, who wanted to keep playing Nosenko and his KGB controllers like a fish on a line. But while Angleton might have inexhaustible patience, Murphy wanted results. Nosenko had involved himself in the investigation of Oswald, which had brought the issue of his status to the attention of the FBI, the Attorney General, and the Warren Commission. Helms, with the concurrence of the Department of Justice, had authorized the "hostile interrogation." It was only a matter of time.

To lull Nosenko into a false sense of confidence, the CIA paid him $60,000 for the information he supplied, began making arrangements for him to become a U.S. citizen, and even sent him on a vacation to Hawaii with Bagley. All the while he was cavorting on the beach, the CIA was constructing a "vault" for him in the basement of what looked like a ranch house a few miles from downtown Washington.

Then, on April 4, 1964, Nosenko was strapped into a lie detector. It was all a carefully rehearsed drama designed to break him. His interrogators told him over and over again that his answers were lies. He asked for Bagley. Bagley came in, examined the lie-detector results, then ordered him stripped and put in a cell. It was only the beginning of his ordeal.

Nosenko spent the next three and a half years in a windowless cell in solitary confinement. He was the prisoner of the CIA. Day and night, the light remained on in his eight-foot-square cell, with guards keeping him under constant visual observation. Every three or four days he was brought in front of interrogators and grilled relentlessly about details of his story. As the weeks dragged on without results, they tried various disorientation techniques, such as gradually setting clocks back and manipulating lighting conditions to convince him it was day when it was really night, thereby confusing his sense of time. At one point, Bagley was convinced that Nosenko was about to break and admit his entire biography was a KGB invention. He muttered something indicating that he could not have held any of the positions in the KGB he had claimed to hold. Bagley held his breath, anticipating that a full confession would follow. When it didn't, he repeated the question. After a long pause, Nosenko replied, "You misunderstood me." He then pulled himself together and stuck monotonously to his story.

The battle went on year after year—Bagley versus Nosenko. Bagley set forth the case against Nosenko in a 900-page report in 1966. "But he never broke," Bagley said, as he ended his story.

Nosenko obviously was out of prison now. When I interviewed him, he was cocky and in high spirits. Not only had the CIA sent him to the *Reader's Digest*, but he said he was working for it as a counterintelligence consultant. What had happened to transform him, in the eyes of the CIA, from a provocateur on a KGB-directed mission, who had been imprisoned, to an accredited defector?

Bagley answered glumly, "I wish I knew." He explained that in late 1967 the Soviet Division was "restaffed." Murphy was abruptly removed as chief and sent to Paris to be station chief there. Bagley, who was then deputy chief, was not promoted; instead, he was transferred to Belgium. Other top officers who had been involved in the Nosenko affair were also switched to other divisions. In the months that followed, the entire case seemed to be turned inside out. The insiders who had developed the indictment against Nosenko were turned out; the outsiders came in. It all happened without warning or explanation. Nosenko, who had been the division's responsibility, was suddenly turned over to the CIA's Office of Security.

Then, when John Hart came to see him, Bagley learned that

Nosenko had been "rehabilitated." He realized that Hart's job was to rewrite the history of the case in order to expunge any suspicion about Nosenko. He had come to see him to pressure him to recant, which Bagley had refused to do. He then learned that the Office of Security man who had handled Nosenko had received a CIA medal.

"For what?" I interrupted.

"The whitewash," he answered bitterly.

It seemed that almost every intelligence official who had been involved with the Nosenko case had had his career wrecked. Angleton, Rocca, Sullivan, Bagley, Murphy: each had been fired or forced into early retirement. The entire counterintelligence staff by now had been scattered to the four winds. Some of these investigators, I also learned, were themselves investigated for their role in the affair. I wanted to know more about this purge—if that is what it was.

In the fall of 1977, even as my book on Oswald was going into final editing, I continued interviewing, and reinterviewing, the CIA officials on Helms's list, which included everyone from the Inspector General who had reviewed Bagley's report to the Deputy Director, who had ordered Nosenko rehabilitated. Now that Bagley had told me the story of the man the CIA had kept locked in a vault for nearly three years, they were willing to give me their versions of what had happened in the inner sanctum of the Soviet Division. Like some medieval palimpsest, which monks constantly rubbed out and rewrote, the Nosenko case was recast over and over again in different reports and revisions between the 1965 Bagley Report and the John Hart report. They had evidently provided different aspects—or were they layers?—to the story, without ending it. All they agreed on was that Nosenko's story about Oswald—the very story that Nosenko had offered to me, with CIA approval—could not be believed.

The reason that the Nosenko affair had hung like an incubus over the CIA for fifteen years was that its central issue, Soviet deception, had never been resolved. Could the Soviets deceive and use for their own purposes American intelligence? What emerged from my interviews was that this question was still lodged, like a paralyzing fish bone, in the CIA's throat.

After my book was published, Bagley gave me one final clue to this mystery. He suggested, almost as if it was an afterthought, that Angleton had not been "completely forthright" with me on one issue.

"What issue?" I asked.

"His prize defector." He explained that the REDTOP who had defected six months before Nosenko in Helsinki had been treated by the CIA differently from any other Soviet defector. Whereas every other defector remained the charge of the Soviet Russia Division, this man had been turned over to the counterintelligence staff. He had become Angleton's personal charge—and source. Angleton believed Nosenko was sent by the KGB to discredit this defector's information, which he had confided to Bagley was crucial to understanding KGB deception. This defector then, not Nosenko, was at the heart of the real mystery. His name was Anatoly Golitsyn.

CHAPTER FIVE

The Golitsyn Secret

For nearly two years, I had been pursuing the shadow of Golitsyn without much success. Then, in the spring of 1980, at an academic conference in Washington, I stumbled onto an unlikely Frenchman who knew all about Golitsyn. He was Philippe de Vosjoli, a former aide-de-camp to General Charles de Gaulle, and, between January 1960 and November 1963, the liaison between SDECE, the French intelligence service, and the CIA in Washington. He introduced himself by saying that he was probably the only French intelligence officer in history "to defect to the United States." Golitsyn was the proximate cause.

He explained that Angleton, with whom he had worked closely, began supplying French intelligence in 1962 with reports that came from SDECE's own secret files. They had been supplied, Angleton explained, by a recent defector from the KGB. This leak meant, as de Vosjoli instantly realized, that the KGB had one or more sources in French intelligence. The defector then provided data suggesting that the penetration not only was widespread but involved de Vosjoli's superiors in SDECE. Then, in November 1963, de Vosjoli was tipped off by a colleague in Paris that he himself would be assassinated on his return to France. De Vosjoli resigned from SDECE, went into hiding, and, with Angleton's help, relocated himself in the United States. The defector who exposed this French conspiracy was Anatoly Golitsyn.

De Vosjoli had not only been fully briefed on Golitsyn, he also retained many of the files about him which the CIA had supplied to SDECE. When I asked whether I could see this material, he suggested that I come to Lighthouse Point, Florida, where he now lives. It was there that I learned the details that helped me reconstruct Golitsyn's story.

Golitsyn organized his defection in Finland on December 22, 1961. He arrived at the American Embassy in Helsinki in the midst of a blinding snowstorm, bundled in a heavy overcoat. He told the Marine on duty that he was a Soviet Embassy official, which was true, and he then asked to see the station chief by name. The request, coming from a Soviet officer, immediately set off alarm bells.

The procedures for dealing with a potential defector were put in effect. After escorting the Russian visitor to an isolated room, the Marine guard alerted the desk officer at the embassy, who relayed the "Mayday" message to the CIA station. Within minutes, the station chief rushed downstairs to meet this short, stocky Soviet "walk-in."

Golitsyn came right to the point. He identified himself as a major in the KGB. To leave no doubt in the mind of his CIA counterpart, he handed over a sheath of secret documents from the files of the Soviet Embassy in Helsinki. He said he would make further information available about the Soviet espionage apparatus if the CIA immediately arranged his safe passage to the United States, along with that of his wife and daughter.

It was an extraordinary offer. The station chief asked Golitsyn if he would consider returning to the Soviet Embassy and acting as an agent in place for the CIA. The standard procedure in the CIA was to do everything possible to persuade REDTOPS not to defect but to become moles.

Golitsyn was adamant. He replied he would not survive if he

returned. The KGB had means of identifying CIA agents in place—and he could disclose them after he was safely in America.

The station chief realized that Golitsyn was suggesting not only that there was a penetration in the CIA but that he could expose it. Unable to persuade him to work as a mole, the chief asked Golitsyn how much time he had to arrange defection.

Golitsyn replied that he had to be out by Christmas Day. After that, his wife and daughter would be expected back in Moscow, and Soviet security personnel, who were being rotated over the holiday, would be back on active duty. This gave them a maximum of forty-eight hours.

In Washington, the frantic search through the CIA's central registry of records produced only a single "trace" on Golitsyn. Peter Deriabin, a KGB officer who had been stationed in Vienna before defecting in 1954, had mentioned Golitsyn to his CIA debriefers as a KGB officer who might be potentially disloyal to the Soviet Union. But before this lead could be followed up in Vienna, Golitsyn was recalled to Moscow.

Now the CIA had been given a second chance. The Soviet Division authorized Golitsyn's immediate evacuation from Helsinki. No matter what diplomatic complications it would cause, it wanted to get this KGB officer in the palm of its hand, and use him to identify and possibly approach other potential defectors in the Soviet diplomatic corps.

On Christmas Day, a U.S. Air Force courier plane landed at Helsinski's snow-covered airport. Servicing military attachés stationed abroad, such flights are routinely exempted from foreign customs and immigration inspection. This was, however, not a routine mission. While the plane waited on the runway, a car pulled up beside it. Its passengers, who carried no luggage, quickly climbed on board. Among them were Golitsyn, his wife, and daughter. Minutes later the plane was airborne again, en route to West Germany.

The first round of interrogations took place at the U.S. Army defector center outside of Frankfurt. Golitsyn was required to write out by hand his entire career in the KGB, from the day he joined in 1948 to the day he defected—listing all the positions he held, promotions he received, and KGB officers with whom he came in contact. Unlike most previous defectors, who had been field agents with limited knowledge about the central apparatus of the KGB, Golitsyn claimed to have been assigned to the KGB's headquarters in Moscow and also to its "think tank," the KGB institute, where intelligence operations were related to overall Soviet strategy.

To determine if his story was true, Golitsyn was next strapped into a stress-analyzing machine, used by the CIA as a lie detector, and relentlessly quizzed about various details of his story—a process known in the CIA as "fluttering." After each session, counterintelligence experts also compared each bit of information he provided with what was already known. By the end of the first week, the CIA was fully persuaded that Golitsyn was a bona fide defector who had indeed held the positions in the KGB he claimed. Arrangements were then made to bring him and his family to the United States.

In February 1962, in an isolated and heavily guarded CIA compound overlooking the Choptank River in Talbot County, Maryland, Golitsyn began an extensive debriefing. To the amazement of his debriefers, he not only revealed knowledge of a wide range of secret NATO documents but identified them by their code numbers. He explained that for convenience the KGB used the NATO numbering system to request specific documents, which would then arrive from their source in France in seventy-two hours.

President John F. Kennedy, apprised of the Golitsyn revelations, dispatched a personal courier to Paris with a letter for President Charles de Gaulle. In it, he warned that the KGB had recruited at least four top French intelligence officers as agents and had then maneuvered them to key positions.

A few weeks later, six French intelligence officers, handpicked by de Gaulle, arrived in Washington. They carried with them specially devised ciphers that bypassed the normal channels of French intelligence, and kept their very presence in the United States a secret from even their own embassy. Their tape-recorded interrogation of Golitsyn, whom they code-named "Martel," took fourteen days, and left them in a paralyzing quandary.

The French intelligence secrets Golitsyn had provided came from the highest echelon of the French government. When the list of those having access to them was narrowed down, suspicion was focused on both the head of French counterintelligence and de Gaulle's personal intelligence adviser. Both were eventually suspended—but no legal case was ever brought against them.

Golitsyn also told of a KGB plan to use the French intelligence service to spy on missile sites in the American Midwest. French intelligence officers who were accredited in Washington would be ordered by SDECE in Paris to use their contacts to gather data—for the benefit of Moscow.

De Vosjoli recalled that he was initially skeptical about this allegation. It implied that the KGB had sufficient control over his own intelligence agency that it could use it as a "false flag" to recruit unwitting agents. He even discussed with Angleton the possibility that Golitsyn was a dispatched defector, sent by the KGB to disrupt U.S.-French relations.

But three months later he received an order from SDECE headquarters in Paris that confirmed, to his dismay, what Golitsyn had asserted. It told him to begin recruiting agents in the United States in a position to report on developments in American missile weaponry.

As de Vosjoli reread the order, he could not believe his eyes. Since he knew that France itself had no need for such information about U.S. bases, and recruiting spies was a very risky business, he queried Paris for further clarification.

The answer instructed him to implement the plan without further delay. He was also warned that it was an "eyes only" operation—and all telegrams concerning the topic must be burned after they were decoded.

At this point, he found out that Golitsyn's other assertions also were proving correct. Angleton told him that the CIA had positively identified through Golitsyn's leads a central figure in a spy ring, code-named "Sapphire." He was considered one of the most promising executives in French intelligence who was working for Soviet intelligence. Days after de Vosjoli passed this information on through channels, this double agent was thrown to his death from a window. De Vosjoli assumed the murder was done to protect others in the ring.

De Gaulle's intelligence advisers became concerned, at this point, that unless the scandal was contained, it would explode into the public domain and possibly bring down the government. It had already caused great strains in NATO. De Vosjoli got the message: they wanted reports, or even gossip, that questioned Golitsyn's credibility.

De Vosjoli reported back to Paris that Golitsyn was becoming increasingly short-tempered with the nonstop debriefings. He heard from Angleton that tensions had arisen over Golitsyn's treatment by the Soviet Division. His case officers there had been determined to have Golitsyn identify as many of the KGB officers who worked in embassies as possible from snapshots they had of Soviet diplomats, but Golitsyn, finding the exercise trivial and demeaning, was refusing to look at any more books of CIA photographs. He also refused the CIA request that he call former KGB acquaintances and attempt to recruit them. He argued that such attempts would be futile because the CIA's Soviet Division itself leaks. The CIA took these problems as signs that Golitsyn was not cooperating.

De Vosjoli next heard that Golitsyn had asked to personally brief President Kennedy on Soviet deception. When informed that such an audience was impossible, Golitsyn became further discouraged that his information was not being taken seriously.

Golitsyn then told the CIA that he wanted to be resettled abroad under a new identity. The CIA's Soviet Division, believing it had "squeezed" Golitsyn of all the information he knew, agreed to this request, provided it could still question him. In early 1963, he left for England. "We were still analyzing his information," de Vosjoli recalled, "when all the trouble began in London."

When I asked about this "trouble," de Vosjoli shrugged. "I heard only echoes." After he resigned from SDECE, he explained, he lost track of Golitsyn. He suggested that I go over to England and ask Stephen de Mowbray about "the trouble." De Mowbray had been the MI6 liaison with the CIA in 1963 and, through Angleton, had become deeply involved in the Golitsyn case.

De Mowbray agreed to see me with surprisingly little hesitation. Subsequently, I learned that Angleton, who apparently no longer wanted Golitsyn to remain a secret, recommended that he talk to me about Golitsyn.

I met him at his country home in Kent, where he had retired after leaving the British Secret Service in 1977. He was a tall, soft-spoken man, with an acid wit and deep contempt for those who didn't understand his intellectual positions. He had joined MI6 in 1958 on the recommendation of Isaiah Berlin, his tutor at Oxford. After he was posted to Washington, he went to work for MI6 counterintelligence, which he called "the queen on the chessboard."

I noted that he had returned to London at about the same time that Golitsyn temporarily moved to London in 1962. Their careers then became intertwined. Had de Mowbray gone back to London to debrief Golitsyn about matters he had not told the CIA or were these two Atlantic crossings pure coincidence?

De Mowbray answered in a mocking tone, "In counterintelligence, we are not supposed to believe in coincidences." He then said, so as to clearly establish his point of view at the outset of the interview, "Golitsyn was not merely another defector. He was, as far as British intelligence was concerned, probably the most important defector in recent history."

I wanted to know why Golitsyn, who had been working at the Soviet Embassy in Helsinki, would be in possession of information that would be so valuable to Britain.

De Mowbray explained that Golitsyn, before being stationed in Helsinki, had been assigned to the division of the First Chief Directorate of the KGB responsible for conducting espionage operations against Britain and other NATO countries in Northern Europe. In preparing for his defection, Golitsyn had memorized English as well as French documents. Many of these documents came directly from the files of MI5, the British equivalent of the FBI. The most troubling of these reports described the breaking of a Soviet code by British intelligence. According to the "bigot list," which identifies those with access to a particular secret document, the contents had been circulated to only five high-ranking officers of MI5. How then could Golitsyn have seen it in Moscow?

De Mowbray concluded that there was only one possible answer: One of these five executives had provided the KGB with the report. The search for that executive, which turned into a mole hunt that was never satisfactorily resolved, began with a secret task force, innocuously called the "Fluency Committee." De Mowbray was one of its seven members (who changed constantly).

Over the course of the next ten years, it gradually eliminated four out of five names on the "bigot list." The remaining suspect was Sir Roger Hollis, the Director of MI5.

Although the Fluency Committee never was able to find direct evidence implicating Sir Roger, such as unexplained contacts with Soviet intelligence, de Mowbray was convinced that he was the traitor. De Mowbray went personally, without any authorization, to 10 Downing Street, identified himself, and asked to see the Prime Minister. To his surprise, he received an immediate appointment. He came right to the point and told him that there was reason to believe the head of the British security service was a Soviet agent. He recognized that this initiative would be the end of his career—and it was. No case was ever made against Sir Roger.

Golitsyn had set this nasty investigation in motion years earlier. During his interrogation by British MI5 officers, he suggested that he had demonstrated to the CIA that it had also been penetrated. But he claimed that the CIA's Soviet Division had never zeroed in on his leads. He had to assume his CIA case officers were either incompetent or unwilling to find a mole in the CIA.

After listening to Golitsyn's story about CIA incompetence, Arthur Martin, who was in charge of Soviet counterintelligence for MI5, called Angleton. Angleton agreed that the Soviet Division had not got the full story from Golitsyn.

Angleton then arranged with Helms to have the responsibility for Golitsyn transferred from the division to his counterintelligence staff. It never had been done before—or since.

Getting Golitsyn back to America was not difficult. A leak was arranged by MI5 to the *Daily Telegraph* revealing that Golitsyn was in England. It had the calculated effect of persuading Golitsyn that his security could not be assured by the British. Three weeks later, in August 1963, Golitsyn returned to Washington.

Angleton was now in charge. His method was not to be a debriefing, but an "elicitation," as he called it. There would be no more exhaustive grillings or repetitive snapshots of Soviet diplomats. Unlike the Soviet Division, Angleton was not concerned with identifying KGB personnel per se or the organization's "order of battle." His primary interest was using Golitsyn to unravel what he called the "logic of Soviet penetration." The need to understand the Soviet method was made all the more relevant by the defection of his old friend Kim Philby to Moscow in November 1963—barely three months after Golitsyn's return.

To assist him with this elicitation, Angleton brought in his new chief of operations, Newton "Scotty" Miler. As his nickname implied, Miler was a dedicated Scotsman, with a reputation for being unflappable. He also had fourteen years of experience as a CIA case officer, recruiting and handling informants in Asia and Europe. While Rocca did research on Angleton's staff and pondered the historical significance of the pieces in the puzzle, Scotty was the man of action, who moved them around the board to test the theories. He was Angleton's right hand. He had worked on the Golitsyn case for ten years, and, in de Mowbray's opinion, he knew "the operational details of the Golitsyn case better than anyone else."

When Angleton had been fired in 1974, Miler had also been forced out of the CIA. He moved to the remote desert township of Placido in New Mexico, where he would be, as he put it, "as far from Washington as possible."

I had interviewed him there previously about Nosenko, but he studiously avoided the subject of Golitsyn. When I called him this time, however, he seemed far more open. Even over the telephone he made no effort to conceal his bitterness toward the new leadership at the CIA. He told me he had been informed that it was "shredding" the yellow sheets of notes he had left behind. Even if it was not intentional, the shredding had the effect of expunging the "institutional memory" of the CIA. After hearing the outlines of what de Mowbray had told me, he agreed to fill in the missing parts of Golitsyn's story.

I arrived at his home in Placido in the late afternoon. Miler had just returned from hunting rabbits in the desert. He had a rugged face, and in his denim jacket he looked more like a cowboy than a counterintelligence expert. We talked briefly about Nosenko. He had just become involved with Golitsyn when Nosenko defected in the winter of 1964.

I asked, "Did Golitsyn know about Nosenko?"

"Know?" he replied coolly. "Golitsyn predicted the KGB would send a man out to discredit him in his first debriefing in January 1962." He pointed out that Nosenko had made his contact with Bagley that June. Nosenko, in turn, had been supported by the stories of a half-dozen other KGB "dangles"—including Fedora and Top Hat.

Miler explained that these Soviet dangles involved nothing more than "an exercise in experimentation—and patience." They worked on the same trial-and-error principle as the fly-fishing lure, he suggested. "If one fly doesn't work, you simply try another kind—until you get one that the fish you are after will snap at in a particular locale." He said that the Soviets had tried numerous lures. "They put one in our path in Paris earlier that year, a drunken diplomat. That didn't work. They then sent another to our embassy in Moscow, but that got screwed up. So they tried Nosenko." Unlike Angleton, who talked in metaphors, Miler didn't mince words. He came right to the point: "The KGB was afraid that Golitsyn could blow everything they were working on. If they couldn't kill him, they had to discredit him or at least muddy the waters. Nosenko, Fedora, Top Hat were all part of that mission."

While Bagley tried to break Nosenko, Angleton's staff focused on Golitsyn's secrets. To build up Golitsyn's confidence that he was now being taken seriously, Angleton arranged for him to brief Attorney General Robert F. Kennedy on the KGB threat. He also invited him to dinners where they would discuss Soviet politics into the early hours of the morning. He treated Golitsyn as a full intellectual partner, and to facilitate the rapport, he had Miler prepare sanitized copies of his prize "serials" for Golitsyn, and then allowed Golitsyn to search for connections between these clues from CIA cases that spanned two decades. He also took Golitsyn with him on trips to Europe and Israel to speak to allied intelligence executives. Golitsyn, encouraged by this attention, proposed organizing a new counterintelligence service outside the CIA.

Miler, meanwhile, was gradually drawing out Golitsyn on the subject of the putative leaks in American intelligence. Golitsyn insisted that the wealth of CIA material he had seen in KGB files could not have come from any single mole or source. He compared the Soviet penetration to a "cancer," saying, "When the patient refuses to recognize it exists, it grows and spreads, with bad cells infecting good cells." The "patient" in this case was both the FBI and the CIA. The "bad cells," he suggested in his analogy, had begun with the Army and CIA recruitment of Hitler's former intelligence officers. He asserted that the CIA had mistakenly assumed that their sources in Eastern Europe were not known to the Soviets, but, in reality, they had been compromised by Germans playing a double game. Instead of arresting these World War II traitors, the Soviets used them as bait to entice CIA case officers into situations where their careers could be jeopardized and they could be compromised. Some of these officers were then recruited, and they produced biographical data on other officers in the CIA, which helped the KGB play on their weaknesses. Golitsyn held that, by the time he had defected, the KGB had maneuvered its "inside men" into key positions in both the CIA's Soviet Division and the FBI's counterespionage office.

Angleton's interest, however, went well beyond the security problem arising from the recruitment of Western case officers by the KGB. He wanted to know why the KGB had focused its attention on particular units of the CIA, such as the operational side of the Soviet Division. The real issue to Angleton was what purposes these penetrations advanced.

Golitsyn explained that they were a necessary part of the deception machinery that had been in place in 1959. Their main job was to report back on how the CIA was evaluating material it was receiving from other KGB agents. With them in place, disinformation became a game of "show and tell" for the KGB. The dispatched defectors, double agents, and other provocateurs, who could be anyone from a Soviet diplomat to a touring scientist, "showed" the CIA a Soviet secret. Then its penetrations would tell the KGB how the CIA had interpreted it. This combination of an inside and outside man, a mole and a fake defector, allowed the KGB to continuously manipulate its adversary.

The immediate remedy was to find the penetrations. With the assistance of the CIA's Office of Security, which has responsibility for ferreting out moles, Angleton arranged a series of "marked cards" for the Soviet Division to test Golitsyn's assertion. The "marked card" is to counterintelligence what the barium test is to medical diagnosis. Information that can be followed, like a bent card, is passed through an intelligence channel to see where it ends up.

One "marked card" in Angleton's series was the exact time and place of a CIA approach made to a Soviet diplomat stationed in Ottawa, Canada. No one else knew about this "approach" except the unit in the Soviet Division to whom this card was passed. The meeting itself was a pure invention.

A surveillance crew was then placed in a position where they could watch the site without themselves being observed. Then, on the day of the contrived meeting, they recorded Soviet security officers watching the site from a car. So this marked card had wound up in the hands of the KGB.

Through a process of elimination, subsequent marked cards narrowed down the possible leak to a handful of CIA officers involved with recruiting REDTOPS and preparing reports on them. Yet, no matter how the cards were dealt out, no single individual could be pinpointed. This development suggested to Angleton that the Soviets had more than one mole in the Soviet Division.

Angleton, moreover, was convinced by these tests that the penetration was in continual contact with the KGB. Time after time, when the division was told about a new operation, the information seemed to reach Moscow in a matter of days. Nosenko himself seemed to have a means of updating his story—even though he was supposedly in isolation. Suspicion fell first on David Murphy. Could the chief of the Soviet Division be a Soviet agent? After he was transferred to Paris, Bagley was investigated and transferred. Five other division officers were considered as candidates for being the mole and reshuffled. Yet the leaks continued. The Philby problem, which had so affected Angleton in 1951, now seemed like just the outcropping of a far deeper phenomenon. Finally, in 1967, Angleton recommended to Helms that he temporarily cut the entire division out of sensitive cases. Helms reluctantly complied.

Angleton, finding that the Soviets were continuing their double-agent operation, advised that the CIA should operate on the premise that it would remain partially penetrated until Soviet methodology was better understood. This advice caused what Miler termed "real strains within the intelligence community."

By the time Miler had finished telling of this fallout from the Nosenko case, it seemed quite an understatement. By 1968, American intelligence was, as Helms described the situation, "a house divided against itself." The Soviet Division was paralyzed by charges and accusations over the Nosenko case. The FBI had broken off its liaison with the CIA. The British security service was in disarray, with its own Director under suspicion as a mole. German, French, and Dutch intelligence were rated "insecure" by the CIA. Pressure was building in the CIA to dissolve Angleton's staff. J. Edgar Hoover characterized Golitsyn as "paranoid" and a possible "provocateur." Why had all this tension flowed from this single defector?

I went back to Angleton for an answer. By then, it was the fall of 1982. He had just given up both smoking and drinking for health reasons and he seemed nervous, if not distracted. After telling him that I had seen his former colleagues, as if he didn't already know, I asked him why there had been so much animosity generated by Golitsyn.

Angleton explained, as if he had been waiting for the question, that Golitsyn delivered a message that the CIA, MI5, SDECE, and other Western intelligence services had great difficulties in accepting. It was that the primary mission of the KGB had been changed in 1959 from conventional espionage, or stealing other nations' state secrets, to an extraordinary form of covert statecraft, where it used its agents and other hidden mechanism to help achieve the geopolitical goals of the Soviet Union. The penetrations and double agents, according to Golitsyn, were all means to a political end. It was this search for political ends, not his revelations about moles, that touched on raw nerves.

These tensions began soon after Golitsyn returned to the United States. He broke off a meeting with Bagley during a discussion about Nosenko, claiming that Bagley, then deputy director of the Soviet Division, "did not begin to understand" what the KGB did.

Golitsyn also came into direct conflict with the division's Covert Action unit, which was writing a book to be issued under the name of Colonel Oleg Penkovsky, an officer in Soviet military intelligence. Colonel Penkovsky had been a double agent from 1961 to 1963 for the CIA and MI6. In 1962, he supplied the CIA with a cache of documents about Soviet rockets that helped the United States assess the military capabilities of the Soviet Union during the Cuban missile crisis that October. Soon after the crisis was resolved, Penkovsky was arrested publicly and presumably executed. Then, under the prodding of Attorney General Robert Kennedy, the CIA began preparing *The Penkovsky Papers*, which, when released as a commercial book, would purport to be a diary the colonel had kept of his spying activities. This project had tremendous support within the CIA because the "diary" would show how the CIA, by recruiting a Soviet colonel, helped President Kennedy accomplish a great triumph: getting Soviet missiles out of Cuba. Golitsyn provided information that undermined this project. He demonstrated, by diagraming hidden Soviet microphones in the U.S. Embassy in Moscow, that Penkovsky's early debriefing had to have been monitored by the KGB. Even if he had been a legitimate traitor then, Golitsyn argued, he would have been forced, in a deal that he could not refuse, to deliver the documents the Soviets wanted delivered to the CIA. He was, in other words, a Soviet postman at the time of the missile crisis.

Angleton agreed with this assessment. There was no question that at some point Penkovsky had come under Soviet control;

the question was when. MI6 counterintelligence meanwhile developed its own analysis pointing to the same conclusion. Even Bagley had doubts about the case.

But Golitsyn went further than merely supplying evidence that Penkovsky, who was about to be turned into an American hero, was a KGB fraud. He attempted to relate the "Penkovsky provocation," as he called it, to a "political end." He suggested that the Penkovsky messages were used to provoke and control the reactions of the Kennedy administration. The missiles were put in Cuba to be bargained away. Khrushchev's strategical goal—manipulating President Kennedy into giving up the Monroe Doctrine by accepting a hostile regime in Cuba, allied with the Soviet Union—had been achieved, according to Golitsyn. The assertion that the United States had lost, not won, did not sit well with the CIA executives who had managed the Penkovsky case—and the book (which became a best-seller in 1966).

Tensions were racheted up nearly to breaking point when in 1964 Golitsyn focused suspicions about British Prime Minister Harold Wilson. The problem began in January 1963, when Hugh Gaitskell, the leader of the right wing of the British Labor Party, died unexpectedly at the age of fifty-six of a rare form of lupus infection. His doctor became suspicious because the symptoms appeared just after Gaitskell had ingested coffee and cookies at the Soviet Consulate in London, and he informed MI5, which brought the case to the CIA's attention. It then developed that Soviet scientists had been experimenting on rats with this particular lupus virus.

Angleton asked Golitsyn whether it was possible that the KGB would engage in this form of political assassination. Golitsyn, after all, had contact in Moscow with the KGB's Department Thirteen, which undertook assassination missions.

"I've already answered that question," Golitsyn said. He referred Angleton back to his original briefing in 1962, which took place before Gaitskell was assassinated.

It turned out, to the amazement of Angleton's staff, that Golitsyn was right. Although it may have seemed of little relevance at the time, Golitsyn had explicitly told his debriefer in 1962 that the KGB was in the process of organizing special actions, including untraceable assassinations. The purpose was to advance Soviet agents of influence in selected European democracies. He also had related how, just before he defected, he had been told by the chief of the Northern European Division of the KGB that "General Rodin" was involved in such an operation. He wasn't sure whether it was to be in England or a Scandinavian country.

Angleton immediately ran a "trace" on Rodin. He was identified as a top officer in the KGB's Department Thirteen. Even more disturbing to Angleton, Rodin was, at the time of Gaitskell's visit to the Soviet Consulate, stationed in London.

Golitsyn, when requestioned by Angleton, recalled that he was also told by his chief that the objective was the elimination of an "opposition leader." He reasoned that since Gaitskell was the main opposition to Harold Wilson's leadership of the Labor Party, Wilson would have been, in the eyes of the KGB, the intended beneficiary of the plot. He suggested further, based on his experience, that the KGB would carry out such an intervention in only two circumstances: first, if Wilson was their man, or, second, if someone in Wilson's entourage was their man.

Angleton opened a file on the British Prime Minister, code-named "Oatsheaf." He concentrated on the activities of Wilson's close associates who had made frequent business trips to Moscow. He found out, through his liaison with the National Security Agency, that when these men were in Moscow, some of their telephone conversations from hotels and limousines had been routinely intercepted. An analysis of these intercepts showed that they had been in contact with well-known KGB case officers. This connection was not in itself incriminating, since Soviet officials put in contact with important Western visitors are often KGB recruiters. But two of these businessmen had become part of Wilson's entourage.

Angleton decided to pass on his Oatsheaf file to the Director of MI5 in case they had additional material on these two advisers. He expected a discreet investigation into the backgrounds of these two associates of Wilson. Instead, he found MI5 was "out of control." Some MI5 officers, including those who opposed Wilson's politics, demanded that he be put under surveillance. Others were appalled at the idea that British intelligence would spy on a Prime Minister. In the end, MI5, after going through this crisis, rejected the proposed investigation.

I understood why the bearer of such messages would not be popular with intelligence agencies, or the governments he served. He was a disturber of the peace. What I found more difficult to understand was why he had presented such a radically different view of the KGB from other sources.

Angleton replied that Golitsyn had been one of a small group of young analysts in a KGB "think tank" who prepared the plans for the massive reorganization of Soviet intelligence that took place in 1959. Aleksandr Shelepin, who then became Chairman of the KGB, was given the mandate to return the KGB to the political mission it originally had under Lenin. Whereas Soviet intelligence had become, under Stalin, an organization mainly concerned with maintaining state security, which involved it in purging dissidents, protecting secrets, and preventing the CIA from recruiting sources, it now was to become an organization capable of manipulating the actions of the United States. Its model was to be the Trust, according to what Shelepin told Golitsyn. This radical change meant that conventional espionage was to be subordinated to deception goals. Rather than blocking contacts with the West, the new KGB would allow the CIA and other Western services to recruit agents, dissidents, and other sources of secrets. But it would use these channels to pass disinformation messages.

Golitsyn's think tank realized that this design, as plausible as it might appear on paper, in practice contained an intrinsic, and potentially dangerous, weakness. KGB officers had to be in continuous contact with CIA officers, either as bait to attract their attention, as postmen to deliver messages, or as double agents pretending to defect. This gave the CIA the opportunity to compromise, entrap, recruit, or even drug the disinformation agent.

The answer it came up with, which then became part of the "Shelepin Plan," was to divide Soviet intelligence into two distinct entities: an outer and an inner KGB.

The "outer" KGB was made up of personnel who, of necessity, had to be in contact with foreigners and were therefore vulnerable to being compromised. It included KGB recruiters and spotters posted to embassies and missions, military attachés, propaganda agents, and case officers who worked abroad. Since they had to be in touch with Westerners, if only to attempt to recruit them as spies, they were assumed to be "doomed spies." A certain percentage of them, by the law of probability, would be compromised—and talk. Golitsyn compared "doomed spies" to pilots sent on raids over enemy territory during World War II who not only were restricted from knowing any state secrets but were purposefully misbriefed in case they were captured and interrogated.

The "inner" KGB was to be where the deceptions were planned, orchestrated, and assessed. It was limited to a small number of trusted officers, under the direct supervision of the Politburo, who planned, orchestrated, controlled, and analyzed the operations. Potential security risks, including officers of Jewish descent, were transferred into the outer service in preparation for the reorganization.

A "China Wall" existed between these two levels. No personnel from the outer service would ever be transferred to the inner service, or vice versa. Nor would any personnel in the outer service ever be exposed to strategic secrets other than what had been prepared for them to divulge as disinformation.

"Consider the implications," Angleton said, pausing for effect.

"If Golitsyn was correct, it meant that we knew virtually nothing about the KGB's capacity for deception."

The idea of two KGBs was indeed staggering. It meant that many targets the CIA were going after as potential recruits—including diplomats, military attachés, journalists, dissidents, and intelligence officers—had little useful information or had been deliberately misbriefed, like World War II pilots. All they would have access to, aside from trivial details about their own espionage apparatus, was disinformation. The same would be true of many "walk-in" defectors. And it meant that the microphones the CIA planted in Soviet embassies would be also eavesdropping on diplomats excluded from the real strategic secrets of the inner KGB. Seen through the new perspective provided by Golitsyn, the KGB turned out to be a different and much more dangerous instrument of Soviet policy.

"It would be impossible to understand the KGB without understanding what changed in this reorganization," Angleton said. He referred me to a 1200-page manuscript that Golitsyn had written, explaining that it was based on a report Golitsyn had prepared for the CIA in 1969. He then added that he could arrange for me to read it.

I spent nearly a week reading the Golitsyn manuscript. It was a remarkably convoluted piece of scholarship. It traced out, in excruciating detail, the multitudinous preparations that had to be made in the Soviet government, the Communist Party, the KGB, and foreign liaison services to facilitate the 1959 reorganization. Golitsyn moved in his narrative, layer by layer, through all the hidden corridors of the Soviet apparatus. He described the personnel that was transferred, the offices that were relocated, and the cover stories that were released to obscure these moves from Western eyes.

What became clear to me as I read through this typescript was that Golitsyn had finally provided Angleton with the great white whale he had been searching for ever since the Philby episode. Yet, over the years, the CIA sources produced no real signs of any Leviathan Soviet deception. Now, with the 1959 reorganization, Angleton had an explanation why it had failed to surface. Like Captain Ahab, Angleton continued to search in an endless sea of data for this Soviet deception—until he was fired in 1974.

CHAPTER SIX

The Last Days of Angleton

On November 9, 1979, when a mob of Iranian students broke into the American Embassy in Teheran, CIA security guards desperately rushed to shred the voluminous classified directives, telegraphs, and other secret memoranda from Washington that had been stored in the intelligence vault there for twenty years. They failed, however, to adequately destroy most of them because the embassy, for financial reasons, used low-budget shredders that cut the paper in only one direction. Iranian women, skilled at weaving Persian carpets, were able to piece most of them back together, though it took over two years of eye-straining work. The Iranian government then published these "Documents from the U.S. Espionage Den" in sixty volumes. The result was that for the first time in history a secret archive of CIA records was made public without its consent. Unlike the material the CIA voluntarily releases, under its own name or through briefed defectors it has put in contact with journalists, these internal directives show the actual method used by the CIA over the years to recruit spies within Soviet bloc governments.

I had never seen anything like these documents. Some were stamped not only SECRET and TOP SECRET but with such exotic labels as NOFORN, which meant they could not be shown to any foreign national whatsoever, not even an allied service; NOCONTRACT, which meant they could not be shown to CIA subcontractors; and ORCON, which meant that they could not be shown to anyone even within the CIA without the written approval of the unit in the CIA that had prepared them. These documents discussed the nitty-gritty of the CIA's espionage business. It was a secret universe in which American diplomats were precisely instructed to report their Soviet counterparts' dining habits, children's schooling, hobbies, sexual proclivities, and even their chronic medical ailments; in which Americans were chosen on their language "fit," medical training, or even height to serve as witting or unwitting "access agents" to steer targeted diplomats into contacts with CIA recruiters; and in which new clandestine skills, such as using invisible ink or other secret chemicals, were taught like school subjects.

I was particularly intrigued by one ORCON, NOFORN directive that had been sent by the chief of the CIA's Soviet Russia Division in January 1973. It was a six-page document entitled "Turning Around REDTOP Walk-ins."* From the context, it was clear that REDTOPS was the CIA's shorthand name for Soviet bloc officials. It directed CIA stations in American embassies abroad to recruit them as spies rather than allowing them to defect, noting that the CIA, through a unit code-named BK HERALD:

> can and does run many resident agents inside the REDTOP countries. We have the capability to mount and support such operations over an indefinite period, and we currently are able to exfiltrate agents, in most cases with their families, from the REDTOP countries when it is time for them to leave.

If the REDTOP was not working where he had access to secrets of interest to the United States, it noted:

> we are prepared to guide and assist him in his career [in the Soviet government], running him in place until he develops the access we need. Our ultimate objective is to have the walk-

*See Appendix B.

in return to his home country and continue his agent relationship while working inside.

Angleton read the directive I had brought him with apparent interest. He was always interested in knowing what had leaked out into the "public realm," as he called the non-clandestine world, if only because it expanded the areas he could discuss.

"What is BK HERALD?" I asked, as Angleton put the document down.

"That is of no importance, it is just a code name that changes all the time," he answered in an impatient tone. "It is the part of the CIA that works against the Soviet bloc."

"By 'work,' do you mean espionage?" I asked.

He nodded, explaining that "espionage tends to be a much unappreciated form of knowledge." It aims not just at acquiring secrets but in doing so in such a way that the theft cannot be anticipated, detected after the fact, or therefore remedied. If it succeeds with this double job, it produces what Angleton called "unexpected intelligence."

In practice, there is only one way that an espionage service can both steal documents and cover all traces of the theft. It must recruit an agent who has legitimate access to the secret data. As Angleton described it, "He must be able to enter the room where it is kept and copy it, without arousing suspicion." Similarly, in the case of intercepted conversations, the agent must be in a position to plant an electronic bugging device—and retrieve it—unnoticed. These requirements usually could be filled only by an enemy national with impressive enough credentials to pass through his own security. In the case of the Soviet bloc, this means a trusted government official has to be secretly hired.

"Think of an espionage service as a highly specialized employment service," Angleton suggested. Like the more conventional "headhunters," an espionage service determines the positions that need to be filled, consults its biographical files, which are well stocked with resumes and photographs, selects potential candidates, and then approaches them with offers that they find either tempting or exceedingly difficult to refuse. But since, unlike their counterparts in the private sectors, these recruiters are asking government officials not merely to change their loyalties to their employers but to betray their nations, they must keep secret the real job they have in mind for the candidates until after they are employed. So they may have to work under an elaborate disguise, or "false flag." The other difference is that when a candidate accepts the offer, he is not allowed to quit his present employer. Instead, as explained in the 1973 BK HERALD directive, he is encouraged to work at two jobs simultaneously: one for his own government and one for his new employer.

Angleton explained that this espionage task is far less difficult than it might seem to an "outsider." It is based on the premise that whereas few individuals would elect to commit treason if they knew what they were doing, not everyone can resist breaking minor rules and regulations when presented with the right set of temptations. It involves not a single conscious decision to betray state secrets but an incremental entrapment. What Angleton called "a subtle web of irresistible compromises."

It took me over a month to finish reading the CIA documents in the Teheran Archive. They illuminated more than the arcane techniques of espionage. When read in chronological order, these documents reveal the extraordinary revisions that took place in 1973, revisions so radical that they appeared to be nothing less than a conceptual revolution in the way that the CIA envisioned its enemy—and itself.

It began in January 1973, when Richard Helms left as the Director of Central Intelligence, and William E. Colby, as executive comptroller, took charge of the Directorate of Plans—which is the clandestine side of the CIA. Colby, who had come from the covert action side of the CIA, not secret intelligence, and who had headed the CIA's Pacification Program in Vietnam, almost immediately instituted a switch in the CIA's policy determining how Soviet bloc officials were recruited.

Up until 1973, CIA directives had assumed that Soviet intelligence services commonly used "provocations." In practice, this meant that Soviet Embassy officials who approached American intelligence officers offering to sell or give away Soviet secrets had some probability of being KGB-controlled dangles. The danger was that they could lead the CIA on a wild-goose chase, expose its sources or methods, or simply embarrass it by contriving an incident. The CIA had thus previously required in its instructions that the bona fides of a REDTOP walk-in be established before he was treated as a source of intelligence.

This procedure was explicitly defined in "Director of Central Intelligence Directive 4/2," signed by Allen Dulles. It states:

> The establishment of bona fides of disaffected persons will be given particular attention because of the demonstrated use of defector channels by hostile services to penetrate or convey false or deceptive information to U.S. Intelligence services.

Since 1954, that responsibility for determining "bona fides" had been assigned to Angleton's counterintelligence staff. Now, however, this doctrine was reversed. The top secret directive entitled "Turning Around REDTOP Walk-ins" was telexed to all CIA stations on January 3, 1973. It ordered that REDTOPS, primarily Soviet bloc diplomats, intelligence officers, and military attachés, be treated differently. It explained:

> Analysis of REDTOP walk-ins in recent years clearly indicates that REDTOP services have not been seriously using sophisticated and serious walk-ins as a provocation technique. However, fear of provocations has been more responsible for bad handling than any other cause. We have concluded that we do ourselves a disservice if we shy away from promising cases because of fear of provocation.
>
> We are confident that we are capable of determining

whether or not a producing agent is supplying bona fide information.

This new policy meant that case officers in the Soviet Bloc Division could make REDTOP recruitments that were not dependent on any prior determination of whether they were provocateurs or not. The assumption was that the value of a "producing agent" could be established from the information he himself furnished.

Further, these new directives reflected a confidence in the CIA's ability to run networks inside the Soviet Union. Previously, the CIA had considered such contacts behind enemy lines to be a dangerous enterprise. Not only did the KGB maintain a full-court press of surveillance, especially around the embassy, but it was known to use double agents to entrap intermediaries who might be used as couriers. But now it appeared the CIA believed it could use these untested REDTOP volunteers as "resident agents" in Moscow. The Soviet Division chief advised all stations: "We have the capability to mount and support such operations over an indefinite period, and we currently are able to exfiltrate agents, in most cases with their families, from the REDTOP countries when it is time for them to leave."

This new confidence seemed to completely override the concerns about Soviet deception. Why did the CIA now believe that REDTOP volunteers were no longer dangles? How could it accept their information, even if it perfectly dovetailed with other such intelligence, if the CIA still believed the KGB had the capacity of orchestrating disinformation messages so that they would appear credible? How could the CIA run networks in Moscow if it still believed that the KGB had penetrations in its Soviet Bloc Division? And why had the job of assessing bona fides been taken away from Angleton's counterintelligence staff? What had happened to Golitsyn?

I decided to raise these questions along with the chronology with Angleton. He had invited me to dine with him at his Army Navy Club in Washington, where he took great pride in the fact that he had held the rank of major in the Army during the brief interregnum between the end of the OSS and creation of the CIA.

I brought the documents from the Teheran Archive with me. When I began to read him the relevant passages from these CIA directives, he stopped me mid-sentence, as if he feared these once top secret words would be overheard. "I'm familiar with those directives."

I asked him what had happened in 1973 to make the CIA so abruptly alter its appreciation of the KGB. "Was there a coup d'état at the CIA?"

"It was more a coup de grâce," he said with a quick chuckle. "It certainly ended the battle over epistemology—for me."

By "epistemology," he meant the theory which allows an investigator to believe that information is either true or false. He explained that in other fields, such as biology, the investigator can safely assume that what he sees through a microscope has not been put there for his benefit (although he might, in keeping with Heisenberg's uncertainty principle, assume that the observer had an effect on the observee). But in the business of secret intelligence an investigator cannot automatically make that assumption. Spies, unlike microbes, do conspire at times to dupe outside observers.

Angleton conceived of deception as the "mirror image of intelligence." They were so closely related that they were like identical twins. The resemblance between these twins was no accident. As Angleton had pointed out with orchids, deception must mimic reality enough to be accepted. Both had the same superficial appearance in what they produced, whether it was a photocopied document, an intercepted conversation, or a report from a defector. Both had the same provenance. And both claimed to have defected from the same parent—the enemy. What made one of these twins legitimate and the other illegitimate was a quality that was not readily ascertainable: the enemy's state of mind. If the enemy was unaware that this information had been taken and turned over, it was bona fide intelligence. But if the enemy had intended it to be turned over, it was disinformation.

An intelligence service works in this view as a kind of adoption service. It attempts to pick out the legitimate twin, provide it with its certificate of genuineness, and then nurture it as a source of information. If it succeeds in choosing the right one, its government will be acting on intelligence that its adversary does not know it possesses. If it fails and chooses the wrong twin, it will become the unwitting ally of its enemy in passing disinformation to its own government. The problem that Angleton had wrestled with for two decades was this crucial choice: How could the CIA know with certainty that secrets it had stolen from its Soviet sources had not been made purposely available to it, to provoke and mislead the American government?

Angleton believed that information could not be its own test. Its validity as intelligence depended on "control," which meant whether or not the Soviets knew the secret had been passed to the CIA. And "control" could only be determined by tracing, and logically testing, every turn in the path the information took in getting to the CIA. In other words, in Angleton's epistemology, the container as well as the contents had to be investigated. This was the issue that had split the CIA into warring camps.

Others in the CIA, such as those Soviet Division executives who wrote the 1973 directive, had a far less complex epistemological approach. They believed that intelligence could be distinguished from deception by judging how well it fit in with other intelligence reports. If it neatly dovetailed with other reports, it was assumed to be valid intelligence.

Angleton traced the dispute back to 1964, when Nosenko was imprisoned and interrogated by the Soviet Division. He had opposed this "hostile interrogation," he explained, not because he believed Nosenko was a legitimate defector, but because he considered it advantageous that the KGB believe Nosenko had been accepted. He viewed Nosenko simply as a Soviet postman, delivering a message. He assumed that he would not have been dispatched on such a mission by the KGB if it did not have an "inside man" in the CIA to feed back to it the CIA's assessment of Nosenko. He had hoped to play the game out, seeing where it might lead.

But Bagley, Murphy, and others in the Soviet Division refused to go along with this cat and mouse game. They believed that they could psychologically break Nosenko and force him to confess he was a disinformation agent. By doing that, they would have settled the epistemology question to their own satisfaction. They would have demonstrated that they were fully capable of telling the good from the counterfeit by brute force.

When his incarceration failed to produce the desired result, the Director, Richard Helms, was left with the incubus, and the messy problem of what to do with a suspect defector. The Soviet Division had divided into factions on this question. Bagley wanted to return him to Russia. Others, especially those in the Report Section who wanted to use the information he had provided, argued that if he turned out to have been a real defector and the Soviets executed him, the CIA would have blood on its hands (as it did in the case of an earlier Polish defector it returned).

Helms finally cut the Gordian knot in 1967 by ordering Nosenko to be "rehabilitated," and assigned the job to the Office of Security, not the Soviet Division. He also ordered, to satisfy Angleton, that all information from Nosenko be labeled that the source was still suspect. To avoid any leaks to the press of the imprisonment, he decided to put Nosenko under contract as a counterintelligence consultant and to pay him for the years he spent in a vault. This compensation rubbed still more salt in the open wounds of Bagley and his supporters—all of whom were transferred out of the division. Bagley groused, when he heard about the payoff: "Nosenko, who came to the CIA at the direction of the KGB, had received $160,000 for deceiving the CIA, while the division officers who had exposed him had been given early retirement, with pensions of one tenth that sum." Their replacements, most of whom were brought in from Vietnam, coined the term "sick think" to describe their colleagues who still believed Nosenko was part of a Soviet deception.

Meanwhile the Golitsyn thesis, which was being developed by the counterintelligence staff, was bringing the epistemological question to a very ugly head. It held that because of the 1959 reorganization, even legitimate defectors and double agents unwittingly could be supplying disinformation if they were excluded from the inner KGB. Golitsyn specifically identified the Soviet bloc UN diplomats, embassy staffs, and military attachés who had been the main target for CIA and FBI recruitment as the group with the least likelihood of having access to real secrets. This view, if accepted, had serious implications for the case officers who had recruited more than a half-dozen Soviet bloc diplomats at the United Nations who claimed to have access to strategic secrets. If they could not have had such access, as Golitsyn asserted, they had to be redefined as disinformation agents. This made the CIA case officers, who had built careers on these sources since 1960, accomplices, albeit unwitting, of Soviet deception planners. And it converted information that had been passed upward to the President into disinformation. In this new light, heroes became villains and victories became defeats. It was the equivalent of, as Angleton put it "stepping through a looking glass."

At the FBI, the Golitsyn thesis was rejected out of hand by J. Edgar Hoover. He had Fedora and Top Hat to think about, both of whom were recruited after the reorganization. They not only claimed that they had access to secrets from the decision-making level of the Politburo, but they furnished them on demand to the FBI. Hoover had personally passed some of this material directly to Lyndon Baines Johnson—he was not about to accept an interpretation that would render this data KGB disinformation. He suggested that the KGB had sent Golitsyn to discredit the FBI. He then refused any further cooperation with the CIA aimed at substantiating Golitsyn's story, even going so far as to withdraw an FBI surveillance team that had been watching a suspect round-the-clock on behalf of the CIA. Eventually, as the recriminations over Golitsyn increased, Hoover broke off all liaison relations with the CIA, which, as Angleton conceded, "damaged" him, since until then his close relations with FBI counterintelligence had been one of his main sources of power in the CIA. Ironically, in 1978, after Hoover's death, events proved Golitsyn was right—at least about Fedora. After it was determined by the FBI that the Soviets had to know Fedora was supplying the FBI with Soviet secrets, he returned to the Soviet Union and received a promotion, which caused the FBI to conclude he had been a KGB-controlled disinformation agent during the years he was supposedly working under FBI control.

The Soviet Division also took strong exception to the Golitsyn thesis, which defined much of its conventional intelligence-gathering process, such as debriefing agents and defectors, as a likely channel for Soviet disinformation. When Bagley wrote his 900-page report on Nosenko, he questioned whether Golitsyn could be believed on information which was not in his original debriefing by the division but which was later developed by the counterintelligence staff. He tried to separate the "vintage" from the "diluted" Golitsyn—especially as it pertained to Nosenko. Angleton strongly objected to this section of the report, which Bagley eventually excised in the final version. The frustration of these division officers was intensified by the secrecy surrounding the dispute. Few of them were briefed on the Golitsyn thesis. All they knew was that their work was being called into question by Angleton and his staff. It had, from their point of view, all but paralyzed normal intelligence operations.

Meanwhile, Angleton was being pressed by Helms to show some "positive results" with Golitsyn. Helms pointed out that he had given Angleton the money and resources he had requested but the result had been more a "mouse" than the expected "elephant." He suggested the test of the investigation should be utility. Could Golitsyn's thesis be used to identify the deceptions of the Kremlin?

Golitsyn himself had never claimed to have participated in any of the actual deception planning. He had only seen the mechanism for executing it being put in place. He did recall, however, that Shelepin gave a lecture in 1958 explaining how the deception machinery could be used to create fake "splits" between members of the Communist bloc. The United States would then be drawn into believing that by helping one side, it could weaken the Soviet Union. After that lecture, Shelepin let it slip that China would be the perfect candidate for such a deception.

Angleton's staff immediately began exploring the Sino-Soviet split that had developed in 1960, just after the KGB reorganization. Could it be a sham, designed to throw the West off balance? The National Security Agency meanwhile produced intercepts, which Golitsyn could not have known about, showing that Soviet intelligence was picking up U.S. bomber data through its space satellites and then relaying it to Chinese intelligence. Using an electronic form of the "marked card" technique, the NSA was able to trace this information moving from the Soviets to the Chinese and then from the Chinese to the North Vietnamese. This evidence meant only that the Soviet Union and China, during the Vietnam War, were coordinating activities on behalf of their mutual ally, North Vietnam. But Angleton took it a step further. He reasoned that if the KGB was able to work with the Chinese in this area, it could do the same in other areas. He asked Golitsyn to set out in writing the case that the Sino-Soviet schism was a strategic deception.

It took Golitsyn until 1968 to draw together all the bits and pieces of evidence. He concluded that the deception he had heard vaguely about a decade earlier was now actually in effect.

Then Helms assembled a committee of Soviet and Chinese experts to hear his case. They were, to put it mildly, unimpressed with Golitsyn's evidence. When various experts pressed him about his theories, he became "overly defensive," as Angleton explained it, and he shouted back demanding to know what evidence they had for disputing his theories. The meeting ended acrimoniously. More important, in the years since Golitsyn had first mentioned the Shelepin lecture, world events moved in a direction that confirmed that the split was real, not fake. There was, for example, a border war between Chinese and Soviet troops on the Ussari River.

Nevertheless, Angleton continued to search for evidence to support Golitsyn. Finally, in 1969, Helms called him into his office and told him that it was now the policy of the Nixon White House not only to accept the Sino-Soviet split as a reality but to exploit it by seeking a détente with China. He was told "in polite terms: drop Golitsyn."

Angleton, who had survived in the CIA bureaucracy for fifteen years by now, understood that Helms, his last real ally, was losing patience. Golitsyn had not produced the promised results. He had to be put out to pasture with a part-time consulting arrangement.

Angleton knew that his own days were numbered when on November 20, 1972, President Nixon asked for the resignation of Helms. Colby, who was now acting executive Director, had been the subject of one of Angleton's counterintelligence investigations, and he made no secret of his animosity. He had little experience in secret intelligence, as opposed to covert actions. He made it clear to Angleton that he rejected Angleton's complicated view of KGB strategic deception. He saw the job of the CIA as a straightforward one of gathering intelligence for the President. He felt that the KGB should not be the focus of CIA operations, that deception was a technical, not a strategical problem. And as far as epistemology was concerned, he had faith that the CIA's polygraph tests could detect false defectors and KGB-controlled double agents.

Colby went to the new Director, James Schlesinger, a professor, who had been Nixon's budget director. He recommended that he fire Angleton, and laid out the case against him.

Schlesinger then called Angleton into his office and went through the criticism of him point by point. Schlesinger told Angleton that Colby had accused him of being overly secretive and having a conspiratorial approach. He blamed Angleton, moreover, for confusing and demoralizing the Soviet Division. On balance, Colby concluded that Angleton's relentless suspicions of Soviet infiltration had proven "more of a liability than an asset."

Angleton, assuming he had been fired, made no effort to rebut this attack. He also recognized that part of it was true. He was secretive; his ideas were complicated and convoluted, with many cunning passages, trapdoors, and contrived corridors—he would say, paraphrasing Eliot's "Gerontion." If they were impenetrable to outsiders, or even his own staff, that was how he dealt with deception as a state of mind. And he had paralyzed the Soviet Division—on purpose.

Just as he prepared to leave the room, Schlesinger called him back. He asked him, almost as a matter of courtesy, what he viewed as the difficulty at the CIA.

Angleton said deferentially that it would take quite some time to even describe the problem—much less the solution. The new director then lit his pipe and beckoned him to sit down. Angleton began talking about the nature of secret intelligence: its epistemology, its vulnerability, and its ultimate value. Three hours went by.

When Angleton emerged from the Director's office, he had not been fired as counterintelligence chief. He had now become the adviser to Schlesinger—just as he had become the adviser to Bedell Smith, Allen Dulles, John McCone, and Richard Helms.

Angleton's reprieve was shortlived. Schlesinger served only four months in the CIA (although he remained close to Angleton afterward and was one of the first to arrive at his memorial service), before he was replaced as Director by Colby.

Colby would not be seduced by Angleton's ideas or his epistemology. Nor had he forgotten Angleton's investigating of his contacts in Vietnam. He realized that Angleton still had vestiges of power—especially in his 180-man counterintelligence staff, some of whose officers had worked with Angleton since the poetry magazine *Furioso* at Yale. He therefore moved expeditiously to reduce the reach and size of Angleton's counterintelligence staff. He first took away its job of determining bona fides, complaining that in the past the CIA had spent an inordinate amount of time worrying about false defectors and false agents. He then began cutting down its liaison duties with other intelligence services—particularly Israel. These liaisons, which Angleton had developed over twenty years, provided him with what was tantamount to his own intelligence service. He could informally suggest an investigation to SDECE, MI6, or Mossad—and they passed the results on to him. Colby also began a reorganization of units and departments that not only undermined Angleton's position in the CIA but made his counterintelligence staff largely superfluous.

During this period of declining power, Angleton had been shaken by the death of his father, Hugh. His ulcer got worse, forcing him into the hospital time and again. His work also lapsed—as Colby stripped him of his mystery.

Finally, in December 20, 1974, Colby found a way to dispose of Angleton that would leave him without any comeback. Seymour Hersh of *The New York Times*, who had been investigating the illicit activities of the CIA, had requested an interview with him. He called him into his office and in response to his questions, confirmed his suspicions. He acknowledged that the CIA had arranged in the late 1950s to open letters mailed from the Soviet Union to American citizens, and named Angleton as the man who had been responsible for this mail-opening program.

Colby next summoned Angleton to his office. He told him that the *Times* was about to publish a damaging story about the mail-opening program, and when this information became public he could no longer afford to have Angleton in the CIA. He asked for Angleton's resignation on the spot. He wanted him out of the Agency before Christmas.

The purge had finally happened. Rocca, Miler, and most of his staff were forced to resign. Major revisions followed, with many of the suspected defectors and double agents accepted as bona fide sources. The "serials" Angleton had labored over were locked in a safe and later, as Miler reported to Angleton, "systematically shredded." (Even the word "disinformation" was subtly redefined; instead of meaning the manipulation of a nation's intelligence system through the injection of credible but misleading data, it came to mean the manipulation of newspapers and television through propaganda.)

When Angleton left the CIA on Christmas Eve, true to his orders, he fashioned three white feathers as symbols of cowardice. He planned to give them to the three top CIA executives under Colby, who had actually authorized and run the mail-opening program that he had been only nominally responsible for. They had allowed Angleton to take the blame. He looked at the feathers and decided instead to use them as fishing lures. The battle within the CIA thus ended without a whimper.

Angleton wanted to hear no more about Washington—or the CIA. He left for the Arizona Desert, abandoning his prize-winning orchids and letting his greenhouse in Virginia fall into disrepair. That next year he went on a long solitary trip to a fishing camp high on the Matapédia River in New Brunswick, Canada. He took with him his collection of over two hundred fishing lures, some of them given to Angleton by Bedell Smith in the early days of the CIA, but most of them painstakingly designed by him. Like all lures, they were meant to misrepresent reality in a way that would trigger a response in the target. He caught more than a dozen salmon. Then he went back to Washington. It was not long after he returned that I first called him, and told him I was interviewing Nosenko.

• • •

Over the next ten years, I would see Angleton whenever I went to Washington in the course of my research. He did not take well to retirement. He continued to testify before congressional subcommittees on counterintelligence but soon lost contact with the new CIA—or so he claimed. He had become involved in publishing a newsletter for retired intelligence officers, but that seemed much more a way of remaining in contact with his old friends than a full-time enterprise. I began to realize how much time he had on his hands when one of our lunches at the Madison Hotel continued on so long that, when the waiters began setting up the buffet for dinner, Angleton suggested we stay. It was the longest meal I ever had. Angleton could be extraordinarily precise, as he was that day (and night), but his stories rarely had a conventional beginning—or end. They were more like peeling away the layers of an onion. What I wanted to learn from Angleton concerned the subject he had raised with Schlesinger: deception. What he called "a state of mind; the mind of the state." Why was it such an intractable problem for American intelligence?

At one lunch in a small French restaurant in a shopping center in Virginia, he brought along a picture from a book of experiments in Gestalt psychology that illustrated what he considered to be the problem. It showed an image that could be seen one of two ways: One either saw the profiles of two heads or one saw a wine cup. It depended on "one's mind-set," he explained. If one expected the heads, they popped into focus; if one expected the wine cup, it appeared. But a person could not hold both pictures in his mind at the same time; they were mutually exclusive concepts. The point applied equally to seeing intelligence or deception in a world picture.

He explained that ordinary standards of evidence cannot be applied to much of the information the CIA receives from inside the Soviet bloc. It is a "denied area," where often it is not possible for American case officers to meet, much less test, the ultimate sources in their chains of agents. What emerges in Washington from the darkness is copies of Soviet state documents and reports of what high-level Soviet officials have said in private. The crucial issue is whether these documents and private conversations from the Soviet inner sanctum represent legitimate intelligence or disinformation. If the material has been intercepted without the knowledge of the KGB, it is considered intelligence; if it has been passed through this chain with the knowledge of the KGB, it is considered disinformation. What separates intelligence from disinformation is nothing more than an assumption about the enemy's state of awareness—an assumption always open to question in the secret world.

As a practical matter, Angleton found in the CIA that a "single mind-set" could not deal with this contingent reality. Like the picture of the two faces—or wine cup—the CIA tended to see the stream of data coming from Russia as either intelligence or deception; but not both. Whatever mode it chose would determine how it interpreted both past and future evidence. The real danger was that the CIA would become trapped in the wrong "mind-set."

The remedy he had proposed in 1954 was for the CIA to have what would amount to two separate mind-sets. His counterintelligence staff would provide the alternative view of the picture. Whereas the Soviet Division might see a Soviet diplomat as a possible CIA mole, the counterintelligence staff would view him as a possible disinformation agent. What division case officers would tend to look at as valid information, furnished by Soviet sources who risked their lives to cooperate with them, counterintelligence officers tended to question as disinformation, provided by KGB-controlled sources. This was, as Angleton put it, "a necessary duality."

I could see why this concept would appeal to every Director from Bedell Smith to James Schlesinger. It was their insurance policy, even though the premium they paid in terms of conflicts and disputed intelligence might be high. It provided a way of guarding the CIA against the nightmare that it would be made an instrument of its enemy. But why had Colby rejected it?

"Colby said he couldn't see the problem," Angleton answered. "Colby believed that the CIA had the technological ability to weed out disinformation—with its satellites, computers, and polygraphs." It could be done by a single mind-set in the Soviet Division, without competition from the counterintelligence. "Colby believed what he wanted to believe. I was fired," Angleton concluded.

Angleton's interest in the "wilderness of mirrors" did not end. He continued to develop and refine his theory of deception, even after he learned in the spring of 1986 that he had incurable lung cancer—and probably less than a year to live.

CHAPTER SEVEN

The Theory of Perfect Deception

In his last years, Angleton saw very little possibility of a nuclear war between the superpowers. The destructive power of these weapons had all but precluded the use of force.

If so, why did the invisible war between the CIA and KGB, which had obsessed him for a quarter of century, matter? What real consequences did deception have for the nuclear world? When I pressed him about these questions, he shrugged and suggested that I read a thin book on Chinese strategy. It was Lionel Giles's translation of Sun-tzu's treatise, *The Art of War*. Since the treatise had been written over two thousand years ago, I took this recommendation as simply another one of Angleton's evasions—until I read the book.

Unlike modern military texts that set out tactics for winning through combat, Sun-tzu argued that the highest form of the art of war is winning without fighting a single armed battle. Victory was achieved by exhausting an adversary's resources, dividing the loyalty of its people, demoralizing its leadership, and ultimately "breaking the enemy's resistance." To achieve this objective, Sun-tzu outlined a system for so misleading a leader about his opponent's capabilities and intentions that he would be completely unprepared to deal with the reality of the situation. It was based on pure deception. He advises: "When able to attack, seem unable; when active, seem inactive; when near, make the

105

enemy believe you are far; when far away, make him believe you are near; when organized, feign disorder; if weak, pretend to be strong, and so cause the enemy to avoid you; when strong, pretend to be weak, so that the enemy may grow to be arrogant."

Sun-tzu recognized that for such deceptions to decisively reshape an enemy's image, it was not enough to stage temporary effects, such as phony campfires, or supply the enemy with disinformation, which he called "false tidings." It was also necessary to control the enemy's own intelligence system.

This "divine manipulation of the threads"—as Sun-tzu termed reaching into and controlling the enemy's intelligence apparatus—involved the close coordination of disinformation, which was sent to the enemy through "doomed spies" who were misleadingly briefed and then sent into enemy territory to be captured, with the penetration of enemy intelligence by "inward spies," or moles. The eventual result was that the enemy's false picture of reality was reinforced by its own intelligence service.

Angleton, like Sun-tzu, based his theory of deception on the vulnerability of the very agencies that were supposed to be proof against it, the intelligence services. He had learned this lesson early on in the Philby affair. "Deception begins and ends with intelligence," he said quietly but with real conviction; he had been pondering the problem, when we spoke about it in 1985, for over a third of a century. Over these years, he had drawn Sun-tzu's "threads" into an elegant, if nooselike concept which he called simply "the loop."

It consisted of two lines of communications that hooked up rival intelligence services—one perpetrating the deception; the other the victim of it. The deceiver uses one set of lines to pass messages to its opposition. In practice, this means that its intelligence service must establish channels, whether human or electronic, that connect it to its adversary's intelligence service. And these must be channels that the victim relies on for its secret information. They can be false defectors, double agents, diplomatic chatter at embassy dinners, inspection trips by military attachés, or even the swathes of territory photographed by enemy satellites.

The deceiver uses the second set of lines to get a fix on the victim's reactions to the messages. At the end of these lines, there have to be moles or microphones in the enemy camp with access to the evaluators of its messages. This feedback, which Angleton had gone into at length earlier, was essential to building up the adversary's intelligence service's commitment to the sources in the disinformation part of the loop. Without it, the deceiver is working in the dark. He can never be sure whether he is tricking the opposition or is being tricked himself. With it, he can amplify and reinforce the parts of the story the opposing intelligence service is prone to believe, and eliminate or revise those that are doubted.

He suggested: imagine a wife, attempting to deceive her husband, who has bribed his psychiatrist into telling her how her husband interpreted all the lies and misleading clues she furnished him. Those he believed, she could elaborate on; those he disbelieved, she could cease providing or modify. Eventually, through trial and error, the wife and psychiatrist would supply the husband with a story that perfectly fit in with what he believed. Through such strategies, as Angleton put it, "the deceived becomes its own deceiver."

Angleton's description of how the deception loop worked against an adversarial intelligence service reminded me of a similar arrangement I had recently seen in the film *The Sting*.

The deception planners in this story were not KGB or CIA intelligence experts but a pair of confidence men played by Paul Newman and Robert Redford. Their particular skill, as the name of their trade implies, is building up the confidence of their "mark" enough for him to turn his money over to them—even though they are strangers. When one of their friends is killed by a gangster, played by Robert Shaw, they use this skill to avenge the murder by duping the gangster into giving them his money.

To accomplish this feat, Newman and Redford, assisted by a gang of a dozen or so other con men, set about constructing a false reality for the gangster. This takes the form of a sham horse-betting parlor, supposedly run by Paul Newman, to which the gangster is led. Next, Robert Redford pretends to defect from Newman's camp and offers the gangster a tantalizing piece of information: the result of the races can be delayed by crooked executives in the telegraph company long enough for the gangster to bet on a sure thing.

As more and more disinformation is fed to the gangster by the group of con men, it reinforces his faith in Redford. And, as the gangster's confidant, Redford is able to feed back to Newman the gangster's reactions. Whenever the gangster has suspicions, Newman can thus adjust the disinformation to allay them. This makes the deception impossible for the gangster to resist and he is fleeced of his money. The deception loop in *The Sting* is illustrated in Table 1.

Angleton asserted that this deception loop was a relatively easy piece of machinery to install. Although a deceiver needed to establish credible disinformation channels, well-placed moles, and secure compartments within its own intelligence service, he found in his experience that both the KGB and the CIA had demonstrated they had the capacity, and techniques, to solve these problems. But he held that the loop itself, though it may control the enemy's intelligence service, was not sufficient to guarantee the success of a strategic deception. For perfect deception, he suggested, two further conditions were necessary.

First, the victim's leadership has to be in a state of mind to want to accept and act on the disinformation it receives from its own intelligence. This might not happen unless the disinformation fits in with the adversary's prevailing preconceptions or interests—which is, at least in the case of the United States, not difficult to determine. Angleton suggested that Lenin showed he understood this principle when he instructed his intelligence

The Theory of Perfect Deception

Table 1. The Deception Loop
The Sting

Disinformation Channels

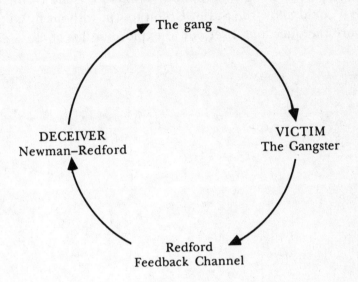

The gang

DECEIVER
Newman–Redford

VICTIM
The Gangster

Redford
Feedback Channel

chief in 1921, in crafting disinformation, to "Tell them what they want to hear."

Second, the victim has to be in a state of mind in which he is so confident of his own intelligence that he is unwilling to entertain evidence, or even theories, that he is or can be duped. This kind of blanket denial amounts to a conceit, which Angleton claimed could be cultivated in an adversary, that one's rival lacks the wherewithal and competence to hide its activities, organize disinformation, and penetrate its ranks. If it proved wrong, it left a nation defenseless against deception.

The issue, as Angleton saw it, was not whether the Soviet Union might attempt to win strategic advantages through peacetime deception—he assumed it would if it could—but whether

the conditions existed, or could be developed, to allow it to succeed. Do these conditions for deception exist today—in the era
of Glasnost? Is there still a "mind of the state" in the Soviet Union
capable of perpetrating a deception? Is there a "state of mind"
here that could allow the Soviet Union to win without fighting?
These are the questions I set out to explore in this book.

PART TWO

The Mind of the State

CHAPTER EIGHT

The Deception Conferences

What was the "mind of the state"—or, at least, the American intelligence establishment? How did it deal with the problem of deception and the issues posed by Angleton?

Between April 1979 and September 1985, I set out to explore and, if possible, answer these questions by attending an unusual series of academic conferences on deception.[1] They were sponsored by universities, foundations, and, in at least one case, the CIA. I wanted to meet the executives of intelligence services in an informal atmosphere in which they would both answer questions and open doors for me. As it turned out, the large contingent from the intelligence community that I had an opportunity to talk to at these small gatherings would not have been accessible to me, or presumably anyone else outside their secret world, under any other circumstance.

From the CIA, there was William Casey, the future Director of Central Intelligence, and William Colby, the past Director; George Kalaris, who had replaced Angleton as chief of the counterintelligence staff; Fred Hutchinson, the CIA's National Intelligence Officer for Deception; Fritz Ermath, the CIA's National Intelligence Officer for the Soviet Union; Larry Gershwin, the CIA's National Intelligence Officer for Strategic Programs; Richard Lehman, the CIA's National Warning Officer; Klaus Knorr, Bruce C. Clark, and Stuart Cohen from the CIA's

National Foreign Assessment Center; Merrill T. Kelly, who headed the DIA's "human systems," which recruited spies; Ray Cline, the former Deputy Director for Intelligence; Theodore G. Shackley, the former associate Director for Operations; Hugh Tovar and Donald J. Purcell, the former directors of Covert Action; Vernon Walters, a former Deputy Director of the CIA and future Ambassador to the UN; and William Johnson, Norman L. Smith, Donovan Pratt, Scotty Miler, William Hood, and Ray Rocca, all of whom had served on Angleton's staff. From the FBI's counterespionage division, there was William Branigan, James Nolan, and Ray Wannall—all Soviet experts. From the Defense Intelligence Agency came General Daniel O. Graham, its former director, and John Dziak, Wynfred Joshua, and Arthur Zuehlke, who were Soviet specialists; from the Office of Naval Intelligence, the former director, Admiral Donald P. Harvey; and from Air Force Intelligence, General George Keegan, its former head. From the President's Foreign Intelligence Advisory Board, there was its former head, Admiral George Anderson.

There were also scientists from the Pentagon, defectors from Soviet bloc intelligence, CIA station chiefs from a half-dozen posts, intelligence liaisons from the British, French, Canadian, Italian, and Israeli services, representatives from the National Security Council, Ph.D.s from exotic think tanks with names such as Pan Heuristics, Mathmatica, Falcon Associates, and R&D, and staff from both the House and Senate oversight committees on intelligence. There was even an active spy, Jonathan Pollard (who was subsequently arrested on espionage charges).

At the first of these remarkable meetings, which was held under the auspices of the Fletcher School of Diplomacy at the Hyatt Regency Hotel in Cambridge, Massachusetts, I was amazed to find that a small group of academics was already developing the subject of deception into an intellectual discipline. It included R. V. Jones, a Scottish scientist and practical joker, who had combined his fields of interest to spoof and deceive German electron intelligence in World War II; Barton Whaley, an MIT trained political scientist and magic buff, who had compiled an 800-page analysis of all the known military deceptions of the twentieth century;[2] Michael Handel, an Israeli professor who had worked out an elaborate theory of surprise that applied to politics as well as war; and Andrew W. Marshall, a RAND intellectual who had now become the director of the Pentagon's Office of Net Assessment, which was funding a large share of the studies on deception.

There was general agreement at the conference on a number of central points about deception. First, no one doubted the power of deception to affect human behavior. It was pointed out that ever since primitive man learned how to dupe prey into coming within his range by placing a lure on the water or mimicking the mating call of birds, deception had been part of civilization. Individuals commonly use deception to make themselves more attractive through cosmetics or deter intruders by leaving lights and radios on when they are not home (or even installing anti-burglar devices that simulate the barking of dogs).

There was also consensus at the conference that governments have a wealth of experience in applying the techniques of deception. Even if these techniques were rarely part of the curriculum of most political science courses, at least outside these conferences, they played an important part in the process through which people are governed. Examples were supplied of how governments, through their manipulation of words, images, music, and other signals that individuals follow and use as a guide to reality, achieve social control. Both democracies and dictatorships, albeit in different degrees, tinker with these closely watched signals, which can be anything from statistics to newspaper headlines. One professor at the Fletcher School of Diplomacy even argued that the modern state uses deception as a "humane and cheap alternative to brute force in regulating the behavior of its populations."

Even in democracies like the United States, deception is a main mechanism of law enforcement, especially in federal crimes. Governments frequently rely on "stings" to catch narcotics dealers, tax violators, influence peddlers, arms traffickers, and even common criminals. These techniques are particularly effective since criminals, lacking the resources to investigate in advance their potential victims or collaborators, must rely on relatively crude indicators, such as their dress, behavior, or credentials—all of which police can easily mimic or forge. In New York City, police routinely disguise themselves as elderly pedestrians, drunks, single women, and other likely victims, and loiter conspicuously—wolves in sheep's clothes—to capture muggers. In Washington, D.C., to round up burglars on a mass scale, police organized their own "fencing" business in a local warehouse and offered higher prices for stolen goods than anyone else. In San Francisco, the U.S. Navy created its own fake defense contractors, which offered payoffs for reordering supplies to entrap Naval employees on the take. In Chicago, police set up a chain of credit card "laundries" offering to surreptitiously convert charges for illicit services made on American Express and other credit cards into ones putatively paid to restaurants. By managing this credit card business, they were able to identify the prostitutes, pimps, panderers, and pornographers supplying the services. The FBI, in its Abscam, dressed as Arab sheiks to test politicians with bribes. In Bermuda, IRS agents created fictional tax lawyers, accountants, and real estate men so that they could be taken into the confidence of other lawyers and accountants arranging tax-avoidance schemes.[3] In Los Angeles, undercover medical investigators randomly visited doctors' offices under the guise of distressed patients to entice doctors into issuing prescriptions for illicit pharmaceuticals. And in the national forests, Fish and Wildlife wardens opened up fake taxidermy enterprises specializing in stuffing endangered species to snare poachers.

The techniques of deception work for the state not only in controlling conventional criminals but in controlling political dissidents. The practice of using agents provocateurs to infiltrate dissident movements was perfected in the late nineteenth century by the czars of Russia. Under the direction of the Okhrana, the czars' predecessor to the KGB, agents masquerading as dissidents would carry out dramatic acts of terrorism, even assassinating their own czarist officials and blowing up their own police installations, to prove their bona fides to the legitimate underground leaders. The Okhrana found that its agents provocateurs could not be weeded out by dissident movements because they could easily pass the only available test: undertaking dangerous missions against the state. Since their successes in this terrorism—as well as their safety—were effectively guaranteed by the hidden hand of the Okhrana, they were in a position to rise to leadership in the underground. This system of pseudo-terrorism was not without its costs. As one participant in the conference pointed out, in 1901, an undercover police agent called Azev supervised the assassination of the Grand Duke Sergei, the Governor General of Moscow. But, even with such embarrassments, the Okhrana gained almost total control of all the leading dissident factions both in Russia and in exile. By manipulating them, it managed to identify almost all the anti-czarists up until the outbreak of World War I—and the czars evidently willingly accepted the costs of this deception.

The agent provocateur system was by no means limited to the service of czars and dictators.[4] The British security service, MI5, employed agents to mimic nationalist terrorists in India, Palestine, and Ireland. France proved equally adept at using these agents in its colonies. The United States managed by the early 1950s to completely infiltrate undercover agents into almost all the key positions in the Communist Party USA. The infiltration was so successful, according to one of the FBI counterespionage experts, that J. Edgar Hoover opposed congressional efforts to outlaw the Communist Party. Hoover maintained that since it was already an FBI-controlled organization, it could help identify and manipulate those who joined it. In this respect, it was not unlike the Trust.

The FBI had institutionalized these deception techniques in its so-called counterintelligence program (Cointellpro) to incite suspicions within many other dissident groups, as I learned from William Sullivan, who had supervised it. By combining inside men—that is, informers—with outside provocateurs, the FBI was able to use the deception loop to immense effect in undermining the element of trust necessary to bond together dissident movements.[5]

Finally, everyone at the conference, including even skeptics, accepted that in time of war governments use deception against their enemies with great effect. Indeed, it seemed a large number of the participants had themselves taken part in deceptions in World War II. Professor Jones, for example, described how he had deceived the Germans about the type of radio direction beacons the RAF was using to bomb Germany by scripting entire conversations that were then passed through double agents to German intelligence. He made it sound easy, explaining in his Scottish brogue, "To deceive, you have to first find what channels of information your adversary has at his disposal, to make sure you provide as many clues as possible, and then either block or discredit those channels in which you cannot supply positive clues."

This method was refined to a fine art in the deception plan that the British used to divide and divert the German enemy before and after its invasion of Normandy in 1944. It could be analyzed in great detail at the conference because, unlike other strategic deceptions, which remain closely guarded secrets, the British government authorized an official history of it.[6]

The Allied strategy was to put all its eggs in one basket and land a million-man British–American–Canadian Expeditionary Force on the beaches of Normandy on D-Day. Before these troops could safely land, however, the Germans had to be given a false picture not only of when and where they would land, but their strategic objective. Otherwise, the Germans would bring all their forces in Western Europe to focus on these beachheads—and possibly overwhelm them.

The deception plan aimed at making the Germans believe, even after the Normandy landings, that the initial landings were part of a two-pronged invasion, with another even greater Allied army poised to land on the beaches of Pas de Calais. If the Germans could be so convinced, they would have no choice but to divide their forces and, even after the invasion, to keep reinforcements farther north to ward off the second blow.

British deception planners had begun working three years earlier toward the goal of establishing this alternative interpretation of Allied activities in the mind of Hitler and the German High Command. The illusionary picture they furnished, bit by bit, when pieced together by German intelligence, was of a huge American army, called the "Fourth U.S. Army Group"—or FUSAG—commanded by General George Patton, stationed in the north of England. Although FUSAG was totally fictitious, the deception planners, called the London Coordinating Committee, strove to focus the attention of German radio interception, aerial reconnaissance, and intelligence analyses so tightly on fabricated signals emanating from the location of the phantom armies that the German High Command would either neglect the real invasion force assembling in southern England, or assess it as merely part of a multi-pronged invasion. As clues, the British deception planners faked thousands of phony messages that appeared to come from various fictional units of FUSAG but actually had been piped across England from real army units. They provided German aerial photography cameras with decoy tanks, landing crafts, and planes at bases in northern England—all of which were fake. They stirred up by wind machines dust clouds that would be misinterpreted. They planted stories in the local press about marriages, engagements, and other vital statistics concerning the officers and men in this nonexistent army. And they scripted false stories—then passed

119

through German agents in England to German intelligence—that were in fact controlled by British intelligence.

The British had developed this capacity to control German intelligence over the preceding four years by capturing some two dozen German case officers, parachuted or otherwise smuggled into Britain, and then having them continue to send radio messages back to Germany—but messages given to them by MI5 agents who were supervising their activities. In this double-cross system, as it was called, the German agents were provided with networks of sources and credible bits of information so that they would be believed by their controllers in German intelligence. Eventually, or at least in time for the deception plan, Germany relied on them as its eyes in England. These double-cross agents, the equivalent of Sun-tzu's converted agents, were thus able to provide reports that falsely confirmed the existence of FUSAG.

The British deception planners also had at their disposal "doomed spies," whom they could expose to information that they wanted to fall into German hands. These were the French, Belgian, and Dutch resistance fighters—whose organizations had been infiltrated by German informers. The probability was that many of them would be captured, interrogated, tortured, or otherwise coerced or bribed to reveal what they knew. They were therefore sent orders to conduct sabotage missions in areas that would be consistent with a second front at Pas de Calais, on the assumption that they would provide German counterintelligence with further evidence of a two-pronged attack.

The feedback came in this case not from a human spy but from the ability of the British to decipher the German military code. Before the war even began, British intelligence agents had obtained through espionage a model of the machine that the German High Command used to encipher all its signals sent out over the airwaves to military units, submarines, and intelligence agents. It was called Enigma.[7] They also obtained through French and Polish espionage agents the manual for this machine and its code settings. By 1941, a team of mathematicians based at Bletchley Park had developed a method of reading these coded messages. The intelligence derived from these intercepted signals was code-named "Ultra." With it, British deception planners could figure out how each of the clues they were planting in German channels were being received by the Germans, and how to modify them to make them more credible. It completed the deception loop (see Table 2).

The German intelligence services were extremely active and technically competent during this entire deception. They photographed English ports and airfields, intercepted messages sent from one Allied unit to another, and successfully penetrated French, Dutch, and Belgian undergrounds. But this merely created more channels for the British to pass disinformation through. In the end, such intelligence gathering, rather than acting as a remedy for deception, became its unwitting ally.

Table 2. The Deception Loop
D-Day Invasion

Disinformation Channels

Captured Double Agents

DECEIVERS
British Intelligence
London Coordinating
Committee

VICTIMS
German High Command

Ultra Intercepts
Feedback Channel

It became clear as the conference proceeded that the British were not the only successful deceivers in the war. Barton Whaley, who had written his Ph.D. dissertation on Hitler's surprise attack on Russia in 1941 code-named Barbarossa, demonstrated that the German High Command had managed through brilliantly orchestrated disinformation to convince Stalin that the massive movement eastward of over one hundred German divisions— an invasion force too large to be concealed—was merely a feint meant to deceive the British.[8] The guidelines for this deception, which were made part of the record of the Nuremberg War Trials, presented a detailed program for gradually sprinkling the fragments of "false intelligence" into channels that were being monitored by Soviet intelligence. When pieced together, these clues were designed to produce "a mosaic picture."

The German logic was that if Stalin became committed to the "picture" that Germany's immediate target was the invasion of England, he would dismiss contrary intelligence that suggested the target was the Soviet Union as disinformation. The German deception planners' problem was engendering that mind-set. They determined that Stalin was predisposed to believing that Hitler depended on his pact with the Soviet Union, and the Trans-Siberian Railroad, to get the fuel, grain, and other supplies he desperately needed, and that therefore Hitler would not turn on Russia until he had knocked England out of the war. To reinforce Stalin's preconception, they sent hundreds of separate messages through double agents, diplomats, compromised codes, and military attachés over a fourteen-month period. They even arranged the construction of expensive German defensive positions in Poland, suggesting Germany was not planning an offense, solely for the benefit of Soviet aerial photographers. The result was that Stalin became so convinced Hitler intended to do nothing more than present him with an ultimatum for more grain—which Stalin planned to acquiesce to—that when Hitler invaded and overran most of Russia, Stalin had a virtual nervous breakdown and was unable to confront the reality of the situation.

But Stalin then went into the deception game himself with a vengeance.[9] Soviet intelligence determined that the German High Command depended on its analyses of the Soviet radio signals it intercepted to track the movements of each and every regiment-size unit of the Red Army. For this purpose, it was not necessary for the Germans to break the Soviet codes, or even know the actual content of the radio communications. They merely had to do "traffic analysis," which means counting and categorizing the signals going back and forth between Soviet walkie-talkies, mobile radios, field transmitters, and telegraph machines. Since each Soviet unit had different types of radio equipment, and organized it differently, its pattern of transmissions, or "signature," could be recognized by German intelligence.

Once Soviet intelligence had worked out exactly the way that this German traffic analysis was done, they used it with devastating effect to deceive the Germans. In the 1942 Kursk offensive against the Germans, for example, Stalin succeeded through communications deceptions in creating even larger phantom armies than the British had in their more celebrated stratagem.

Japan also used deception to dupe the United States about the true state of its military competence.[10] The main channel that the Japanese used to foster this misperception was their air shows. When Western military attachés were invited to Japanese air bases in 1941, exhibitions of flying incompetence were purposely staged for them. And they were then informally told by Japanese Air Ministry officials that the air force was having difficulties training Japanese pilots to fly solo—which reinforced American preconceptions about Japanese incompetence. While concealing its modern Zero fighter, Japan displayed its antiquated and obsolescent planes. As one of Japan's leading strategists later explained, "Foreign observers saw only what we allowed them to see." The picture that emerged, and was duly reported to Washington and London, was of a primitive Japanese Air Force, lacking the technology for refueling in midair, precision bombing, and long-range missions. This left the United States and Britain unprepared for a Japanese Air Force that had superior planes, the ability to extend its range through midair refueling, and pilots trained to torpedo ships in presumably safe harbors. By December 1941, U.S. intelligence had concluded that Japan did not have the capacity to launch torpedoes from airplanes in shallow water, and therefore the Naval Command assumed that its fleet would be safe from torpedoes in the shallow waters of Pearl Harbor.

The real surprise was not the time of the attack on Pearl Harbor on December 7, 1941, but the technological ability of the Japanese. This was demonstrated the next day when the United States left its only wing of bombers unprotected on Clark Air Force Base in the Philippines—even after the attack on Pearl Harbor—and it was destroyed by Japanese bombers that had been unexpectedly refueled in midair. Such Japanese strategies succeeded only because of a false picture of Japanese incompetence that persisted for the first year of the war.

The United States, in turn, deceived the Japanese. It used highly sophisticated electronic wizardry and Hollywood props to create the illusion it would attack the northern Japanese islands in 1945.

Moreover, the technique of using the "double cross system" to take over an opponent's espionage service, though publicly revealed when Sir John Masterman, an Oxford historian and former British counterintelligence officer, published a report he wrote for MI5 that documented how British intelligence "actively ran and controlled the German espionage system in this country," was not a British or even recent invention.[11] Sun-tzu noted, "The enemy's spies who have come to spy on us must be sought out, tempted with bribes, led away and comfortably housed. Thus they will be converted spies available for our service." And while

MI5 was occupied turning all the German agents in England into disinformation agents, the German Abwehr was engaged in exactly the same game in Holland, Belgium, Turkey, and France, duping both the British and Americans.[12] The Abwehr was, in turn, deceived by Soviet intelligence operating an extensive double-cross system in the Balkans in which it sacrificed military units in order to build credibility.[13] Without belaboring the point, it appears everyone deceived everyone in World War II.

After reviewing the plethora of material on these wartime deceptions, only one relevant question remained: Could the same techniques be used in peacetime to win without fighting?

CHAPTER NINE

The Goldhamer Inventory

"The British and French will come in and squash us like
flies."

    —Air Marshal Hermann Goering

"Not if we buzz loudly enough."

    —Adolph Hitler

Andrew Marshall, with his large bald head, horn-rimmed glasses,
precise but soft voice, and pipe that refused to stay lit, was the
embodiment to me of the defense intellectual. When I first met
him at the conference in Cambridge, he told me that his Office
of Net Assessment was interested in non-military as well as military uses of deception, and he mentioned that in 1974 he had
commissioned a study that dealt with projecting misleading images of national strengths and weaknesses to win strategic advantages in peacetime.

 I then went to see him at his office in the Pentagon, which
was located adjacent to the suite of the Office of the Secretary
of Defense. As I looked at the giant maps on the wall, he explained that his job was to take as many factors into account as
possible in weighing the relative strengths of the United States

and the Soviet Union, and provide the Secretary with an ongoing assessment of the gap between the two.

"Is the capability for deception put in this equation?" I asked.

He answered, relighting his pipe, that he had made that a consideration but that "not everyone in the Pentagon" agreed with him about the relevance of deception. He pointed out that it is far more difficult to gauge than tanks, ships, submarines, or nuclear warheads. And assessing the effectiveness of deception in peacetime presented even greater difficulties since "what is successfully hidden is not found."

When I reminded him of the study he had discussed in Cambridge, he confirmed that it had indeed provided some very illuminating examples of peacetime deceptions that had decisively worked, especially in the 1930s. Unfortunately, Dr. Herbert Goldhamer, the political scientist who had played the "leading role in the program," and for whom Marshall had the highest regard, had died in August 1977—leaving the study unfinished. He reflected for a moment and then added that he had given Goldhamer's widow, Joan, a grant to put her husband's relevant notes in a three-volume, 1100-page inventory for the Office of the Secretary of Defense.[1]

His assistant, presumably with Marshall's approval, subsequently sent me the Goldhamer Inventory. I found in the fragments, as Marshall had suggested, data that when pieced together showed how Hitler had used deception as a peacetime stratagem: first, by projecting false strength to deter Britain and France from intervening; second, by dividing his enemies; and finally, by projecting false weakness to slow down their own military preparations.

In 1933, the situation was as follows. Hitler had no real prospect of conquering Europe by force. The German Army had neither the manpower nor the ordnance to realize his vaunted ambitions. Less than a decade earlier, it had been completely defeated and disarmed. The Treaty of Versailles, which ended

World War I, still restricted Germany from possessing any offensive weapons or fortifying its borders. It was specifically prohibited from stationing any armed troops, even military police, in its own Rhineland, which was to be an undefended buffer between it and France. Nor was Germany allowed to possess an air force. Its navy was limited to a few antiquated patrol ships. Its skeleton army was little more than a police force. It was barred from having any tanks, armored cars, heavy artillery or other mobile weaponry, and from drafting any soldiers.

Even though it had managed to evade some of the treaty restrictions, Germany still had little offensive capability.[2] In the West, it faced France, which had the largest and best-equipped land army in the world, and Great Britain, whose all-powerful fleet could blockade German ports at will. In the East, Germany was hemmed in by Czechoslovakia and Poland, both backed, through a series of alliances, by France, England, and the Soviet Union. Hitler's immediate objective was to break out of this bind. Since he had no chance of accomplishing this through military means, he substituted fraud for force.

But how could Hitler win without fighting? Any massive rebuilding of the German armed forces, which would openly violate the terms of the Versailles Treaty, would invite an invasion or blockade by the Allied powers, who were its guarantors. Given the defenseless state of Germany's borders, this would put a premature end to his "Thousand-year Reich." To deter the Allied powers from intervening until Germany was fully rearmed, Hitler therefore had to invent an illusionary threat of retaliation. For this purpose, airpower was a perfect bluff.[3]

Until then, military officers had had little experience with aerial bombardment. Although the few bombs dropped during the final days of World War I resulted in little actual damage, they caused panics and riots—and a legacy of fear for the next two decades.[4] They also caught the imagination of the postwar peace movement, which raised the specter of the total destruction of Europe. The concern was heightened by scientists who, taking the worst case possible, greatly exaggerated their effect. In England, for example, it was estimated that a mere 40 tons of gas sprayed from bombers would end all life in London; while in Paris, the head of the fire-fighting brigade announced that fifty incendiary bombs would reduce the French capital to a mound of ashes. Politicians also did little to allay popular fears by repeatedly pointing out that while the military was relatively safe from attack—the French Army behind the Maginot Line and the British Navy protected by the English Channel—there was no apparent protection against bombers for the civilian populations.

Hitler evidently realized that these widespread fears of annihilation could be played upon to deter Great Britain and France from intervening in Germany. Even though Germany had no bombers in 1933 capable of reaching England—and it would not have them for at least another eight years—Hitler had the means of immediately establishing the reputation, if not the reality, of the Luftwaffe's strength: strategic deception.

Here German staff officers already had considerable experience. The word "disinformation" was in fact coined by the German High Command (OKW) during World War I.[5] Whereas deception had always been part of German military tactics at the field level, the development of the radio forced these tactical deceptions to be centrally coordinated. The OKW thus set up a special unit, called the Disinformation Service, to coordinate the forged radio traffic that was likely to be intercepted and misread by British, French, and Russian intelligence. Its outstanding accomplishment had been in dividing and disrupting the Russian war effort against Germany. In April 1917, with 10 million Russian soldiers still arrayed on the Eastern Front against Germany, the German deception staff organized one of the most successful pieces of planned subversions in modern history. General Walter Nicolai, of German military intelligence, arranged a special train to take Lenin and thirty other revolutionaries from Switzerland, where they had been in exile, to the Russian border, where they would be smuggled in. As he made clear to his superiors, the purpose of this exercise was to undermine the Russian war effort against Germany. His intelligence service, which had been in close contact with these revolutionaries in Switzerland, had correctly assessed that while they were only a tiny faction in Russian politics, they would work conspiratorially to disrupt the new provincial government. And indeed, within a year after it had been insinuated into Russia by German intelligence, the Lenin faction managed to seize power in a coup d'état. It then moved to withdraw Russia from the war with Germany. While Lenin and his colleagues were unwitting instruments in the German design, they received substantial clandestine support from the German Embassy—both in terms of money and intelligence— which greatly facilitated their coup.

Even though the Disinformation Service was officially disbanded after the war, its officers and techniques, working as part of the German High Command, played an important role in the peacetime deception that successfully evaded the arms prohibitions in the Versailles Treaty and, by so doing, concealed the training of a cadre for a future German Army.

This gigantic subterfuge, code-named "Operation Kama," took place mainly in the Soviet Union. As ironic as it seems in retrospect, Lenin had secretly agreed in 1921 to help Germany rearm in return for industrial equipment and patents. By 1926, nearly a third of Germany's military budget was funneled into the Soviet Union through a dummy export-import corporation called GEFU, which was the acronym in German for Industrial Export Corporation. Through a chain of equally fictitious subsidiaries, GEFU organized plants in Leningrad and Moscow to manufacture forbidden weapons, such as poison gas and bombs. It also leased clandestine bases on the Ukrainian plains to test aircraft and train German pilots. As the scale of this operation increased in the late 1920s, Germany developed many of the offensive tactics, such as the Blitzkrieg and dive bombing, with which it would later surprise its host. This curious collaboration between ideological enemies, which continued for eleven years, required elaborate deception. German pilots killed in crashes were shipped back in crates labeled machine parts. Fighter planes were disguised as advertising planes, towing behind them, as they flew back to Germany, banners recommending beer. Officers who had nominally resigned from the German military during their training in Russia were nominally reemployed on their return as pilots for Lufthansa, the commercial airline.[6]

Although the deception ended in 1933, this covert enterprise had provided Germany not only the nucleus for an air force but also a highly experienced apparatus for planning and implementing sustained deceptions.

The first step in Hitler's strategic deception was turning weakness into what appeared to be strength. The few German fighter planes, which still were not even operational, had to be converted through the techniques of disinformation into an apocalyptic threat. This required, in turn, a channel through which the German deception planners could place bits of information—some true, some false, but all misleading—directly into the hands of Western intelligence. The conduit they selected was British Air Intelligence, a newly formed adjunct to the British Secret Service, which ironically had the job of ferreting out the secrets of Germany's airplanes.

The head of this new espionage service, Wing Commander Frederick W. Winterbotham, was a thirty-six-year-old former Royal Air Force pilot who had already attempted to maneuver a British agent named William de Ropp, who was working in Berlin as a salesman for Bristol Aircraft, into a position of access in the German Air Ministry. To further the intrigue, Winterbotham himself had feigned sympathy for Hitler (to whom he was personally introduced), and had also offered to help the Luftwaffe buy British aviation equipment from de Ropp.[7] Taking advantage of this double agent, German intelligence officers provided British Air Intelligence with Luftwaffe secrets—but secrets especially selected so as to exaggerate German aeronautical advances in such crucial areas as speed, range, and bomb-carrying capacity.

To reinforce this sporadic stream of disinformation, the Germans also allowed British air attachés to inspect airfields at appropriate times. Within a few years, this arrangement evolved into a system of quasi-formal inspections by two RAF vice marshals and two British intelligence officers. The Luftwaffe fully understood that whatever facts it chose to provide to these observers would become an important part of Britain's and its Allies' assessment of German capability. As one Luftwaffe executive later noted: "Naturally we were aware that these officers were expected to furnish their espionage chiefs with reports . . . which would ultimately reach the top government circles of all the major powers."[8] They also realized that the basic data the observers would report on—the number, speed, and range of warplanes—could be manipulated for the desired effect like peas in a shell game.

German airports now became the modern equivalent of Prince Potemkin's one-dimensional villages in eighteenth-century Russia. Just as those legendary facades were moved each night on barges and reassembled in the morning on another site to impress Catherine the Great with the number of villages in her empire, the small force of advanced Luftwaffe fighters was flown from base to base for the benefit of visiting delegations of foreigners. In 1938, for example, every fighter plane in the Luftwaffe was ordered to a single airfield in advance of the arrival there of a French general. The same fighter planes were thus counted over and over again in British, French, and American intelligence estimates.

In addition, the German aircraft factory at Oranienburg was converted into a veritable showcase to impress foreign visitors. The stage-managing used to exaggerate the performance of the Luftwaffe often involved carefully rehearsed dramas. For example, when General Joseph Vuillemen, the French Air Chief of Staff, visited Oranienburg in 1938, he was shown an airfield "carefully packed with aircraft, assembled each day from other fields to give him a vastly inflated figure of German air strength."[9] Then, to create the illusion of speed, he was taken up in a courier plane that had been specially prepared to fly extraordinarily slowly without stalling. Although he did not realize it, the plane deliberately slowed down to less than 35 miles an hour. At this moment, a test pilot shot past in an experimental plane, disguised with military markings as the vaunted Heinkel fighter. In a staged conversation with other Luftwaffe officers, his pilot suggested this plane was now being produced daily on three production lines.

Not realizing how slowly his own plane was flying, or that the plane that streaked by was not the Heinkel fighter in current production, General Vuillemen was, as he later conceded, "shattered." He assumed—incorrectly—that the Luftwaffe had achieved a technological breakthrough in speed that left the French Air Force totally helpless. "If war breaks out, there won't be a single French aircraft left after fourteen days," he told the French Ambassador in the car on the way back to Berlin. As one historian noted, Vuillemen was so "gulled and swindled by [the] series of Potemkin villages" that he returned "convinced that war would mean the ruin of Paris."[10] Even though Charles A. Lindbergh, the celebrated American aviator, had more experience with such stunt-flying tricks, he was just as thoroughly hoodwinked by the tours the German air staff organized for him of aircraft factories. Lindbergh, assuming that the efficiency and precision he witnessed in these selected showcases were typical of other German production lines, concluded—and reported to Allied intelligence—that Germany was mass-producing warplanes at a rate well beyond that of France, Britain, or America. As his wife later observed, "There is no doubt that [German Air Marshal Hermann] Goering did 'use' Lindbergh to show off his air production, anticipating that stories of its strength would spread abroad and delay opposition to Hitler's aggressive program."[11]

Hitler also used international air competitions to reinforce this illusion of invulnerability. For example, at the Zurich International Air Meet in July 1937, the Luftwaffe entered a silver-colored, pencil-shaped bomber with the same military markings as the German planes that had recently bombed Guernica in the Spanish Civil War.[12] It was called the Do-17, which suggested it was a German bomber in mass production. As French and British military observers clocked its speed, it zoomed ahead of all the other fighters entered in the competition. This led Allied intelligence to conclude that Germany had a long-range bomber that could not be overtaken by their fighters. At this stage of military aviation, in which neither radar-controlled guns nor antiaircraft missiles had yet been developed, a bomber that could outspeed fighters was virtually invulnerable.

The Do-17, however, was not then, and would never be, an operational bomber. It was a prototype, designed to awe and intimidate the observers from foreign intelligence services. Its engines, handcrafted out of rare alloys for the competition, were not available for any other Luftwaffe planes. As Herbert Malloy Mason, Jr., describes in his authoritative *Rise of the Luftwaffe:* "this particular flying pencil had been specially fitted with a pair of the scarce DB 600A, 1000 horsepower engines, and handily won the Alpine Circuit competition with a maximum speed of 280 miles an hour—faster than any of the foreign fighters present . . . [but] astonished French and British air observers had no way of knowing that production versions of the bomber were coming off lines with lesser engines and speeds."

Germany, in fact, had decided even before the competition to suspend production of the Do-17 and all other strategic bombers because of shortages of imported materials. The primary mission of the handful of long-range bombers built in these prewar years was not to bomb but to break records at air meets—and to intimidate potential enemies. Hitler even had a so-called Amerika-Bomber tested, with a range of some 9,000 miles, to threaten

New York in this image war, although only a single such plane was ever constructed.[13]

The deception of trained observers worked in part because seeing turned out to be believing. The trick of showcasing simply involved substituting the atypical for the typical. What they saw at airfields, factories, and competitions was real, but it did not represent what it purported to represent—operational warplanes. As Don Quixote points out, "Facts are the great enemy of truth."

To be sure, the gross overestimate of the Luftwaffe threat was not entirely the result of a German manipulation. "In addition to the systematic bluff organized at [the] top level," notes a former Luftwaffe leader, "there was also willing self-deception . . ."[14] He observed that when British and French air attachés were shown the exterior of empty hangars, they were more than willing to jump to the conclusion that they were crammed full of ultra-modern fighters.

At higher levels in the chain of Allied intelligence, there was also a predisposition toward accepting the reports of Luftwaffe air supremacy. Indeed, advocates of British airpower used them to make their own case for dramatically expanding the budget and manpower of the Royal Air Force. If German bombers outflew all the RAF fighters, they could argue that there was an immediate need to develop faster British interceptors—no matter what the cost. And if Germany was mass-producing its bombers, they could cogently argue that England needed a similar crash program. German deception planners thus found receptive, if unwitting, allies in their efforts to shape a convincing image of an omnipotent Luftwaffe.

In the orchestration of the deception, the leitmotif of disinformation, played directly into the ears of British intelligence, echoed and confirmed by staged exhibitions, was reinforced in the media by the constant drumbeat of propaganda. To inspire mass hysteria over the possibility of the bombing of civilian targets, the German propaganda mill supplied a constant flow of horror stories to the Western press about the devastation wreaked on cities during the Spanish Civil War. It especially exploited the German raid on the small fishing village of Guernica, with gory pictures and newsreels showing bomb damage.[15] This had the desired effect of magnifying the Luftwaffe threat in a spate of scare stories in the Western press. In London, *The Times* created a near panic by reporting that the Luftwaffe had deployed a four-engine bomber that could carry 5 tons of bombs across the Channel—in fact, the Germans had no such bomber—while in Paris, politicians warned of a worker's revolution, and establishment of a new Commune, if Parisian factories were bombed.[16] (Indeed, when the war finally began, it was common to exaggerate civilian casualties in a single air raid by 3,000 percent or more.) Churchill measured the success of this German propaganda campaign by the fact that 750,000 hospital beds were set aside for air-raid casualties in 1939–40, whereas only 6,000 were actually needed. He later wrote, "The picture of air destruction was so exaggerated that it depressed the statesmen responsible for the pre-war policy."

Hitler fully understood that deception depended more on the appearance of overwhelming numbers of planes than on their operational reality—at least so long as enemy intelligence continued to count, and miscount, the aircraft parked at the "Potemkin village" airfields. Under these circumstances, it mattered little that most of the planes were not adequately armed for combat. As late as 1939, when pressed by his Air Minister for emergency funds to equip the air force with ordnance, Hitler turned down the request, commenting tellingly: "Nobody inquires whether I have any bombs or ammunition, it is the number of aircraft . . . that counts."[17] As the historian A. J. P. Taylor concluded, "pretending to prepare for a great war and not in fact doing so was an essential part of Hitler's strategy."[18]

The first real test of this strategy came when Hitler reoccupied the demilitarized Rhineland in 1936 with a mere three thousand soldiers armed with nothing more than rifles and light machine guns. It was a clear violation of the Versailles Treaty. Hitler realized at the time that he had no chance of success if France, the guarantor of the treaty, chose to intervene with its vastly superior army—or air force. As he put it, "We would have had to withdraw with our tail between our legs, for the military resources at our disposal were inadequate for even a modest resistance."[19]

What he was counting on to deter the French and British was not, however, military resources but their carefully cultivated fear of reprisal bombings by the Luftwaffe. To prepare the climate for this coup, Hitler did everything he could to give an air of reality to the phantom threat. Mason recounts that "the Luftwaffe temporarily requisitioned every available civilian aviator—including even student pilots—and then filled the skies over the Rhine with as many aircraft as it could muster. The same planes, with hastily repainted insignia, repeatedly flew around in circles over the Rhine to multiply the illusion of numbers. In reality, the dreaded German air force amounted to no more than a squadron of fighters, not one of which was capable of combat."[20] The few planes that had both ammunition and guns lacked the synchronization gear necessary for firing through the prop.

Nevertheless, in a performance for the benefit of its enemies, the High Command telegraphed ominous orders to its phantom air units and overseas missions over lines that it knew were being tapped by the Allies. These messages suggested that Hitler was preparing an Armageddon-type raid on Paris in the event of French intervention in the Rhineland. The bluff succeeded: Without a shot being fired, Hitler was able to remilitarize—and fortify—Germany's Western Front.

Behind his dazzling shield of phantom bombers, which had now proved its power to intimidate, if not totally blind, Britain, France, and the other guarantors of the Versailles Accord, Hitler proceeded to unilaterally scrap the treaty, remobilize the German Army, and, in March 1938, incorporate the 6 million people of

Austria in his "Thousand-year Reich." He then demanded, in an ultimatum in the spring of 1938, the entire Sudetenland portion of Czechoslovakia—which, with its hundreds of miles of underground fortifications, was the only defensible part of that country. Britain and France were thus faced with the choice of either ceding to Hitler their ally in Central Europe or fighting Germany, with its presumed air superiority.

Hitler was prepared at this time to wage a war of nerves but, as his generals warned him in the summer of 1938, not one involving tanks and planes. In both these crucial categories, German forces were blatantly inferior to those of France and England. Yet he had so successfully manipulated his adversaries' intelligence reports that they had erroneously conceded the German Army superiority on land and the Luftwaffe near invincibility in the skies. In Paris, French liaison officers passed the word to their British counterparts, as one full colonel put it, that "there will be no war, since we are not going to fight."[21] According to their assessment, the French Air Force was "powerless" to contain the German air threat, and the French military had decided that they could not risk the threat of reprisal bombings. Since Britain could not go to war with Germany without France— or dispute this assessment—the fate of Czechoslovakia was sealed.

In Munich, on September 30, 1938, Britain and France accepted Hitler's terms.[22] Czechoslovakia was dismembered and its Sudetenland made part of Germany. Less than six months later, the Czech President was summoned to Berlin and told that Luftwaffe bombers were waiting on runways for the order to turn Prague into rubble. He hastily signed the document turning the remainder of his country into a German protectorate.[23] So Czech air bases, an hour away from the heartland of Germany, rather than being available to refuel Allied bombers in the event of war, now became advance bases for the Luftwaffe in Eastern Europe. The thirty-five well-equipped Czech divisions, which only months before the Allies had counted on to pin down German divisions, now became part of the German order of battle. And the giant

Skoda arms industry, the most modern in Europe, was now available to supply the German Army. This sudden advance into the Balkans also left Hungary and Rumania—with its vital oil fields—no alternative but to join Hitler's axis. Through the Bomber bluff, Hitler had significantly altered the balance of power in Europe.

Hitler himself made no secret about the role that deception and propaganda played in this victory.[24] He explained to an audience of German editors in late 1938:

> I myself became aware of the enormity of this success when I stood for the first time in the middle of the Czech fortifications [in the Sudetenland]. Then and there I realized what it means to take possession of fortifications representing a front of almost 2000 kilometers long without firing a single shot of live ammunition. . . . This time, by means of propaganda in service of an idea, we have obtained 10 million human beings with 100,000 square kilometers of land.

The systematic twisting of facts indeed had ruled the day. The problem was not that England and France lacked intelligence agents in Germany, but that they were misled. They were fed—and shown in sham demonstrations—data that led to disastrously wrong conclusions.

In choosing appeasement instead of confrontation, the Allies had, as they learned in retrospect, been intimidated by a phantom threat. They, not Hitler, had the superior forces. Whereas they had assumed that the Luftwaffe was invincible in the air—it had, according to one authoritative estimate, as many as twelve thousand planes ready for war—it was not even capable of defending Germany. In all, it had a mere four hundred fighters, and as Mason points out, "what only the Luftwaffe High Command knew was that nearly half this number was earmarked for use in the east, leaving the rest of the Reich perimeter spread too thin to counter any serious air offensive by the R.A.F. or the French."[25]

The bomber threat was also mainly illusionary. The dreaded four-engine strategic bombers had not yet even gone into production. Almost all of the three hundred bombers available in the West were tactical dive bombers, without the range or bomb-carrying capacity to threaten London or Paris. And on the ground, the five German combat divisions were no match for fifty mobilized French divisions. Against such odds, Hitler could—and did—win only by not fighting. Napoleon's dictum that "The reputation of one's arms . . . is everything and equivalent to real forces" applied, as Hitler demonstrated, in peace as well as war.

After his costless victory in Czechoslovakia, Hitler turned his full attention toward Poland—a country half the size of France that now remained the only obstacle to Germany's total domination of Eastern Europe. Its integrity was guaranteed by the Soviet Union—to whose own defenses it was vital—as well as by France and Britain. And while phantom bomber terror might again be used to deter the French and English from coming to the aid of the Poles, it was not likely to restrain the Red Army. Not only was Moscow well out of range of the Luftwaffe, but the bombing of civilians held little terror for Josef Stalin, who had himself ordered the mass executions of millions of his own citizens. As early as 1937, Hitler realized that he needed a different kind of deception that would disrupt and, at least temporarily, weather the Red Army.

THE STRATAGEM OF SUBVERSION

Just as, twenty years earlier, the German High Command had disrupted the Soviet Union through the provocative stratagem of returning Lenin, Hitler found a similar opportunity in 1937 to use deception to undermine the Soviet military.

It began when a German agent, pretending to cooperate with Soviet intelligence, reported to his superiors in German military intelligence, the Abwehr, that he had received an unusual—and curious—request from his controller in Moscow. They wanted him to attempt to search German intelligence files, to which he had access, to determine if there existed any trace of a plot by Soviet and German generals to overthrow Stalin. Although no such plot existed, the Germans pressed their double agent to find out more about this Soviet concern. As it then turned out, the request came from Stalin, who seemed obsessed with the idea of a conspiracy against him, and on the verge of launching a purge of the Red Army. By piecing together other clues from their informants, the Abwehr determined that the most probable target was none other than M. N. Tukhachevsky, one of the Soviet Union's greatest heroes, and one of the four ranking marshals of the Red Army.

Reinhard Heydrich, the chief of Hitler's security service, immediately saw the potential damage that could be done to the Soviet military if these suspicions were fanned. As he put it to his deputy, by encouraging such a purge, "a blow could be struck at the leadership of the Red Army from which it would not recover for many years."[26] All that was needed was credible disinformation that would persuade Stalin that there was indeed a conspiracy to overthrow him.

Heydrich's staff, after months of research, finally found an archive of old intelligence records that seemed perfect for this deception. They had been compiled ten years earlier, during the era of covert German-Soviet cooperation by "Group R," which had supervised the training of German officers in Russia during Operation Kama. The dossiers on Soviet officers in this archive included the routine assessments done by German intelligence officers of their political views, capabilities, and vulnerabilities. In completely innocent encounters in training facilities, bars, and restaurants, the Germans had duly reported many of the comments, complaints, and jokes made by Soviet officers. It was standard, and essentially trivial, intelligence intended at the time to provide a picture of the weaknesses and strengths of the Red Army. Yet now, a decade later in a different context, these dossiers became part of the plan to wreck the Soviet military. Hitler personally approved the plan, but insisted that it be kept secret from even the German Army.

Heydrich, with two squads of trusted intelligence officers, discreetly removed the decade-old Operation Kama dossiers from the archive and, with the help of specialists, began to reorganize the material. Exculpating documents were removed, pages were renumbered, dates were changed, and new entries were added to the chronological record of contacts between Germans and Soviet officers. Special attention was given to those Soviet officers, such as Tukhachevsky, who had risen in the intervening years to positions of command. The resulting dossiers were not for the most part out-and-out forgeries but ingenious rearrangements that gave innocent chatter among soldiers the appearance of secret liaisons between conspirators. The entire process of sorting through, abridging, and editing the material took four days.

The next step in the deception was to allow—and induce—a Soviet espionage agent to "steal" the doctored dossiers. To alert the Soviet secret police to the existence of this poisoned file, German intelligence began leaking clues about it to numerous double agents in Central Europe. For this purpose, it was not necessary to determine whether their primary loyalty was to Germany or the Soviet Union. The assumption was that at least some of these agents would report the existence of the treasure trove to Soviet intelligence.

The bait apparently worked: in early 1938, Soviet intelligence began pressing their recruiters to find a source in German intelligence with access to this file. Then, in Czechoslovakia, a German official, pretending to be a traitor, approached the intelligence chief at the Soviet Embassy and offered to deliver the sought-after file for three million rubles—a staggering sum that German intelligence hoped would add to the credibility of the documents.

After a flurry of coded cables, Stalin authorized the payment of the three million rubles (though, as the Germans learned later, the banknotes had been counterfeited). Less than a day later, the dossiers were delivered and flown to Moscow in a special courier plane.

Stalin, presuming that this documentary evidence resulted from his agents' penetrating the secret archives of German intelligence, used it to build a case against those he suspected in the Red Army. Thousands of the officers named in the dossiers were called in and brutally interrogated about what they had said to the Germans some ten years earlier. If they omitted mentioning any of the meetings cited in the dossiers, or denied their involvement, they were confronted with their dossier and then arrested. If, on the other hand, they admitted the meetings but claimed they were innocent, they were also arrested. The investigators ignored the context—that Soviets were assisting, on Lenin's orders, German rearmament—and forced officers to implicate their superiors. It took little more than a year to expand the investigation to the top command of the Red Army.

Finally, in May 1938, Marshal Tukhachevsky was confronted with his dossier, summarily imprisoned, tried—and executed one week later. The purge of the army that followed resulted in the execution or imprisonment of no fewer than twenty thousand officers, more than a third of those then on active duty.[27] The victims included three out of five of the Soviet marshals, thirteen out of fifteen of the commanding generals, over half the commanders of Soviet divisions, and seventy-five out of eighty members of the Supreme Military Council. By 1939, when the purge ended, these losses had crippled the Red Army.

Whether Hitler had caused this catastrophic purge or merely added fuel to the fire through the diabolic gift of the Kama file, he took full advantage of it. He offered Stalin a deal he was not in position to refuse: a non-aggression pact. On August 23, after hectic negotiations in Moscow, the Molotov-Ribbentrop Treaty, named after the foreign ministers who signed it, was announced to a stunned world. The secret codicils to the treaty sealed the fate of Poland: In return for the Soviet Union's not opposing Hitler's planned invasion of western Poland, Hitler agreed not to enter eastern Poland, which Stalin would then be free to seize. This agreement also meant that Germany could ship across Russia on the Trans-Siberian Railroad from Japan and Pacific ports the strategic materials it needed, and thereby greatly mitigate the threat of a British blockade of German ports. Nothing now stood in Hitler's way.

On September 3, 1939, after staging a fake Polish attack on a German outpost, complete with corpses dressed in German uniforms, Hitler's Panzer divisions raced across Poland.[28] Within a week, they surrounded the Polish capital of Warsaw. England and France, not accepting Hitler's transparent pretext of defending against a Polish attack on him, declared war on Germany as was required by their treaty obligation. Both, however, still deterred by the Luftwaffe threat, did nothing more to help the Poles than drop propaganda leaflets on three German cities.

On September 17, while German troops were mopping up isolated pockets of resistance, Soviet troops moved in and occupied their allocated zone in eastern Poland. Hitler's first war was over, without the promised Allied intervention, two weeks after it began.

Although France and Britain officially were now in a state of hostility with Germany, the situation remained, as it was aptly called, a "phony war." Both sides peacefully withdrew to their own lines, and virtually all shooting and bombing stopped.

This hiatus provided Hitler with the opportunity he desperately needed to complete his rearmament. Even after the conquest of Poland he was still unprepared for a real war. The navy was still awaiting the delivery of submarines. The army had exhausted much of its stockpile of ammunition and fuel in the Polish campaign. The air force still lacked everything from bombers to navigation equipment. The highly-touted western defenses, the so-called Siegfried Line, also still had not been completed—leaving Germany exposed to a French counterattack. According to even the most optimistic assessment of his High Command,

Germany needed months to consolidate its victories in Poland and Czechoslovakia, and redeploy its forces in the West. It was thus decidedly to Germany's advantage to prolong the phony war.

To accomplish this without unduly provoking France and Britain to accelerate their own rearmament programs, Hitler's deception planners created a false dissident group in Germany. Its purpose was to convince the British government that a conspiracy of anti-Nazi generals was on the verge of overthrowing Hitler. And, to succeed, they needed several more months without war to complete their preparations. If, on the other hand, Britain attacked Germany, their anti-Nazi colleagues would be forced to defend their homeland and consequently there would be no coup d'état. The implications were that war in Europe could be averted, and England and France could win their objectives without fighting, if only they delayed their attack. It was a message that presumably the British would want to hear—and believe.

THE STRATAGEM OF WEAKNESS

German intelligence had already prepared a suitable channel for passing this disinformation to the British: the British Secret Service. Through dogged surveillance, Germany had managed to identify all the principal British intelligence officers in Holland. Moreover, it found out that some of the top British officers there had been illegally making money for themselves by selling visas to Jews wanting to emigrate to Palestine, and therefore were vulnerable to blackmail. By skillfully exploiting this corruption, it further succeeded in recruiting one of The Hague station's key men—Jack Hooper.

By 1939, with the unseen help of German intelligence, The Hague station had developed into the principal link between anti-Nazi groups in Germany and the British Foreign Office. It was headed by Major Richard Stevens, a young officer with no previous experience in the dangerous game of foreign intelligence.

He was joined by Captain Sigismund Best, an English business-man in Holland, who had developed his own independent net-work of German spies. As it turned out, most of Best's agents, code-named "Chair," "Table," and other pieces of furniture, did not actually exist. He had invented his secret sources, like the character in Graham Greene's *Our Man in Havana,* to get extra money from the British Secret Service. Fully apprised by Hooper of the inexperience and petty corruption of British intelligence in Holland, the German deception planners had little difficulty in manipulating its activities.

They knew, for example, that Stevens and Best were under orders to attempt to recruit a German Air Force officer as a spy. And they accommodated them by sending them a candidate: a German counterintelligence expert masquerading as a disaf-fected Luftwaffe officer.

Major Sohm, as he called himself, made contact with Best that October. He claimed to be one of a group of disaffected German officers. To demonstrate his access to the highest level of the Luftwaffe, he provided Best with several secret documents. As the deception progressed and the documents were accepted by the British as genuine, Sohm identified a dozen anti-Nazi Ger-man generals as the principals in his conspiracy. He then passed on the message to Best that they wanted to set up secret talks with the British government to end the crisis on a status quo ante basis. If the British agreed to these negotiations, the generals further proposed to arrest Hitler as a sign of their good faith. The British Secret Service, falling for the offer, then arranged, through Stevens and Best, for one of the generals in the plot to fly to London.

Throughout this deception, the Germans had a source in Lon-don in a position to feed back to them the British assessment of their messages. He was Charles Howard Ellis, a senior officer in the British Secret Service, known to his friends as "Dickie."[29] The Germans had recruited him through a double agent in the late 1920s when he was stationed in Paris, and he had continued to sell them secrets when he was returned to England. Assigned in headquarters to the sensitive job of translating purloined top secret German documents in 1938, he was privy to the evaluation of the material received from the dissident generals. His reports were then relayed back to German intelligence through the double agent in Paris who recruited him. Through Ellis, and possibly other sources, the German deception planners were able to establish that the British placed considerable value on their fake dissidents, and play out their hand accordingly.

Later that spring, Sohm informed Best that any renewed Allied military actions on the Western Front would delay, or even end, their plot to arrest Hitler. He pointed out that many of the generals involved in the conspiracy would, in the event of an attack, put their duty to defend the German fatherland above their distaste for the Nazis. The remaining dissidents would then risk betrayal—and arrest. If, on the other hand, the British refrained from seriously engaging the Germans for one or two months, he suggested that the dissidents would overthrow the Nazis.

This intelligence was immediately relayed to London. To politicians who feared German bombings of cities and generals not eager to become involved in a land war in Europe, the prospect of winning without fighting was beguiling. In any case, the British military wanted more time to prepare for war. The dissident offer, if nothing else, furnished a persuasive rationale for the British to do what they wanted to do: defer military countermoves to the Polish invasion until after the summer.

Meanwhile, Hitler gained the time he needed to consolidate his gains in the East, and prepare his invasion of Holland and Belgium. In November 1939, with the fiction of the dissidents becoming increasingly more difficult to maintain, German intelligence decided to liquidate the deception with a demoralizing blow. On the pretext of arranging still another meeting with his generals, Sohm lured Best and Stevens to the village of Venlo in Holland, where they were kidnapped at gunpoint by German agents and driven across the border to Germany. Even after the Venlo Incident,[30] as it was called, which revealed Sohm as a German agent, the British still hung to the hope for several months that the dissident generals in Germany he claimed to represent might be real—and planning a coup d'état.[31] This illusion was dashed that spring when Hitler launched surprise attacks in rapid succession against Holland, Belgium, Denmark, Norway, and France—and, in little more than a month, completely dominated Europe.[32]

The concepts of deception that Hitler used to win the peace in Europe, though dramatic in consequences, were hardly original. Their tactical design came from the standard operational practices of German military intelligence in World War I, and their strategic design was contained in Sun-tzu's precept: If weak, feign strength; if strong, feign weakness. When Germany was too weak to defend itself, it pretended to have a secret weapon— the Luftwaffe bombers—which deterred its enemies from attacking it. Subsequently, in 1939, when it became strong enough to mount a surprise attack, it pretended that there was a split between the Nazi government and the generals which lulled its enemies into complacency. And when confronted with the threat of the Soviet Army in the East, it pretended that it was collaborating with Russian officers, which deeply divided the enemy. In each case, it shaped the deceptive message to tell its foe what it wanted—and expected—to hear. In shamming a strategic bombing force, Hitler provided the French and British air forces with the budgetary rationale they themselves needed in order to expand. In faking a dissident movement within his own ranks, Hitler played on the disinclination among the Allies to engage in an unrestricted war. In faking conspiratorial files for key army officers, Hitler provided Stalin with the evidence he wanted for his purge. The deceptions thus found willing, if unwitting, allies in the victims.

Moreover, these deceptions relied on their adversary's intelligence services to unwittingly provide them with a direct channel for their disinformation. Whatever channels the messages originally used—whether fake dissident movements, military attachés, or double agents—the messages quickly passed into the hands of the adversary's intelligence officers, as they were intended to do, and then, through them, to the government leaders. Paradoxically, if Britain, the Soviet Union, and France had not run espionage networks, they would have been more difficult to dupe.

Finally, the Germans had the requisite sources of feedback deep inside British intelligence to assure that the deception was not precipitously detected. Whenever British suspicions were aroused, a German "inner spy," or mole, was in a position to warn the deception planners. They could then either change the channel used for the disinformation to one that had not been discredited or, as in the case of the Generals' plot, they could abruptly disconnect it by arresting the principal contacts on an entirely different pretext. In any case, with all these elements in place, deception cost very little to implement (Stalin even paid for the privilege of being deceived) and was by any measure a far less risky enterprise than war—as Hitler learned in the next four years.

It was the war, not the peace, that Hitler lost. Up until then, he demonstrated a frightening capacity to change the balance of power through peacetime stratagems.

CHAPTER TEN

The New Maginot Line

Peacetime deception had been effectively used in the 1930s to dupe the Western Allies. Could it be equally effectively used against the United States today?

The answer given by the American intelligence establishment is no. According to their public statements, modern technology combined with satellites in space constitutes an all but infallible defense against strategic deception. Bobby Ray Inman, who served first as Director of the National Security Agency, which plays the lead role in collecting electronic intelligence, and then, until 1982, as Deputy Director of the CIA, for example, has stated that American intelligence operates under the assumption that the Soviet data intercepted by these American satellites "came in relatively pure," that is, untainted by deception.[1] He explained: "The vastness of the [American] intelligence 'take' from the Soviet Union, and the pattern of continuity going back years, even decades . . . [make Soviet deception] impossible." He reasoned further that if the Soviets exposed false information to any one sensor (for example, the telescope on a satellite), the attempted deception would be picked up by other sensors (the data-intercepting antennae on a satellite), so the only way the Soviets could deceive the United States would be to create electronic as well as visual "Potemkin villages." But he ruled these

150

out as "impractical" because even if they were technically practical, they would exhaust all the economic resources of the Soviet Union.

This confidence was also shared by Admiral Stansfield Turner, who headed the CIA up until 1981. He suggested in his biography that the telescopes, antennae, and other sensors in space are capable of "seeing," "hearing," or otherwise "detecting" virtually everything of consequence that happens in the Soviet bloc. He predicted: "we are approaching a time when we will be able to survey almost any point on the earth's surface with some sensor, and probably more than one . . . we should soon be able to keep track of most activities on the surface of the earth, day or night, good weather or bad."[2] To Turner, this new technology makes the United States not only virtually omniscient but free from dependence on conventional spying.

The extent to which these satellittes and other exotic intelligence-gathering machines had been adopted by the American government as its Maginot Line against deception was driven home to me at a conference I attended at the Air Force Academy, Boulder, Colorado, in June 1984. At almost the last moment, through some misunderstanding or error, I was asked to be the moderator of a panel on "Intelligence and the Allocations of Resources."[3] When I accepted, I had no idea what topic was actually covered by this innocuous title.

I found the conference room at the Air Force Academy packed with generals and admirals, and, as the first paper was read, it quickly became apparent that the subject that had drawn these staff officers was not a mundane one. It concerned the effectiveness of new and super-secret technology for intelligence gathering. The issue on the agenda was how the money for it, which was hidden in the Pentagon budget, should be divided among the CIA, the NSA, the National Reconnaissance Office, which was responsible for running "overhead" photography satellites, the Special Navy Control Program, which was responsible for tapping into undersea Soviet cables with submarines, and other units of the military which sounded to me like random letters from the alphabet. It was all part of an entity called the National Intelligence Program, a term I had not heard before, which was important, as I also learned at the meeting, because it constituted over 90 percent of America's multi-billion-dollar intelligence budget. This program was administered, at least in terms of its budget allocations, by a small group called the Intelligence Community Staff, working jointly under the Director of Central Intelligence and the Secretary of Defense. Three of the other members of the panel who, unlike me, had top security clearances, worked on or with this staff, which explained the turnout. William Lackland was the deputy director of this staff; a second, Peter C. Oleson, represented the Secretary of Defense on the staff; and the third, George "Chip" Pickett, Jr., had been the liaison between the Senate Select Committee on Intelligence and the staff. Among them, they had a great deal to say as to which programs were funded. The fourth member of the panel, William Johnson, came from the CIA and had served on Angleton's counterintelligence staff. He, however, fell silent after Lackland described his specialty, espionage, as "nickel and dime stuff . . . not really worth talking about."

The three technocrats talked about intelligence in almost janitorial terms, as if it were simply another maintenance service provided by government. Over and over again, Lackland talked about "vacuum cleaning," which meant, as he somewhat impatiently explained when I asked, "sucking in data from wherever you can find it." In other words, signals were indiscriminately recorded with the idea that they might later be analyzed. At one point he suggested that "the entire electromagnetic spectrum could be vacuum-cleaned." For the better part of an hour, they elaborated on the "reach" of this high-tech equipment, which they wanted to extend not merely to the Soviet Union but the entire world.

"But couldn't the Soviet Union anticipate and take measures against this kind of surveillance?" I interrupted. As moderator,

I attempted to steer the discussion toward the issue that interested me: I suggested that Angleton had argued that intelligence cannot be easily separated from its twin, deception, if the sources and methods of collecting it from an adversary are anticipated by him.

Lackland answered, without missing a beat, "Even if the Soviet Union knows about it, there is nothing they can do." He acknowledged that conventional intelligence was predicated on a chance "snapshot," and it was conceivable that someone might try to deceive the camera by posing if he could anticipate where and when the photograph would be taken. But he insisted that with state-of-the-art space surveillance so many snapshots were taken, through so many different mediums, that the subject could not alter his image. So what if he knew his actions were being watched and listened to; he was "impotent" to deceive this omniscient surveillance.

It became clear as the discussion progressed that this trio was not merely describing a technology but a new philosophic doctrine or even, in Angleton's term, a new "epistemology of intelligence." It blurred the distinction between unanticipated and anticipated intelligence on the grounds that the quantity of data "vacuum-cleaned" made the target's state of knowledge irrelevant.

Under these premises, systematic deception was treated as if it were little more than a sick joke. When I pressed the issue about how one could know "the state of mind" of the enemy, for example, Lackland and Pickett responded with another technological solution: the staff had approved funding for research on ESP "mind-reading" projects which, if successful on Soviet leaders, would provide another field for vacuum cleaning.

The assertion that these technical systems, even without ESP, gave the United States an invulnerable shield against deception, if true, justified the projected expenditure of over $50 billion on them in the next decade. It also fit in well with the values of the reorganized American intelligence community. If these satellites systems could yield the answers to all relevant questions about the Soviet Union's strategy and plans, the CIA and NSA could do their job by processing a steady flow of predictable information from legal sensors in space, which required no risks or embarrassments. They could also project budgets on stable expectations of what hardware was needed through the millennium, predicated on the life span of satellites; provide routine coverage of Soviet sites specified by arms control treaties; and, in accomplishing these tasks, measure success by the quantity of intercepted photographs and signals.

But whereas this new technological doctrine may have satisfied many of the bureaucratic requisites of the intelligence establishment, it seemed to arouse considerable hostility from the generals and admirals in the room. One Air Force general asked pointedly, "If these systems are so all-seeing, why the hell didn't we receive warning about the Soviets going into Afghanistan?" Others cited warning failures in Europe and the Persian Gulf. An admiral recalled a U.S. Navy experiment in which a task force of ships knowing the precise orbit of U.S. satellites were able to so successfully zigzag out of their range that they crossed the Atlantic "invisible" to satellite coverage.[4]

Lackland, Oleson, and Pickett dismissed these examples as mere "glitches" in the system, but many in the audience seemed unconvinced. Afterwards, in less formal circumstances, I discussed these problems with some of the generals. I subsequently brought the matter up with Senator Malcolm Wallop, who had served on the Senate Intelligence Committee, and Angelo Codevilla, his staffer who had dealt with space intelligence (and who had also been at the Air Force Academy conference).

They had great admiration for the technological ingenuity of these intelligence-gathering machines which could identify virtually any target under the right conditions. But they pointed out that when all the bureaucratic jargon and mystery is stripped away, satellites are nothing more than platforms for observing or listening to an object that is at least one hundred miles away. They had their limitations.

Moreover, as Senator Wallop noted, there are only a handful of American observation satellites in the sky at any one time. The two main types are two Key Hole satellites, called the KH-11, a photo reconnaissance satellite, which takes detailed pictures over Soviet territory; and four signal satellites, code-named Aquacades, which are permanently stationed over Soviet territory to intercept radio and other electromagnetic signals. In addition, there are a few special-purpose satellites for tracking specific targets, such as the heat generated by Soviet missile launchings. And in December 1988, the United States added a satellite code-named Lacrosse that employed radar to "image" targets. This limited array of satellites, backed by tens of thousands of analysts at the National Reconnaissance Office, National Security Agency, and CIA, constitute the "eyes" and "ears" of American space-based intelligence.

The two KH-11 spacecraft are each 64 feet long and weigh 15 tons apiece. They fly across some Soviet territory every ninety minutes at altitudes of from 150 to 330 miles. At this relatively low altitude, their telescopes take pictures of preselected targets. Unlike earlier satellites, which took pictures on film (which then had to be ejected and recovered), the KH-11 transmits these pictures electronically, relaying them through other communications satellites to the Special Missile and Aeronautics Center at Fort Meade, Maryland. Here, within seconds, they are enhanced by super-computers into photographs with sufficiently high resolution to identify not only individual pieces of military equipment but, through insignias and numbers, the unit to which they belong.

But the KH-11 satellite still can only "see" with any meaningful clarity in the daytime and in good weather. It cannot take photographs at night, which is half the time, or through clouds, which cover over 70 percent of the Soviet Union at any one time.

Moreover, as Codevilla pointed out to me, these satellites not only do not "cover all that they can theoretically see, but they cannot even cover the square kilometer directly on their ground track." This is because their telescopes can focus with any clarity along a thin swath of territory. So, by any standard, the two KH-11 satellites can see only a small fraction of what is happening in the Soviet Union at any one time—and because of weather and other technical factors, not what they necessarily want to see. The difficulty in identifying a new site under the best of circumstances is illustrated by how long it took U.S. intelligence to photograph the giant Soviet radar at Krasnoyarsk in 1983. Even after the United States had learned of the radar station's construction and approximate location through other means (and it was the height of a thirty-story building), it took U.S. satellites more than two months to pinpoint the site and find appropriate weather conditions to photograph it.

To compensate for this fragmented vision, the CIA, through the National Reconnaissance Office, builds what it calls "mosaics," which are composed of hundreds of separate pictures taken at different times of the same site. The assumption—which is problematic—is that the gaps between the individual pictures, both in time and space, are irrelevant.

There is, however, a far more important limit on the KH-11, or any other satellite: it cannot see what is going on inside buildings or under roofs. And it is indoors where secret developments tend to take place. The KH-11 has never managed to photograph a single SS-18 or any other Soviet fourth-generation missile.

All that the KH-11 can be relied on to see is the outside of permanent structures, such as missile silos, radars, and factories, or weapons, such as aircraft carriers, that are too large to hide or move out of range. It peeks in on only a very few Soviet activities—and the Soviets can pull the shade down on these "windows" at any time.

The Soviets can control exactly what is seen because of the totally predictable orbit of the KH-11. Unlike World War II

156

reconnaissance planes or the U-2, which could arrive at unexpected times and change directions, satellites are tracked by computers from the moment they are launched. The KH-11 does have rocket engines, which allow it to modify its orbit (to the extent that the minuscule amount of fuel it carries lasts), but Soviet radar can detect these changes.

The Soviets also know precisely what the lenses can see, not only by knowing the laws of optics but through espionage. In 1978, the KGB acquired the KH-11 manual from an ex-CIA officer named William Kampiles. It explains all the operating procedures, transmission features, and capacities. Since then, the KH-11 has in no way been secret.[5]

Nor is its path. The verification procedures in the SALT arms control agreement have had the paradoxical effect of making the routes of the KH-11 highly predictable. Because the Soviets know which missile sites under construction must be continuously monitored by the United States, they can determine the angle at which the satellite's telescope is pointed, and the range of its camera on each pass. Soviet intelligence has even used its liaison with the SALT compliance commission to test the full capacity of the KH-11—by simply staging minor violations of SALT under different conditions to find out exactly when they can be detected by the satellite.[6]

Moreover, since 1966, the Soviets have employed a sophisticated warning system to alert all secret sites, such as missile-testing ranges or weapons-testing laboratories, exactly when they will be exposed to the lenses of American spy satellites. Not surprisingly, they are then able to bring indoors or otherwise cover objects they wish to hide. Missiles, for instance, are not loaded during the brief interval when the KH-11 passes.

With this Satellite Warning System, the Soviet deception planners deal with U.S. surveillance, when the alarm sounds—just as a politician uses a photo opportunity—to put in the path of the satellite lenses what they want to be photographed. To accomplish this deception, they need not forge comprehensive Potemkin villages; they need only add or alter the data which American analysts rely on to gauge relevant activities. According to the KGB defector Aleksei Myagov, Soviet military counter-intelligence, in conjunction with the KGB, has since 1968 been given the mandate "to prepare and carry out . . . special measures for disinformation of the enemy," which include deceiving space surveillance.[7] Another more recent defector, Viktor Suvorov, has provided detailed accounts of how the Soviet Army displays fake military equipment for the benefit of the satellite. The coordination of these "special measures" to deceive and confuse U.S. satellite cameras was even put under a special staff, known as GUSM, originally organized by General N. V. Ogarkov.[8] When an American satellite is due to pass over a secret site, GUSM has three options: It can permit it to be photographed in its true state; it can try to hide or disguise this site; or it can use the opportunity to expose some other feature or equipment on the site, real or fabricated, which will mislead the United States.

No greater skills are needed today to camouflage objects subject to satellite photography than were needed to deceive aerial photography in World War II.[9] Though it is a vastly superior technology, the space-based telescope takes a picture from 100 to 330 miles away, whereas the aerial camera used in World War II took a picture from a distance of a mile or less. The additional power of the telescope simply compensates for the additional distance. As can be calculated, taking pictures from an altitude of 100 miles away with a telescope that has a focal length of 64 feet (the maximum that will fit in the KH-11) permits observation of objects down to six inches in size, in perfect air conditions, which is approximately the same resolution as the aerial cameras used by German planes in the 1940s. Yet Soviet deception planners demonstrated their ability to dupe German aerial photography in World War II even to the extent of creating phantom armies and fortifications.

The concept was known as *Maskirovka*, or mashing, which involved hiding real objects through camouflage while at the same time displaying spurious indicators of nonexistent objects to confuse and distract foreign intelligence sensors. The *Soviet Military Historical Journal* cites more than twenty major military successes between 1941 to 1944 that proceeded from such techniques. As the camouflage problem is now no different and they have no doubt improved these techniques, the duping of satellites cannot be considered a technical impossibility.

If an adversary knows where, when, and how he is being served, there is no way to prevent him from putting misleading messages in the path of the surveillance. Since the KH-11 operates under such conditions, if only because of the predictability of its orbit, it can serve as a channel of communications for GUSM as well as an observation platform for the CIA. This severely limits its ability to serve as any sort of shield against Soviet deception.

Of course, satellite photography is only one component—the "eyes"—of America's surveillance of the Soviet bloc. The other mainstay is the "ears"—signals intelligence satellites stationed some 22,500 miles high, in geosynchronous orbit, over Soviet territory.[10] Although this is too far away for photographs, their antennae continuously "vacuum-clean" emissions coming from Soviet VHF, UHF, or microwave broadcasts, the telemetry from missile tests, communications between aircraft, telephone relays, and most other electronic transmissions. Unlike the KH-11, these satellites travel at approximately the same speed as the earth, remain positioned over important targets for long periods of time, and can intercept signals broadcast from them in any weather, day or night. They then relay these intercepted signals, through the "down link" in Pine Gap, Australia, to NSA headquarters at Ford Meade, Maryland, for processing. But their activities are neither secret nor unexpected. Soviet intelligence learned their capabilities—and vulnerabilities—in 1975, when a

TRW employee, Christopher Boyce, delivered to the KGB hundreds of technical documents describing the way these satellites (then code-named "Rhyolite") operated.[11]

Signals intelligence satellites are, moreover, easily identifiable by Soviet radar—if only because of their football field–size antennae. The Soviets can be expected to know, at any given time, their position and the direction in which their antennae are pointing. They can then figure out their potential targets simply by checking which of their own radio emissions would intersect with the antennae. Then, as Codevilla pointed out in his analysis of space intelligence, those responsible for Soviet communications security can "either shift the [compromised] communication to a safe channel or transmit knowing someone is listening."[12] If they choose the latter course, they can encrypt the data, which will make it meaningless to the listener, or else use the opportunity for deception, which means adding material that will mislead the listener.

Even though the United States deploys other highly specialized reconnaissance satellites that pick up radiation, heat, magnetic impulses, and other "signatures" from Soviet radar, nuclear blasts, and missile launchings—and even though the amount of data processed is no doubt "vast"—the focus is extremely narrow, limited to tiny slits in Soviet security such as unencrypted broadcasts or equipment left outdoors.

For example, the new radar satellite, code-named Lacrosse, can detect objects through cloud cover, and at night, by bombarding them with high-frequency signals and then deducing from the way the "blips" bounce off it, the shape of the object. But the amount of Soviet territory that can be analyzed this way by a single satellite is minuscule—even compared with the KH-11 satellite. Moreover, it has little value as clandestine or unexpected intelligence since radar "reads" an object, like a blind person reading braille, by touching it with blips, allowing the Soviets to know exactly what was being spied upon by the satellite.

And because it can be anticipated, radar can easily be deceived by distorting angles and surfaces.

Codevilla and Wallop estimated that "thousands of satellites would be needed to do what Stansfield Turner claimed we do routinely: keep track of everything important on the face of the earth!"[13] And even most of these exposures can be controlled by the Soviets if they believe it is worth the expense and effort to shut the slits or bias the information leaking out of them. In wartime, when it is more difficult to control exposure, especially if there are major military movements or missile launchings, space-based intelligence is truly invaluable. It may also be extremely helpful, and convenient for both sides, to verify arms control treaties. But in peacetime, because the peepholes can be more tightly controlled, the handful of American satellites cannot be assumed capable of exposing many kinds of activities— and especially those which the Soviets valued enough to keep secret.

This led to a further concern. The intelligence executives I spoke to seemed to be unconcerned with obtaining unanticipated intelligence about the Soviet Union. Indeed, they did not believe this arcane form of spying was necessary. If so, and if, consequently, Soviet intelligence could expect where, when, and how American satellites would be looking and listening to its activities, could it also use these highly valued American intelligence machines as channels for deception?

CHAPTER ELEVEN

The Telemetry Double Cross

Could high-tech satellites be double-crossed in the same way that human spies were in the celebrated double-cross systems of World War II?

I pursued this line of inquiry in Los Angeles with Amrom H. Katz, whom I had been introduced to at the first deception conference as America's foremost authority on space reconnaissance.[1] He had begun his career in 1940 at the Air Force's Aerial Reconnaissance Laboratory, and then he played a major role at RAND in the development of America's space-based reconnaissance. Later, in 1973, he headed the Bureau of Verification and Analysis, which had the responsibility for verifying the SALT treaties. Like others involved in arms control negotiations, he used the euphemism "National Technical Means," or NTMs, to describe spy satellites.[2]

Katz, a short, assertive man, spoke with a precision about his science that at times was its own kind of poetry. He began by cutting right to the heart of my question about space surveillance. He asked suggestively: "Why not apply Heisenberg's principle to NTMs and assume that the observer inevitably affects the actions of the observed?"

"And the Soviets know that they are being observed?" I asked.

"It would be foolish to assume otherwise," he answered, reasoning that "the laws of physics apply equally in both hemispheres," and what the Soviets cannot deduce from theoretical physics they can ascertain by experimenting with their own satellites, which operate at similar altitudes and conditions as their American counterparts. He pointed out further that aside from what they had learned through their espionage successes the Soviets also had the ability to test the limits of American satellites merely by staging an infraction of the SALT accords and then seeing whether or not it was detected. "I doubt there is much mystery that remains about what we are observing." He suggested that rather than catching either side by surprise, the satellites provided a mutual channel for communications. They permit each side to disclose data the other side needs to know, he argued, adding, "Disclosure is part of deterrence." He reminded me that in the satirical film *Dr. Strangelove*, the Soviet deterrent, a "Doomsday" bomb designed to end life on earth if the Soviet Union is attacked, failed because the Soviets had not informed the United States about it.

Satellites allowed each side to disclose not only whatever "Doomsday" deterrent it might possess but whatever other information it wanted foreign observers to be aware of, such as its compliance with the SALT Treaty. "What it needs to keep secret is another problem." NTMs, at least in this mode, acted as a sort of collaborative "show and tell game." Indeed, Katz pointed out that when the United States considered shuttling missiles around between silos in the mid-1970s, it included in the plan a provision for sliding open the roofs of both the empty and full silos when Soviet satellites passed overhead so that they could accurately count the missiles.

But if that was the case, why couldn't the Soviets use this "game" to show information which, even if it was not factually inaccurate, would mislead American intelligence? I asked, "Does anyone worry about satellites being double-crossed?"

Katz quoted what he called Crow's Law, which had been developed by a British bureaucrat called Crow, and held: "Do not think what you want to think until you know what you ought to know." He said, "I have a colleague at RAND who can possibly tell you what you ought to know. He has been working on this problem for years." He was William R. Harris, an international lawyer at RAND and a consultant to the Senate Intelligence Committee, who was, as Katz put it, "fascinated with turning things inside out."

I met Harris for breakfast at his home at Pacific Palisades the next morning. He was young, energetic, articulate, and extremely guarded in what he said, preferring to speak in the hypothetical realm. He explained that he held very high "code word" security clearances for his work at RAND and had to be very careful in what he said. He was also an almost obsessive intelligence buff, who compiled a three-volume annotated bibliography on spies and deception while he was at Harvard University in 1968.[3] In 1976, he had worked on a project at RAND to reassess data that had been intercepted from the Soviet Union. And he knew, even before I had broached the subject, of the double cross in which I was interested.

Before we had finished our first cup of coffee in what was to be a long, caffeine-drenched day, he came to the point. "In the 1960s a mistake was made by us in assessing Soviet capabilities," he began. "It was a mistake of such stunning magnitude that we are still reckoning with the consequences today." He explained that this error, which persisted for the better part of a decade, involved drastically underestimating the ability of the Soviet Union to produce intercontinental missiles that had the pinpoint accuracy necessary to threaten America's land-based missile force. This occurred when U.S. intelligence, employing its "most advanced sources and methods," concluded that the Soviet Union was precluded from achieving such accuracy in the foreseeable future because it had not mastered the key component in the guidance system, and, given this deficiency, the Soviets were basing their future strategy, which could continue into the next millennium, on targeting their missiles on cities, which required far less accuracy, instead of missile silos. If so, the Soviets had a defensive deterrent, since they could retaliate against American cities, but not a strategy for striking first and destroying American missiles on the ground which were (and remain) clustered in a half-dozen sites. On the basis of this intelligence, "We made unwarranted assumptions about both the invulnerability of our missiles and Soviet weakness," he concluded.

It seemed incredible to me that America's entire strategy could be based on some deficient part in some rocket. I asked him, moving from the grand to the prosaic picture, "What was this key component?"

He answered, "The accelerometers," holding his thumb and forefinger about three inches apart, indicating the tiny size of this part. He explained that accelerometers act as a sort of high-precision gyroscope that, by measuring the pull of gravity, indicates exactly how fast an object is accelerating at any moment. From this information a computer can then calculate the object's precise position and speed. This is crucially important on missiles because it allows a computer to determine when to release the warheads, which then, with no further guidance, proceed by gravity toward their targets thousands of miles away.

"But what about our satellites and other NTMs?" I asked, borrowing the lingo from Katz. "Couldn't we ascertain something as evident as how accurate Soviet missiles were . . . ?"

He jumped in with his answer before I had finished my question. "We did rely on NTMs. That's the point. The data that led to the error came from NTMs."

He explained that the United States had been intercepting the measurement data broadcast back to earth, or telemetry, from Soviet rockets when they were tested. For this purpose, even before it orbited its signals satellites, the United States used antennae in Turkey, Iran, and Pakistan. Among this telemetry, which was broadcast back unencrypted in the 1960s, was the data from each of nine accelerometers sent back on separate channels. Analyses showed striking variations between different accelerometers supposedly measuring the same value. The CIA task force studying these interceptions was perplexed not only by this inconsistency but by the fact that the Soviets were using redundant accelerometers. The Soviets were using nine accelerometers whereas three would be enough—one to measure each of the three axes. The assumption the CIA made to explain this discrepancy was that the Soviet accelerometers were so inaccurate and unreliable that the Soviets did not trust their measurements. Instead, the Soviets had to resort to a primitive system of averaging the data from multiple accelerometers on each axis and using that result. (The United States had considered a similar method before it developed more accurate accelerometers.) The CIA thus found that the Soviets showed no intention of designing accurate missiles, a conclusion which fit in with what America wanted to believe about the Soviet Union.[4]

This conclusion proved to be wrong in 1968 when the Soviet stunned American strategists by testing MIRV and other highly sophisticated missiles which demonstrated that they had mastered the accelerometer problem, despite the telemetry data. How could such a contradiction be explained?

When the data was reanalyzed, it was then determined, as Harris put it, that "only the systematic biasing of telemetry by the Soviets would produce the apparent large errors in guidance." The Soviets had, in other words, allowed some of the accelerometers to broadcast inaccurate data, which evidently was not used for purposes of guidance, and this bad data, when averaged in with the relevant data, produced the "systematic bias" that so disastrously misled the U.S. strategic design.

There still remained the question of whether or not the deception was deliberate. "Did Soviet intelligence know the United States was intercepting its telemetry?" I asked.

"There is no doubt about that, it was hardly a secret," Harris answered. The Soviets had captured a large cache of their own telemetry data on a downed U.S. transport plane which had strayed over Soviet territory in 1957, and in 1960, Bernon Mitchell and William H. Martin defected from the National Security

Agency to Moscow. Both had been working on telemetry analyses and no doubt told the KGB exactly how the United States intercepted Soviet telemetry.[5]

Soviet intelligence had great experience in double-crossing communications interceptions. It had used it as a technique of disinformation ever since the Bolshevik Revolution. For example, in 1921 when British intelligence agents obtained the Soviet diplomatic code from a spy in its Estonian mission and used it to decode its messages, Soviet intelligence, rather than changing this betrayed code, used it to misinform British intelligence about Soviet arms shipments to rebels in British India. It sent messages in this code to its Teheran Embassy suggesting that it was ending its clandestine arms traffic, knowing they would be read by the British. By doing so, it provided evidence that the British Foreign Office needed to sign a trade treaty with the Soviet Union.[6]

Stalin also used this double-cross technique in 1940 when he discovered that Germany, though then supposedly an ally, had tapped into the cable link between Japan and the Soviet Union, and deciphered the code through which messages were sent to its embassy in Tokyo. Although he could have easily changed from using the compromised diplomatic code to virtually unbreakable "one-time" pads, in which the code is switched every message (which were being used at European embassies), he decided instead to allow the Germans access to this link. He then arranged for Soviet intelligence to insert disinformation messages in the cable traffic.

"The same concept applies to double-crossing telemetry signals," Harris suggested. In this case, the Soviets simply had to add to each missile being tested extra gauges that were biased in one direction or another so that they would broadcast back data that would appear to be inaccurate to American eavesdroppers. Since Soviet scientists knew which gauges were dummies, they could simply ignore the biased data. But the United States, not knowing what this data reflected, had no way of excluding the bogus data from its calculations.

Why would the Soviets go to such trouble to deceive the United States? Harris explained that Soviet planners had a very good reason for deceiving the United States about the accuracy of a new generation of missiles, the so-called SS-7s, that their Yangel Design Bureau was developing in 1958–59. If U.S. intelligence had realized that the guidance systems on these missiles were good enough to pinpoint and destroy in a surprise attack all eighty command centers necessary to launch U.S. land-based missiles, the United States would have compensated for this by either placing their missile force on moving trains—a plan then under consideration—or further hardening the silos to make them less vulnerable. In either case, it would have defeated the peremptory threat of the Soviet SS-7. But by distorting the telemetry, and making the SS-7s appear to be inaccurate, the Soviets furthered their potential for winning a Pearl Harbor type preemptive war.

Harris pointed out that by the early 1960s the "KGB not only established a field office at the Tyura-Tam Missile Test Center [where the SS7s were tested], but actually controlled access to missile guidance and calibration facilities at that test range." The KGB was thus able to manage the "indicators" through which the CIA decided the degree of lethality of these weapons. Moreover, he noted that there was no downside for the Soviets to this deception. "The recorded mis-calibrations, before flight testing, of one or more of each set of redundant instruments, could result in a test series in which the Soviet strategic rocket forces could estimate the actual guidance errors" while deceiving the United States at the same time.

After I returned to New York, I dug out an old file of notes. Harris was not the first person to have brought up accelerometers. I recalled that Willam Sullivan had mentioned them in regard to another matter shortly before he died in his hunting accident in 1976. It did not seem relevant at the time, but when I reread the file I realized it fit in with what Harris told me.

Sullivan had described how Vadim Isakov, a Soviet diplomat working for UNESCO in New York, led the FBI "on a merry chase of arms dealers" around the country in the early 1960s— even though he knew he was under surveillance. He was trying to buy, among other things, accelerometers. Eventually, in 1965, he led his FBI shadows to an arms dealer in New Jersey, who agreed to sell him accelerometers, and he was promptly arrested. Sullivan's point was that it was a "set-up" designed to focus American attention on these devices (which he did not describe further).

When this Soviet interest in accelerometers was passed on to the CIA science and technology task force, it requested the FBI to see what the two FBI double agents at the UN, Fedora and Top Hat, knew about Isakov's mission. Both men reported that they had received a questionnaire from Moscow that urgently requested information about American guidance controls, which meant accelerometers.

Fedora then returned to Moscow on home leave. When he came back to New York, he had some further data for the FBI. He said that he had learned that Soviet scientists were having great difficulty gauging the exact moment to separate warheads from missiles. They needed to know, according to Fedora, how American scientists had solved this problem.

Sullivan had no doubt that Fedora was a Soviet-controlled agent (which was later confirmed when he returned to Moscow). He was therefore suggesting that Moscow was feeding Washington disinformation about the inaccuracy of its guidance system through double agents.

When I told Harris about Fedora's role, he hardly sounded surprised. He added, "It wasn't only double-agent channels that were used" to reinforce the biased telemetry. There was a third channel, but he insisted that he "absolutely could not discuss it."

By this time, I could make a fairly educated guess, especially in light of my prior conservation with Katz, that this third channel was satellite photography. After all, as Katz had explained to me, ever since World War II, photo reconnaissance experts had studied bomb and artillery craters to determine the accuracy of weapons. It would be an obvious use for satellites.

I raised this issue with a staffer on the Senate Intelligence Committee who also had an interest in deception. He answered matter-of-factly, perhaps assuming that I knew more than I did, that the National Reconnaissance Office used crater analysis to confirm the relative inaccuracy of Soviet missiles. It tasked satellites, when weather conditions permitted, to photograph the Soviet missile-testing range in Siberia the day after test firings. He pointed out that the Soviets certainly knew the craters were being photographed and even left telephone poles they used as aiming points in place. So it was a relatively easy matter to deduce how far the warheads went astray.

This "crater impact analysis," I further learned, provided results of wildly off-the-mark missiles that dovetailed with both the data from the intercepted Soviet telemetry and Fedora's reports. These three Soviet channels, all confirming each other, further convinced American strategists that they were right in downplaying the likelihood of highly accurate missiles.

He then went on to explain that in the early 1970s unexpected intelligence revealed dramatically different results. For a brief period, the Soviets did not realize that what they assumed was a signals satellite was actually photographing its missile range. The photographs this satellite took, obviously anticipated by Soviet intelligence, revealed Soviet bulldozer crews working at night filling in some craters and excavating others, and also moving around the aiming points. Presumably, these alterations were being made for the benefit of the expected American satellites that were scheduled to pass over the sites the next day. The comparison of the real craters with the doctored ones revealed the purpose of the satellite deception: as in the case of the doctored accelerometers, it was to underrepresent the accuracy of Soviet missiles. If nothing else, this suggested that "vacuum-cleaning" different channels would not expose a deception so long as the Soviets orchestrate what is seen and heard in other channels. In this case, the clues dished up by three channels—telemetry, double agents, and satellite photography—only served to make the deception more credible. And through this orchestration the United States was misled about the accuracy of Soviet missiles over a five-year period.[7]

Once the Soviets realized that the United States had caught on to the faking of the craters, they not only ended this activity but the reports from Fedora and his associates suggesting Soviet missile inaccuracy dried up. And, soon afterwards, the Soviets began encrypting the telemetry from their accelerometers so that it was no longer available to the CIA. It now seemed persuasive that, before and after the fact, the Soviets were coordinating what the United States saw—and didn't see—in these channels. Could it be anything else than a well-planned double cross of U.S. intelligence? It certainly had disastrously misled American strategists.

The Soviets had the capacity to orchestrate such a deception. The Soviet missile command had been reorganized in 1959, and a special staff, GUSM, had been given the responsibility for the security of its secret testing. But there still remained one element missing in the deception loop—feedback.

In order for GUSM to have organized such a massive deception in 1961, and sustain it for six years in the mind of American intelligence, it would have to have a "window," as Harris put it, to see how its tricks were being interpreted. It had to be certain, for example, that the CIA had accepted the "averaging method" of calculating telemetry (a method that had been conveniently disclosed by a Soviet scientist at a conference monitored by the CIA). It had to be sure that the CIA had swallowed the bait about the accelerometers and that the National Reconnaissance Office had taken the telephone poles among the craters to be aiming points. And it had to be sure that the United States did not have an unanticipated source of intelligence (as it subsequently developed) that would expose the deception. This window would require a mole who had access to some of America's most secret and exotic intelligence.

I took this problem to Colonel Thomas D. Fox, whom I had met in 1975 when I was doing research on narcotics control and he was working for an elite anti-drug task force.[8] He had headed the counterintelligence of the Defense Intelligence Agency in the late 1960s and he had a labyrinthine memory for all the convoluted trails left by moles in the defense establishment. I now wanted to know from him if any had been in the position to provide feedback for a telemetry double cross.

"One candidate, who had both the position and access, would be Whalen," he began, as he recounted his history from memory like a computer file. Lieutenant Colonel William Henry Whalen had been the highest-ranking American military officer to be convicted as a Soviet agent. He had joined the Army, at the age of twenty-five, in 1940. After sustaining injuries in a car accident in 1941, he became a special service officer, assigned to the Office of Chief of Staff, Intelligence Division, in Washington, D.C. This division is the private intelligence service of the Joint Chiefs of Staff, which has access to virtually all military secrets. In the late 1940s, he was assigned responsibility for finding, and resettling, German rocket scientists in the United States—which involved maintaining "liaisons with industrial research, scientific, and scholastic organizations." For this work, he received a top secret and cryptographic clearance. Then, in the mid-1950s, he served in Japan, helping to organize communications intelligence systems. From 1955 to 1957, he returned to Washington and worked with the Foreign Liaison Office in the Pentagon. His job there involved delivering "cleared" information (including disinformation) to Soviet military liaisons. Fox speculated that this was where he came to the attention of Soviet recruiters.

In any case, as Army intelligence later pieced together, Colonel Sergei Edemski, the Soviet Army attaché, began cultivating Whalen with dinners and small cash gifts in the guise of presents for his child. When he found Whalen receptive to taking money, he gradually increased the amounts. Since he had apparently learned through another undetermined Soviet source in the Pentagon that Whalen was not reporting these unorthodox social contacts, he intensified the pressure on him. He asked, for example, Whalen's help in getting some unclassified manuals—which would greatly help him impress his Soviet superiors. When Whalen complied, further compromising himself, Edemski then began requesting more useful data. At this point, Whalen realized that the Soviets could not only destroy his career but put him in prison. He had little alternative but to continue his relationship with Edemski.

In July 1957, Whalen was promoted to deputy chairman of the Joint Intelligence Objectives Agency which, among other tasks, assessed secret intelligence received from scientists. And, in 1959, he was chosen as the intelligence adviser to the Army Chief of Staff—one of the highest intelligence positions in the country. From these two vantage points, he could claim a "need to know" virtually whatever intelligence was relevant to the Joint Chief of Staff's planning and allocation of military forces. This included satellite, communications, and electronic intelligence gathering. Whalen continued passing such information on to his Soviet case officers until 1962. This would have been the critical period for feedback for the telemetry deception. "He certainly told the Soviets about the conclusions we were drawing from the telemetry intercepts," Fox concluded.

Fox added that Whalen had been caught by the FBI through surveillance. He confessed, was arrested, tried, and convicted of conspiring with a Soviet agent in 1966.[9]

So Whalen could have provided the window the Soviet deception planners needed initially. But who provided it after 1962?

"The Soviets might have gotten what else they needed from Jack Dunlap," Fox suggested. Unlike Whalen, Jack E. Dunlap was merely a sergeant in the National Security Agency. But he had access to the "kings of the kingdom" as the chauffeur for

Major General Garrison B. Coverdale, the chief of staff of the National Security Agency. Fox explained that at NSA headquarters at Fort Meade, Maryland, where the total product of U.S. electronic interceptions—the data vacuum-cleaned from antennae in space satellites, naval spy ships, and planted listening devices in hostile countries—is processed and analyzed, security is based on preventing anyone from taking any data from the base. Everyone is searched at the gates—with one exception. As the driver of the chief of staff's car, Dunlap was permitted to drive on and off the base without being searched. It was, according to Fox, the only vehicle that could leave the base without being inspected.

Dunlap also opened up a small business which vastly increased his access. Since his car had unique "no inspection" status, he volunteered to help senior officers at the NSA pilfer from the base various items, such as typewriters and furniture, which they wanted at home. At least six of the officers accepted the offer and, with Dunlap's help, continued smuggling articles out for at least two years. A later investigation even found that one NSA colonel had tutored Dunlap in methods of circumventing other NSA procedures.

All this time Dunlap was a Soviet agent, having been compromised and recruited in Turkey in 1957. While pretending to be merely assisting his superiors get their effects off the base, Dunlap and his KGB controllers got virtually the complete run of America's most secret intelligence base. The pilfering ring not only provided Dunlap with the keys to offices and combinations to safes; it also gave him a plausible rationale for his after-hour visits. Dunlap was thus able to deliver to his Soviet contacts microfilmed copies of virtually all the instruction books, repair manuals, mathematical models, and design plans for the machinery used to encrypt American codes.

Then, in 1961, he was given responsibility by the chief of staff for shuttling secret data back and forth between Fort Meade and the CIA counterintelligence officers on Angleton's staff who were cleared on a "need to know" basis to see these interceptions. This afforded Dunlap the opportunity to ascertain—and feed back to his Soviet case officers—the questions that CIA counterintelligence was asking about data intercepted from the Soviet Union. He could have, up until 1963, delivered what Fox called the "methodology" for this intelligence.

But that could not be determined by military intelligence. On October 10, 1963, before the evidence came to light showing he was a Soviet mole, Dunlap died in his car in his garage from asphyxiation, an apparent suicide.

Fox told me that there had been a full-scale NSA postmortem investigation by General Joseph P. Carroll that I could obtain under the Freedom of Information Act, which I did.[10] I then went to see Angleton since, according to Fox, Dunlap had been acting as a liaison with Angleton's counterintelligence staff shortly before his death.

After reading through the Carroll Report, which he had obviously seen before, Angleton said glumly, "The real tragedy was that Dunlap was never debriefed." I recalled that a number of other Soviet agents had apparently killed themselves before they could be interrogated. There were three such cases in Germany alone in 1968. "Making murder look like suicide is no trick," he said with an enigmatic shrug.

Angleton did not want to talk about Dunlap's contacts with his staff, saying, "That was not the problem." He explained that in 1962, when Dunlap was carting NSA data by the trunkload to his Soviet case officers, the NSA was involved in the installation and security arrangements for the CIA's new central computer. This system not only connected up the CIA's own archives but provided electronic channels to safely transmit data to outside agencies in the intelligence community. Since this computer was a prime target of Soviet intelligence, Angleton feared that Dunlap might have given away the computer's safeguard design. If so, the Soviets could "breach the computer from the outside" and monitor, step by step, the way the CIA "conceived of an intelligence problem." He then suggested that in the late 1960s his counterintelligence staff and the Office of Security developed incontrovertible evidence that such a "breach" of the computer system had indeed occurred. The Soviets thus had their feedback (see Table 3).

**Table 3. The Telemetry Double Cross
1962–67**

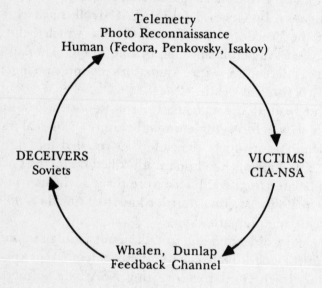

Disinformation Channels

Telemetry
Photo Reconnaissance
Human (Fedora, Penkovsky, Isakov)

DECEIVERS
Soviets

VICTIMS
CIA-NSA

Whalen, Dunlap
Feedback Channel

CHAPTER TWELVE

The War of the Moles

> Having inward spies means making use of officials of the enemy . . . to find out the state of affairs in the enemy's country, ascertain the plans that are being formed against you, and disturb the harmony and create a breach between the sovereign and his ministers.
>
> —Sun-tzu, *The Art of War*

After learning about Dunlap, I wanted to know why U.S. intelligence was vulnerable to penetrations. Not only must such a mole be in the right place at the right moment, he must be willing to betray his country, very possibly at the risk of his life. What were the conditions that allowed the KGB to find these "inward spies"?

Earlier in my research, an officer in the CIA's Soviet Bloc Division outlined to me what he claimed was a novel that he wanted to write. It was called "The Letter."

It begins when a young CIA officer working out of the American Embassy in Berne, Switzerland, receives an anonymous letter warning him that one of his superiors in the CIA is a Soviet mole. The writer adds that he will personally contact the officer within the week and provide him with secret documents that will establish his bona fides. The letter writer makes one final request: he asks the CIA officer to keep even the fact that he has received the letter a secret from his superiors, lest it leak back to the mole and the KGB.

The case officer ignores this injunction. Instead, following CIA procedures, he informs his superior about the letter. Several months later he receives another letter from the mystery writer explaining that his initial letter has leaked to the KGB, precipitating a Soviet security investigation. To prove that there was indeed a penetration into the CIA station, he also encloses the name of an Eastern European diplomat the CIA was planning to recruit that month. The writer notes that if this letter is passed up through channels, he will undoubtedly be discovered and arrested; if not, he will contact the CIA officer.

The CIA officer, convinced by this information that indeed there is a mole in his own chain of command, decides this time to follow the instructions in the letter. This time he ignores the rules.

Weeks go by. Then, at a large reception, a Soviet diplomat identifies himself to the CIA officer as the letter writer. He explains that he is a KGB counterintelligence officer who wants to defect to the United States. He points out that, having revealed himself, his life now depends on the discretion of the CIA officer. And he offers a bargain that is difficult to resist. He will supply an entire cache of documents about Soviet intelligence operations that will pinpoint the Soviet moles in the CIA. In return, all the CIA officer has to do is help conceal his identity until the mole complex is exposed.

The CIA officer replies that he has no real choice in the matter: whatever documents he receives from him will have to be passed up through channels.

The KGB officer then suggests a way out of this bind. The documents could be turned over to his superiors, but, to throw the inevitable KGB investigation off his tracks, the CIA officer would misreport the time of the meetings by a day or so. He argues that this misreporting, which would be leaked back to the KGB, will allow him to establish an alibi.

The CIA officer accepts the deal. He figures in return for trivial lies to his superior that will not be noticed, he will protect his source's life. The documents he gets will then expose the moles, which will make him a hero.

The documents begin flowing in, and the case officer suddenly finds himself an important man in the Soviet Division. He is even taken to a briefing of the President.

But his source, who is becoming progressively more valuable, then begins to complain that the KGB security investigation is closing in on his section. Even with the time discrepancy, he says he will come under suspicion if he continues to supply material. He now needs the CIA officer's help in diverting attention away from him. He asks him to make a trip to Vienna and report that his source was there (even though the Soviet officer will remain in Switzerland).

The CIA officer, anxious for the next batch of documents, agrees to this harmless deception. He gets the documents in Switzerland, holds them secretly in a girlfriend's apartment, then travels to Vienna, where he hopes he will be picked up by Soviet surveillance. On his return from Vienna, he gets the documents and hands them in to his superior—as well as a fake report about his contact.

As more and more secret material comes in, his "mole" assumes progressively greater importance to the CIA. Accordingly, the case officer has to go to greater lengths to maintain the fictional identity of his source, which by now involves falsifying expense vouchers, as well as the times and places of meetings.

Finally, when the CIA case officer is sufficiently entangled in this web, his "mole" suddenly turns the tables on him. He shows him a complete dossier that has been ingeniously compiled on him by the KGB during this entire episode. It includes everything from photographs of him in places that he was not supposed to be, with a Soviet diplomat whom he has never mentioned in his reports, to bank books showing that money has been deposited in his name in bank accounts.

The CIA officer, realizing how incriminating this dossier would look to his superiors, listens in stunned amazement as the Soviet intelligence officer now makes him a proposition: becoming a Soviet mole. If he accepts, the Soviet recruiter says, the KGB could make him Director of the CIA. If he refuses, his dossier will be leaked to CIA counterintelligence.

The CIA case officer decides to break off his contacts with his Soviet accomplice, and admits to falsifying the records of the case. But his superiors do not believe him—and a new nightmare begins as he tries to prove he is not a mole. This was as far as the author had gotten in his outline.

Angleton said, when I had finished recounting this plot to him, "That is not a novel; it is what had happened in 1962."

The only difference was the ending. The CIA officer who had gotten himself entrapped through a combination of zeal, ambition, and compassion was forced to resign, since even with lie detectors the counterintelligence staff could not be certain about his story. Angleton understood he had become a successful banker.[1]

The ease with which a trained, loyal, and experienced CIA case officer could be entrapped interested me. The recruitment of a mole appeared to have been refined to a science by intelligence services. As Angleton explained it, the making of a mole is far less difficult in practice than it appears to the public. It is based on the premise that whereas few individuals would elect to commit treason if they knew what they were doing, few can resist breaking minor rules and regulations when presented with the right set of temptations. What it involves then is not a single conscious decision to betray state secrets, but an incremental entrapment in a subtle web of compromises. Intelligence services, with the aid of psychologists and social behaviorists, have refined the procedure to a precise science. It requires three conditions: access, vulnerability to compromise, and the inability to resist blackmail.

• • •

Access, or the opportunity to approach a target without arousing suspicion, is rarely a problem in the intelligence game. Enemy intelligence officers, especially those charged with espionage operations, are continually in contact with one another. It is, as Angleton put it, "part of their mission." The main job of a CIA officer is, after all, to recruit an Eastern bloc intelligence officer. Conversely, the main job of a KGB officer is to recruit a CIA intelligence officer. The CIA's Soviet Division, which is in charge of this espionage activity, stations most of its officers in American embassies around the world and in the UN, under the guise of American diplomats. The KGB's American Section of its Foreign Service (or First Chief Directorate), which performs a similar mission for the Soviet Union, posts its officers under diplomatic cover at most of its embassies abroad—and its UN Mission. Since the diplomatic cover tends to be transparent, they both know who the other is (and, if there is any question, both sides maintain archives of snapshots to identify their rivals).

At diplomatic receptions where Western and Eastern bloc intelligence officers often home in on one another like long-lost friends, both sides attempt to assess each other's vulnerabilities. In these exchanges, it is not uncommon for a CIA and KGB officer to pick each other as targets for recruitment. As this game continues, the rival intelligence officers may invite one another to dinner, family outings, sporting events, or other social occasions. They can even dangle bits of information to each other—so long as these are "cleared" by their own intelligence service as "bait." The only restriction on this activity, according to Angleton, is that each officer file a full written report of his contact with the enemy.

In addition to such diplomatic contacts, opposition intelligence officers frequently call each other "cold" to establish contact. To heighten their counterpart's interest in them, they often feign dissatisfaction with their work, financial difficulties, or a sexual vulnerability. These ritualistic flirtations involve a sizable part of both the American and Soviet espionage services. Angleton estimated that, any given time, there are several hundred intelligence officers "in the deer park," as he called this pool of case officers and targets.

The second condition, vulnerability, is more difficult to find. Not all the targets can be compromised, but intelligence services have techniques for selecting those in the pool with weaknesses that can be exploited. The "target" somehow must be tempted into doing something that is an infraction of his country's rules and regulations—no matter how trivial. The lure can be whatever appears to interest him, including money, sex, drugs, friendship, career advancement, or any combination of the above. In 1966, a study prepared for the Assistant Army Chief of Staff for Intelligence, entitled "Motivations to Treason," concluded that bribes were by far the most often used inducements. (Ironically, the Intelligence Chief's own deputy, Lieutenant Colonel Whalen, was later convicted for passing classified American secrets to Soviet intelligence officers in return for money.)[3] Bribes need not be direct. They can take the form of loans to relatives, consulting fees, gambling tips, inside information on a stock, or participation in a profitable business venture. Nor does the person dispensing the benefit have to reveal for whom he is really working. Or the bait can be sexual—custom-designed to fit almost any human weakness or perversion.

While it may be more convenient for a nation to find a recruit predisposed to its cause—as Philby, Burgess, Maclean, and Blunt were sympathetic to the Communist cause—it is not necessary. Acting under a "false flag," a KGB recruiter can assume, Proteanlike, any affiliation to which his target is predisposed, no matter how antithetical it is to communism. Angleton recalled cases in which KGB officers pretended to be Israeli officials, NATO military attachés, and even neo-Nazis. Once these officers violated the reporting requirements of their service, they were compromised and blackmailed into service for the real principal—the KGB. Since any "false flag" can be adopted, any intelligence officer who believes strongly enough in any cause or movement is vulnerable.[2]

Because of the peculiar symbiotic relations of intelligence service, recruiters can also use the desire for career advancement to compromise rival intelligence officers. "Careers are made on sources," Angleton said. They can offer to make or break their career in their own service—because rival intelligence services often depend on each other for their successes. For both the CIA and the KGB, the ultimate prize is a source in the enemy's camp. And almost invariably these "sources" are enemy intelligence officers. An intelligence officer who finds—and controls— such a source in the rival camp greatly increases his own prospects for advancement. To the extent that such a source is considered valuable, so is the case officer who often has exclusive access to him.

Whereas money, sex, ideology, and ambition provide the means for compromising targets, the lever used to convert a man into a mole tends to be blackmail. The point of the exercise, as Angleton explained it to me, "is to get the recruit in the palm of your hand, and, once he has nowhere else to go, gradually squeeze him." The aim is to compromise the prospect enough so that cooperating appears to be a lesser danger than not cooperating. To execute it, the case officer may require months of surveillance and preparation, and employ teams of specialists. Whatever lure is used, the point of the sting is to make it impossible for the recruit to explain his activities to his superiors. He is compromised, not so much by his original indiscretion, but for failing to report it.

A CIA document I found in the Teheran Archive explains this recruitment practice: "From the view point of Soviet Intelligence, any American who agrees to an unofficial and personal relationship with a Soviet, and conceals the fact from his (or her) superiors has already taken a first compromising step." Every move by the KGB is intended to deepen the guilt. "By accepting

the small aspects of clandestineness which are gradually introduced, such as not calling the Soviet at his official number or
agreeing to meetings at unorthodox times and places, the American compounds his original compromise. . . ." It continues, "The
effect of this process is to draw the American into a 'confidential'
relationship, from which the American gradually comes to realize
he cannot withdraw except at the cost of acute embarrassment—
or perhaps severe personal consequences—by disclosing the
compromise to his superiors."[4] When he is in so deep that he
cannot plausibly explain his actions, he will be confronted with
the loss of whatever he values most: his career, his reputation,
or even his family. The alternative is to supply information to
the enemy. Initially, he may be asked only for completely innocuous documents, such as an embassy's Christmas card list,
but supplying it gradually increases the blackmail threat.

Still, for the purposes of getting feedback, it is not enough
merely to recruit moles. They must be in precisely the right place
at the right time. This is no easy matter, since intelligence agencies usually are divided up into tight compartments, with strict
rules and "bigot lists," specifying which members of the intelligence service are allowed to see the secret material within it. A
mole cannot therefore glean the information his principals need
by casually wandering around an intelligence agency and chat-
ting with his fellow officers in corridors; he has to have a "need
to know" clearance for it. To get such privileged access, a mole
must be maneuvered and advanced through the bureaucratic
labyrinth until he is in the right compartment. The real problem,
according to Angleton, was managing the careers of moles by
remote control so that they wound up burrowing into the right
compartments. Such compartments are, for example, the CIA's
Reports Sections, where agents' reports are collated and analyzed; the counterintelligence units, where reports are vetted and
challenged; and the liaison committees representing different
agencies, where U.S. intelligence operations are coordinated.
And since the KGB is unlikely to find a single mole that meets

all its requirements, it needs moles it can maneuver from position to position.

Here again the peculiar symbiotic relationship of the KGB and CIA provides each side with a means for advancing their mole into the necessary compartment. Both sides can give the other a Trojan gift in the form of a highly placed source. The KGB, for example, can allow the CIA to recruit another one of their agents, who becomes the "outside man." Then the "outside man" gives the mole information that in order to investigate takes him to new areas. The classic example of this outside-inside gambit was Heinz Felfe.[5]

Felfe was recruited by Soviet intelligence in 1951, when he was a minor investigator in the West German intelligence service. At the behest of his Soviet case officer, he applied to his own counterintelligence section, and his transfer was approved the following year. He had responsibility there for investigating the credentials of refugees pouring in from East Germany. To build his career, Soviet intelligence allowed him to detect six East German agents among these refugees. Each of these agents then agreed to be "turned" and provided Felfe with the intelligence questions they had been sent into West Germany to answer. They, moreover, all agreed to work for him as double agents.

While these coups made Felfe a hero in the eyes of his superiors and led to his rapid promotion—he became Deputy Director of the West German counterintelligence service in 1959— they had also expanded his access to see information from other West German departments and agencies and pass it on to the KGB. For instance, the KGB sent him a refugee agent into West Germany and, like a chess sacrifice of a pawn, allowed him to be caught by the West German police. This sacrificed agent had in his possession a list of prominent NATO names. When it was turned over to Felfe, the list thus gave Felfe a "need to know" rationale for investigating the names on it, which required working with the CIA and other Western intelligence services. As this case expanded, he further extended his reach. By the late 1950s, his KGB controllers had maneuvered him, through his supplied "sources," into a position where he was able to feed back to them the assessments of allied intelligence services of the disinformation being furnished through refugee sources. He even visited CIA headquarters in Washington. (He was not exposed until 1963.)

How prevalent are penetrations in the CIA? Although the number of legal actions brought against present or former officers for working for hostile intelligence services is relatively small—twelve since 1948—the question of KGB penetration is not a question that can be answered by resorting to the legal record. As Angleton explained, the counterintelligence technique employed by the CIA when it discovers a potential "turned" employee is not to arrest him and hold a public trial, since the KGB will learn their agent is compromised, as well as other valuable clues from the legal proceedings. The KGB will then have the opportunity to replace a known agent with an unknown one. The alternative that is followed, according to Angleton, is to quietly transfer suspects from highly sensitive compartments.

Intelligence services do not need a 100 percent success rate in advancing moles. If one candidate fails to get the right job, another can be substituted. With even a one-in-ten success rate, intelligence services can, according to Angleton, establish the feedback they need for deception. Moreover, studies of the penetrations of NATO services, sparked by Golitsyn's defection, were not reassuring. The facilities with which the Soviets recruited and maneuvered moles in the British, French, Canadian, and West German services, which were only secondary targets in the intelligence war, made it difficult for Angleton to believe that the KGB would not have applied equal resources to penetrating the services of its "main enemy"—U.S. intelligence. "There was no reason to presume CIA officers were invulnerable to recruitment," he pointed out.

The CIA was an ad hoc group, pulled together from many

different organizations in the late 1940s. Its personnel was anything but homogeneous: some had Ivy League backgrounds, others had Russian or Eastern European backgrounds and had been chosen because of their language skills. Many of its officers had served in Russia during the war, or were liaisons with underground fighters in Eastern Europe who were allied with the Communists. If the Soviets had followed the same procedures they did against the British, a significant proportion of these officers would have been targets of recruitment operations. Once a higher-level candidate had been compromised, the data that the KGB acquired from low-level penetrations, such as Marine guards, secretaries, embassy bugs, and purloined documents, could be used to support the recruitment.

Yet, when Angleton and his counterintelligence staff reexamined their files in the early 1960s, they found that the reporting of these contacts was so "sporadic and chaotic" as to raise questions whether there was any "quality control at all," as Angleton explained the problem. Even if it were assumed that none of these officers made a conscious decision then to commit treason, it did not necessarily follow that no one would not have committed indiscretions or accepted some favors from their ally. And so, Soviet intelligence would have some leverage to pressure them, even years later, into other irregular acts.

In the cases of both Whalen and Dunlap, the KGB showed that even an obscure agent could still tap into crucial intelligence assessments at the highest level. It simply took advantage of their liaison role within the ganglia of different agencies in the "intelligence community." Since the liaison level is where intelligence jigsaw puzzles are pieced together by the different agencies, it became, ever since Philby, a prime target for infiltration. Angleton cited the case of David Barnett, who had served as a CIA officer for twenty years in Asia as a secret operations officer. The KGB recruited him after he left the CIA, and attempted to place him on the Senate Select Committee on Intelligence. At the CIA, Barnett, as a field officer in Indonesia, had only limited value: he could betray CIA sources and methods where he was stationed, but this would not lead to any penetration of the centralized assessments being made of data intercepted from the Soviet Union. At the Senate Select Committee, which had oversight responsibility for all the intelligence agencies, reviewing methods as well as results, he could provide the feedback necessary for Soviet deceptions. (Before he could actually do any damage, Barnett was arrested, tried, and convicted for collaborating with Soviet intelligence officers.)

Angleton's point was that the core business of intelligence services was establishing and running moles in the enemy camp. Like other modern businesses, such as advertising, they had developed the techniques to accomplish this task (though it was antithetical to their work to spell them out). If nations like the Soviet Union, United States, Britain, France, West Germany, and Israel did not believe, after studying the secret data, that the job of recruiting, compromising, and managing moles was at least do-able, they could not justify the continuation of their espionage services—the KGB, CIA, MI6, SDECE, BND, and Mossad. The KGB, moreover, had already demonstrated with Philby, Whalen, and Dunlap that it could find and breach the nerve-center compartments in American intelligence. So it would be only prudent to assume that the Soviet Union had, or could obtain, the feedback necessary for strategic deception.

The picture pieced together by Angleton, as bleak as it was for the CIA, suggested that the KGB also could be infiltrated by the CIA. Wasn't penetration a two-edged sword? Had not the United States also recruited its share of Soviet intelligence officers in the war of moles?

Angleton acknowledged that the CIA had its share of successes. CIA documents in the Teheran Archive, moreover, made it clear that the CIA's Soviet Bloc Division was fully confident that it had "the capability to mount and support . . . operations" in the Soviet bloc that included managing the careers of its moles in government positions and even evacuating them to safety if they got in trouble. And, as it was pointed out at the deception conferences, there had been over one hundred defectors from the Soviet bloc since the end of World War II, most of whom had been recruits, if not actual moles, of the CIA and its allied services.[6] But, as it turned out, with the notable exception of Lieutenant Colonel Peter Popov, a Soviet military attaché whom the CIA maintained as a mole for nearly eight years, the life span of the moles recruited by the CIA has been relatively short. Even Oleg Penkovsky lasted only seven months before he came under KGB surveillance.[7] And almost all were from the pool of Soviet officials permitted to travel abroad—such as diplomats, military attachés, and intelligence officers, which Golitsyn had identified as the "outer" KGB. In none of these hundred-odd cases cited had the CIA succeeded in advancing a mole to a critical position in Soviet communications intelligence, intergovernmental liaison, or central assessment before he had defected. Soviet intelligence, on the other hand, succeeded in recruiting and running agents in virtually every strata of American activity of interest to it. The moles who have been uncovered in the United States have been, aside from intelligence officers and diplomats, nuclear scientists, rocket-technology experts, defense systems engineers, cryptographers, telemetry analysts, congressional staff members, economists, mathematicians, archivists, translators, antisubmarine warfare experts, medical researchers, journalists, computer operators, and business executives.

These differences appeared to proceed not from any lack of sophistication or skill in the CIA but from fundamental distinctions between open and closed societies. It was what one think tank analyst at the deception conference referred to as "the asymmetries."

To begin with, the Soviet Union does not need to rely on either its espionage service or its satellites for basic intelligence about the state of mind of the American political leaders, debates over U.S. national security policies, or the technological developments they depend on. It can openly garner such material from newspapers that keep close contact with the elites, such as *The New York Times* and *The Washington Post*; television programs, such as the MacNeil/Lehrer Newshour and ABC's Nightline, on which policy makers debate each other; trade publications like *Aviation Week*, in which defense contractors vie with one another to release information about their projects; and congressional reports and debates, which spell out priorities in policy. To supplement and test these data, Soviet bloc diplomats, journalists, and other researchers in the United States can use public libraries, archives, and university services such as University Microfilms to obtain on microfilm reference books, Ph.D. theses, telephone directories, scientific treatises, and government data released on prior Freedom of Information Act requests. Soviet intelligence can also, for the price of a computer search, consult data bases, such as Lexis, Nexis, and Facts On File. It can take advantage of UN research facilities, which interconnect with most economic data bases, or even make its own Freedom of Information Act requests. (Not surprisingly, Eastern bloc countries make a vast number of such requests.) In addition, it can send observers to almost all government hearings, which are by law open to the public. And whereas its own officials are restricted, it can often acquire the insights from zealous investigations of American journalists, congressional staff members, and special prosecutors—not to mention defectors from the bureaucracy who "go public" in books, magazines, and Senate hearings because of their objections to policies.

Aside from the plethora of information available in the public domain, Soviet intelligence systematically intercepts telephone conversations of Americans it is interested in, through means that are both legal and internationally acceptable. It can use, for example, antennae on its embassy in Washington, D.C. (which, after all, is not subject to U.S. laws), or its antennae in Cuba (which pick up all trans-Atlantic satellite calls), or its satellites in space, which are sanctified as "national technical means" by the SALT Treaty. These interceptions are effective for two reasons:

First, unlike the Soviet Union, the telephone is universally used in the United States, and virtually all targets of Soviet intelligence make and receive calls. Second, dialing is now mainly computerized, which makes it relatively easy to distinguish phone calls made to selected numbers such as the office or home number of policy makers, congressional staffs, Defense Department employees, defense contractors, scientists, or lobbyists. And, unlike the Soviet Union, telephone books are readily available. Soviet diplomats can even buy mailing and telephone lists of government employees from American market research services. This ubiquitous telephone vulnerability means that even Americans who avoid leaking to the press or testifying before Congress can be listened to by Soviet intelligence.

The extraordinary mobility of employment in the United States, even for those holding classified secrets, makes it exceedingly difficult to control this leakage of information. The rapid movement of technicians, lawyers, and academics back and forth between the private and public sectors renders it virtually impossible to segregate telephone users. And when government officials move into the private sphere, they cannot be compelled to speak over "scrambler" telephones. Nor, since there is no Official Secrets Act, can ex-officials be prevented from revealing secrets to journalists preparing books or, with the exception of CIA employees, from writing their own memoirs. Even when an employee leaves a job in which he has access to secrets and moves to another position, he still may hear "echoes" about the project from friends and acquaintances, which he may pass on to others. The huge consultant industry in Washington, which has had its share of corruption, is based on ex-employees having informal access to important information about American defense policy. Just as corporations buy such insights by retaining consultants, so can Soviet intelligence through "false flag" companies.

American deception planners, to be sure, could use these public channels for disinformation by planting, and orchestrating, fake stories in news media, congressional testimony, biographic disclosures, and even phone conversations. But this possibility is severely mitigated by the sanctions and opprobrium that arise from government attempts to manipulate the American media. The concern that limits government actions is not the disinformation, which may be an acceptable objective, but the "blow back" when it is reported by American news organizations. When, for example, the Reagan White House planned to use disinformation to undermine Libyan ruler Muammar Qaddafi, career civil servants and military officers immediately assessed the risk in terms of their own careers. Lieutenant General John H. Moellering, representing the Joint Chiefs of Staff, protested that the use of this disinformation could be exposed. He asked, "What if the [memorandum] ever got out?"[8]

As it turned out, the plan was leaked to Bob Woodward of *The Washington Post,* presumably by the "Middle East experts" at the CIA and Pentagon who were "aghast," as Woodward reports, at the prospect that the disinformation would "blow back" to the American media. When he published the story on the front page, the media were predictably outraged, and the careers of those involved were permanently stained. The lesson was that disinformation is a very dangerous enterprise; no one could be sure that enemies or rivals in the present or future administration would not leak a plan. For many in the American bureaucracy, the risk of exposure outweighs any advantage. While Soviet intelligence cannot totally discount the possibility of disinformation being inserted into public channels, it can reckon that this is done only in rare circumstances given the penalties imposed on it by the American media.

Whereas the United States must use its intelligence resources to piece together a mosaic about Soviet intentions, the Soviet Union, which has licit access to the vast public realm of data about America and its allies, can concentrate all its espionage energies on penetrating the few compartments that still remained sealed. And here too, because of the differences in society, it has a distinct comparative advantage. Whereas the CIA has to operate in the tightly controlled police states of the Soviet bloc, the KGB operates mainly in the open societies of the West.

From the point of view of running espionage agents, the freedom of nationals in a target country to travel beyond national borders is itself a significant advantage. Such freedom does not exist in the Soviet Union. Soviet nationals cannot travel abroad without special permission and, if they possess secrets, security clearance. And, in many cases, they cannot even travel internally to other cities in the Soviet Union. So if the CIA recruits an agent in Russia, it then must attempt to equip and service him inside the country—in cities where American or allied diplomats are stationed—under the full surveillance of the Soviet state police. In Moscow, for example, the CIA has to operate out of a base in the U.S. Embassy which, as of 1988, had so many embedded microphones in its structure that, according to one CIA officer, working there was "the electronic equivalent of working in a fish bowl." Even the sealed rooms and encrypting machines on which they depended for the security of their communications were compromised repeatedly by the KGB, which, by recruiting entire teams of Marine guards, was able to gain entry to the embassy. Moreover, when American diplomats left the embassy compound, they found themselves under relentless surveillance. They were irradiated with microwaves, sprayed with chemical tracers, and followed by dogs. They also had to contend with the fact that the KGB had learned through a CIA defector, Edward Lee Howard, some of their most important trade craft for communicating with potential Soviet traitors and turning them into agents in Moscow. The chances of maintaining contact undetected under such difficult circumstances are not high.

The KGB, on the other hand, has no such disadvantage. Since American citizens, even with security clearances, are free to travel almost any place in the world at their own discretion (even without passports in Mexico and Canada), KGB case officers can arrange their rendezvous in locations where the chances of surveillance are minimal. In many cases, they are instructed to fly to Austria, where through connections the KGB maintains with the local security service, neither they nor their spies were at much risk. Americans can even go as tourists to Eastern Europe without arousing suspicion.

A second difference that benefits Soviet espionage is the almost unrestricted mobility of employment in the United States. In the Soviet Union, individuals cannot simply leave one job and apply for another. They need permission from their superior, as well as from Communist Party officials and police officials. For the CIA, this means that once a Soviet national is recruited in Russia, he cannot be easily maneuvered into a job where he will have access to needed secrets. For example, if a dissident academic or disaffected municipal employee is recruited, there is not a great probability that he can get a job in a sensitive military position—and even a request for such a transfer might place him under suspicion. In the United States, however, where job turnover is relatively high, the KGB would have little problem advancing its moles to positions in which they would be helpful. Individuals need not explain why they are leaving a job, other than in terms of self-betterment or a change of interest. No one needs justify his or her shift from job to job or from private to government employment. Aside from largely perfunctory FBI security checks, there is virtually no bar to getting jobs with access to sensitive information.

Finally, constitutional safeguards in an open society, meant to protect its citizens from government power, have the side effect of making it safer for hostile espionage services. In Russia, there are virtually no restrictions on what security police can do if they even suspect an individual is in contact with a foreigner. They can surreptitiously open his mail, bug his telephones, break into his residences, get his medical records, intimidate his friends, or detain him without obtaining any prior court approval. This carte blanche authority, which in many ways defines a police state, greatly increases the tensions and risks of an espionage agent.

In the United States, the police have no such unrestricted

authority. They need court warrants or, in some cases, the Attorney General's approval, to place a bug on a telephone or search a residence. Investigations are impeded by a suspect's right to invoke the Fifth Amendment, and the rights of his spouse, lawyer, accountant, psychiatrist, and doctors not to reveal privileged information about him. Moreover, the espionage laws themselves place the burden of proof on the government. It must prove to a jury, beyond a reasonable doubt, not only that a defendant provided secrets to the KGB but that he did so with the intention of damaging the United States. In the case of Richard Craig Smith in 1985, the defendant was acquitted of espionage, although he admitted selling Army secrets to a KGB officer, because the government could not prove he believed he was helping the KGB.[9]

Confronted with these asymmetries, it is understandable why the CIA has proved far more successful at encouraging Soviet agents to defect than in persuading them to continue working as double agents. And although defections may be trumpeted in the press as CIA accomplishments, they do not add to the capabilities of the CIA to breach the Soviet compartments that would yield feedback on a continuing basis. This meager product has, in turn, led to cutbacks in the money allocated to espionage. Admiral Turner, for example, eliminated over a thousand positions in the clandestine services in the late 1970s which resulted in shrinking espionage activities by 40 percent, according to one former member of Angleton's staff. For the espionage branch, it was a vicious cycle: the fewer the officers, the easier it was for the KGB to reduce their effectiveness; and these poorer results, in turn, justified further personnel cuts.

It was becoming increasingly clear to me why the participants at the Air Force Conference laughed at American espionage "as nickel and dime stuff." Yet, without moles, how could the United States counter Soviet penetrations?

CHAPTER THIRTEEN

The Denial of Deception

"When an intelligence service believes it is invulnerable to enemy deception, it is most vulnerable."
—James Jesus Angleton

The final deception conference I attended turned out to be the most revealing. It was held on September 26 to 28, 1985, at the U.S. Navy Postgraduate School at Monterey, California. The subject was supposed to be Soviet Strategic Deception. But the CIA, which was helping to fund the conference, as I later learned, had its own agenda: the presentation of a thesis that effectively denied the possibility that the CIA could be duped by the KGB.

This antideception argument was outlined in the opening session by Richards Heuer, a CIA consultant and former case officer. It asserted that the CIA had debriefed more than one hundred Soviet bloc intelligence service double agents and defectors in the postwar years, and that through this constant contact with Soviet intelligence services it had come to "understand the KGB better than any agency of the U.S. government." This premise was accepted by others in the large CIA contingent sitting around the table, which included Fred Hutchinson, its National Intelligence Officer for Deception, and Arnold Horlick, its National Intelligence Officer for the Soviet Union.

Heuer next explained that from this "knowledge base," the CIA had deduced "the operational rules of the KGB" that prescribe what the KGB can and cannot do in the intelligence games it plays with the CIA. These "iron laws," imposed by the Soviet hierarchy, could not be broken or bent. In a sense, they were like the convenient "Indians don't fight at night" axiom in cowboy films.

One such "operational rule," according to the CIA, is that Soviet intelligence officers are not permitted to disclose Soviet secrets in documentary form to the CIA. This meant, Heuer asserted, coming to the point, that the KGB could not use Soviet secrets "as chicken feed" in order to advance or make credible a disinformation agent. This stricture proceeded from, as Heuer put it, the "Soviet passion for secrecy." "If there is one thing more important to the Soviets than deceiving the enemy," he concluded, "it is protecting their own security."[1]

At this point Heuer was interrupted by questions from surprised participants who had prepared papers on Soviet deception. Did he mean secret information was never used to support a deception scheme? What if events, such as satellite reconnaissance, would disclose the secrets anyway in the near future?

"Secret documents cannot be passed by the KGB under any circumstances," Heuer insisted categorically. This imputed KGB rule thus gave the CIA an ironclad means of testing the bona fides of any Soviet source. If the documents he handed over contained authentic secrets, they could not have been deliberately disclosed by the KGB; and hence he was genuine.

The rule supposedly applied not only to the present but to the past, so the CIA was able to reassess all the cases of defectors and double agents where deception was suspected by Angleton and his counterintelligence staff—such as Nosenko, Fedora, and Top Hat. All these suspected Soviet sources had given secret information, so they could not have been under KGB control at the time. Through such retrospective analysis in the late 1970s, the CIA was able categorically to conclude that it had never been deceived by a Soviet double agent on any issue of strategic importance—nor had any Soviet disinformation been passed through it for at least the past ten years.[2] The head of the clandestine part of the CIA, David Blee, had already advanced the denial thesis to a point where, as he explained to members of the Senate Intelligence Committee, the CIA "no longer attempted to prove the bona fides of individual sources"; instead, it relied on its ability to verify the data they provided.[3] If the data was accurate, the CIA assumed that its source was valid. And Admiral Turner, Director of the CIA up until 1981, blamed the "paranoia of the CIA's counterintelligence staff" for the intelligence failures of the CIA in the 1960s and 1970s, all of which had been since remedied by the CIA.[4]

But how could the CIA be so certain it had correctly inferred the KGB's "operational rules"? The defectors and double agents, as it turned out, were not unimpeachable. As Heuer acknowledged, many of them were not from the Soviet intelligence services at all but from Eastern European and Cuban intelligence services, where they could not be expected to know the operational rules of the KGB. These allies might indeed have been instructed never to give away Soviet secrets to build an agent's credibility—but this would not mean the KGB itself did not make exceptions. Of the Soviet defectors, most were either military or foreign service officers of such low rank that they could not be reasonably expected to know KGB policy in such sensitive areas. Others had actually defected before the KGB was created in 1953. And, of the KGB double agents who might be in a position to know operational rules, some prominent ones, such as Fedora and Igor, not only had returned to Moscow and the KGB fold— and had been accordingly assumed to be disinformation agents— but they had been determined through other U.S. intelligence surveillance techniques, which Soviet intelligence apparently had not known about at the time, to be under KGB control when they conveyed their messages to the CIA. Finally, and most important, the information provided by those with access to the

KGB was far from unanimous. Not only had Golitsyn said that the KGB had license to provide the CIA with secrets; if they were cleared by a KGB committee, he also furnished massive details about a reorganization in the KGB, as we have seen, that separated the deception staff from intelligence officers who were to be stationed abroad. This would account for the lack of knowledge other defectors had about Soviet deception policy. So how could Heuer and others at the conference be so confident of the KGB's "operational rules"?

The answer emerged toward the end of the conference. One top CIA executive explained that the CIA had recently acquired a KGB defector who overrode all these objections. He had served in the KGB up until August 1985, making him current with its practices; then, holding the rank of General-designate, he was in the "top compartment" of Soviet intelligence, one of the six highest-ranking officers in the KGB headquarters at Dzierzhinski Square. He was, as became public several weeks later, Vitaliy Sergeyevich Yurchenko. The CIA was so confident that Yurchenko ended the issue about deception that it sent me his biography in the KGB. From this, and interviews with intelligence officers involved with him, I pieced together his story.

Yurchenko, a forty-nine-year-old Russian sporting a Stalinlike mustache, appeared to be a remarkable catch. According to the biography the CIA compiled on him, Yurchenko had been a staff officer in a Soviet submarine brigade in the Pacific before he joined KGB counterintelligence in 1960. From 1961 to 1968, he worked for the KGB on submarine security. Then, from 1969 to 1972, he was transferred to Egypt, where he was in charge of preventing the recruitment of Soviet officers by Western intelligence services. After becoming deputy chief of the intelligence department of the KGB's Military Intelligence Directorate in May 1972, he specialized in running "dangles," an operation that continued until 1975, in order to test Western intelligence services, learn their procedures, and confuse and demoralize their operations. Because of his successes, he was transferred to Washington, D.C., where he served as the security officer at the Soviet Embassy from August 1975 to August 1980. Aside from being responsible for neutralizing the efforts of the CIA, FBI, and NSC to penetrate the Soviet Embassy—which again involved sending dangles to the FBI—he handled "foreign visitors . . . volunteering their services to Soviet establishments."

The CIA came in contact with Yurchenko in Washington in 1980, and, as a matter of course, made him a cold-turkey offer to become a double agent for the CIA. There was no reason to expect him to accept the gambit, but it was done on the remote chance that sometime in his career he might run into difficulties that would cause him to reconsider. In August 1980, as scheduled, he returned to the Soviet Union.

In Moscow, he had (according to his CIA debriefing) a meteoric rise within the KGB. In September 1980, he had joined the First Chief Directorate and was made the chief of the counterintelligence department, which investigated suspected espionage by KGB staff personnel. Here he was responsible for, among other things, investigating the credentials of foreign agents recruited by the KGB—which involved using "special drugs" on occasion. He also said he had the task of investigating suspected cases of treason among KGB personnel and of supervising "the indoctrination of [KGB] counterintelligence [officers] going abroad."

Then, in April 1985, he was promoted to deputy chief of the department specifically responsible for organizing espionage operations against the United States, which included not only supervising Soviet agents but coordinating their efforts with those from other Eastern bloc countries.

Less than three months after reaching this pinnacle of success, Yurchenko, using an address supplied to him by the CIA five years earlier, contacted the CIA and offered to supply it with information. If his incredible offer—and self-reported career—was authentic, it was the coup that CIA had been waiting for.

Not only was he the highest-ranking KGB officer ever to volunteer his services to the West, but he was a man uniquely qualified to definitively answer the questions that had plagued American intelligence about Soviet deception.

Although his motive was still unclear, General-designate Yurchenko indicated that he was prepared to divulge the KGB's most closely guarded secrets: its sources and methods. He offered to rendezvous with CIA case officers in Rome the last week in July 1985.

This offer could not have come at a more propitious time for the CIA. Western intelligence services had recently had a string of disastrous losses that required an explanation only a source within the KGB could provide. Earlier that summer, the KGB had arrested a CIA agent named A. G. Tolkachev, who had been considered one of their most valuable sources in the Soviet Union. As an electronics expert employed by an elite Soviet think tank that researched problems of military aviation and space detection systems, Tolkachev was in a position to pass on to the CIA technical data on the state of the art of Soviet ground-and-space-based radar, which revealed the extent to which American submarines and planes were vulnerable to detection. During the same period, other CIA agents, suspecting they had been compromised and were on the verge of being arrested by the KGB, came in out of the cold. First, in India, Igor Gheja, the third secretary of the Soviet Embassy, whom the CIA was secretly developing as a potential mole, defected from his post; next, in Greece, Sergei Bokhan, a Soviet military intelligence officer who had provided the CIA with valuable insights into Soviet efforts to infiltrate the Greek military, sought protection at the American Embassy; then, one month later, in England, Oleg Antonovich Gordievsky, the political counselor at the Soviet Embassy and a KGB officer, who had been selling Soviet secrets to British intelligence over the years, hastily organized his escape (abandoning his wife and two children).[5]

In less than three months, the careers of four well-placed spies for the West were abruptly ended. While the defections could be treated in the press as victories for the CIA, they were not. They all represented KGB successes in closing down sources of information. As the secret 1973 CIA memorandum entitled "Turning Around REDTOP Walk-ins" explains:

> While [intelligence] defectors can and do provide critical information, there are very few cases in which the same individual would not have been of greater value if he returned to his post and remained in place. . . . Our ultimate objective is to have the walk-in return to his home country and continue his agent relationship [with the CIA] while working inside.[6]

Yurchenko could provide answers to how these agents were compromised. He could also describe the KGB apparatus in North America for recruiting its agents and identify moles who had been infiltrated into American intelligence. The CIA therefore wasted no time in dispatching to Rome one of its most experienced officers in the Soviet Division, Colin Thompson, as well as a team of debriefers.

The initial interrogation took place in a safe house on the outskirts of the city during the last week of July. Yurchenko then surprised Thompson: Instead of returning to Moscow, as expected, he said that he wanted to defect to the United States. The CIA, needing his information, had no choice but to accede to this demand.

On August 1, Yurchenko formally applied for political asylum at the U.S. Embassy in Rome. The next day he was bundled aboard a military courier plane and flown to the United States. Officially, he entered the United States on CIA parole.

Yurchenko was installed in an isolated two-story house, surrounded by woods and a lake, some twenty-two miles outside of Washington. As the questioning proceeded, he told his CIA interrogators that the KGB had uncovered the Western agents, not through any inside information, but through new and innovative surveillance techniques. He described how the KGB sprayed an invisible dust on Western diplomats in Moscow, which they would then unwittingly get on whatever paper they touched. When they posted clandestine letters to agents, the KGB could detect the dust with machines in the central post office and trace them to their recipient. The CIA—and State Department—had already detected this dust, but Yurchenko now gave a plausible explanation for its use.

The Tolkachev affair could not be fully explained by this KGB dust spraying of diplomats. The CIA had used a newsman rather than a diplomat to make contact with his contact, who was known as "Father Roman."[7] But Yurchenko added that a former CIA officer, known to him as "Robert," told the KGB about the CIA's procedures for contacting its agents in Moscow.

He explained that the ex-CIA officer had visited the Soviet Embassy in Washington in 1983, and subsequently traveled to St. Anton, Austria, for a meeting with the KGB. These details immediately focused suspicion on a thirty-three-year-old ex-CIA employee who had been spotted by FBI surveillance at the Soviet Embassy in Washington in 1983. He was Edward Lee Howard.

Howard had joined the CIA in 1981, and was trained for an embassy job in Moscow—where he would meet and service agents. But before undertaking the assignment, during his lie-detector examination, he made a damaging admission about drug taking and, in June 1983, his brief career at the CIA ended. Several months later he was spotted at the Soviet Embassy, and when he was informally asked about the visit, he admitted that he had gone there with the idea of giving them secrets.

Now, with the additional details about "Robert," the FBI again questioned Howard. He acknowledged that he had met with several Soviet officials in St. Anton. Although the date of the meeting indisputably identified Howard as "Robert," it was not altogether clear that he was in a position to have betrayed Tolkachev—who had not yet been recruited when Howard left the

203

CIA in 1983. Before this contradiction could be resolved through further interrogation, Howard disappeared from his house in Sante Fe and defected to Moscow.

Yurchenko also volunteered one further tantalizing bit of information about another ex-KGB source. This was a former employee of the NSA who had come to the Soviet Embassy in January 1980 and sold the KGB vital information about the NSA's facilities for listening to the activities of Soviet submarines in the Sea of Okhotsk. The NSA had known for years that Soviet intelligence had learned of these listening devices, but now it had a plausible explanation for how they were compromised. The ex-NSA employee was quickly identified as Ronald Pelton, who was subsequently tried and convicted for espionage.

Yurchenko's revelations were exactly the evidence the CIA had been looking for to end the long and debilitating debate about moles in the CIA. He claimed that its agents were not compromised by traitors within, but by Soviet chemical surveillance that was easily defended against. The only recruits the KGB had made were two ex-officers—Howard and Pelton—neither of whom was of any further use to the Soviets. Moreover, all the KGB's attempted recruitments of CIA personnel, which came under Yurchenko's purview, had failed. Even more reassuring to the CIA, Yurchenko claimed that the KGB had not managed to dupe the CIA with any "dangles" and it had not sent any false defectors. The KGB therefore had neither channels nor feedback from Western intelligence services. And when pressed, Yurchenko confirmed the CIA hypothesis that the KGB followed predictable operating rules.

By mid-October, Yurchenko was taken to meet Director William Casey, who agreed to give interviews on this defector to news media and authorized a book by him, along the lines of the CIA's earlier covert best seller, *The Penkovsky Papers,* to publicly demonstrate the CIA's successes over the KGB. As part of this drive, John McMahon, then the Deputy Director of the CIA, took this as evidence that the KGB lacked the wherewithal to deceive influential senators and congressmen. On October 31, he briefed the Agency's perhaps most influential critic, Senator Malcolm Wallop, the Republican senator from Wyoming.

Wallop considered it ironic that McMahon brought him this news on the seventh anniversary of the CIA's "Halloween massacre"—in which hundreds of top career officers had been fired or reassigned. He considered that reorganization part of the "progressive degrading" of the CIA's capacity to detect Soviet deception.[8]

McMahon now told Wallop that his concerns were ill-founded. Yurchenko was a "fact" demonstrating that the KGB, because of its self-imposed restrictions, had failed at any long-range penetrations of American intelligence. Without such feedback, it could have little hope of successfully deceiving the CIA.

Wallop was not entirely satisfied with this "one-man proof," as he put it. He asked whether the CIA had considered the "alternative hypothesis" that Yurchenko had been sent by the KGB to misinform the CIA. After all, he pointed out, Yurchenko was telling the CIA what it wanted to hear.

McMahon replied that that was "impossible." Other collateral information Yurchenko provided about Soviet recruits, which he said could not be discussed outside the secure rooms in the CIA, would prove "beyond a shadow of a doubt, Yurchenko was a genuine defector." McMahon stated, therefore, "no other hypothesis is necessary." He then dramatically concluded by saying: "I would stake my career on Yurchenko's bona fides." It was a statement that he would have cause to regret in forty-eight hours.

But while Deputy Director McMahon and other CIA executives were making the case public, Colin Thompson and his team of interrogators were finding the "take" from Yurchenko progressively less impressive. As scientists closely analyzed what he had said about KGB "spy dust," they found that the radioactive properties of the material deteriorated too rapidly to make it feasible for the KGB to use to ferret out letters in the central post office—perhaps days after the diplomat mailing them had been sprayed with the dust. Moreover, using all its exotic technology, U.S. intelligence could find no evidence that the Soviets screened mail in this manner or even had the equipment in place. Nor, as the cases in India, Greece, and London were reanalyzed, did it appear the agents there could have been traced through spy dust. As the evidence came in, much of it through techniques the KGB could not have anticipated, it seemed increasingly plausible that the spy dust story was a red herring.

Moreover, the two former American intelligence officers Yurchenko gave away turned out to be agents whom the KGB had reason to believe had blown covers anyway. Howard had failed his lie-detector test, had been spotted by the FBI outside the Soviet Embassy, and had admitted to CIA security in 1983 that he had made telephone contact with a Soviet official. The KGB, presumably learning this from Howard during his debriefings, would (correctly) have assumed he was too compromised for any future intelligence use other than to give away other agents.

Similarly, the KGB could have assumed that Pelton had been compromised five years before by the two phone calls he made to the Soviet Embassy in Washington. The KGB certainly was aware that its telephone lines were constantly monitored and tapped by the FBI, which thus had advance warning that an American ex-intelligence officer would be coming to the Soviet Embassy to divulge secrets. It could further assume that the FBI, from its photography and visual surveillance of visitors to the embassy, would determine his general physical characteristics—Caucasian, mustached, middle-aged, and male—and, with these clues, it would only be a matter of checking through the few hundred photographs of recently discharged men who fit this description before the FBI would come across Pelton (who had left the NSA five months earlier). Moreover, he could be (as he in fact subsequently was) positively identified from his voice on the FBI's tapes. Further, even if the KGB had not concluded that these contacts compromised Pelton in 1980, the fact that he had failed to show up at a scheduled meeting in Vienna with the

KGB in April 1985 would probably have indicated that, if not caught, he had little further value to the KGB—aside from diverting attention away from still active KGB agents in American intelligence. So Yurchenko had merely told the CIA during his debriefings what the KGB could presume the CIA already knew from other sources.

Even more suspicious, after delivering his initial messages in July and August, Yurchenko clammed up about the Soviet's illegal network in Canada and the United States. He claimed, for example, total ignorance about the existence of dozens of elaborate hiding places for messages that Soviet illegals had prepared for spies. This was all part of the "wiring diagram" that Yurchenko, as the KGB's section deputy chief for North America, should have known like the back of his hand. The more he was pressed, the more recalcitrant he became. Even the offer of a million-dollar contract, in which he would collect generous bounties for each Soviet mole he identified, failed to move him to reveal KGB operations. Instead, he repeated, as if by rote, that the KGB had not made any other recruits during the five years that he was in charge of the KGB's counterintelligence unit.

Despite his tenacity, the CIA interrogators had other evidence demonstrating his claim was untrue. Both the CIA and Canadian counterintelligence had dispatched "dangles," who allowed themselves to be recruited during Yurchenko's tenure. Since all these double agents would have been known to Yurchenko if he held the position he claimed, his failure to name them—even when led in their direction by the CIA—raised very serious questions about his authenticity.

As they pondered these problems, Thompson and others from the Soviet Division were no doubt aware of the parallels between Yurchenko and Nosenko twenty-one years earlier. Like Yurchenko, Nosenko had claimed to work in KGB headquarters in Moscow—a position, in both cases, which the CIA had no independent way of verifying. And like Yurchenko, Nosenko came with a message that implied that there was no mole, or other serious leak, in the CIA. He too had cited chemical "spy dusts" painted on the soles of shoes as the explanation of how the KGB had uncovered an important CIA agent in Russia. He also gave away, like Yurchenko, burned-out ex-agents who no longer had access to secrets. But once Nosenko had been imprisoned, the CIA could find no way of proving or disproving the theory he was a dispatched agent.

As Yurchenko grew more recalcitrant and the interrogation sessions ground to a halt, his CIA handlers were determined not to make the same mistake. Instead of attempting to confine his movements, they decided to test his intentions.

When Yurchenko asked to see a Soviet acquaintance in Canada—the wife of a high-ranking Soviet diplomat in Montreal, with whom he maintained he was having a romantic liaison—the CIA decided to accommodate this extraordinary request, even though KGB defectors on parole are usually prohibited from contacting Soviet citizens, both for their own safety and to prevent them from giving any signals to former comrades. Yurchenko was permitted to make contact—although the exchange of words did not lead to a meeting.

The game between Yurchenko and his handlers finally drew to an end November 2—exactly three months to the day after his arrival in America—on a cold, rainy Saturday afternoon. If they did not actually return him to the Soviet Embassy, they gave him every opportunity to go. First, they took him to a clothing store in the nearby town of Manassas and bought him a coat, hat, and umbrella. They also left him at a phone, where he made two long-distance calls to the Soviet Embassy and advised the Soviet officer on duty he was returning. Then he was handed over to a lone CIA officer who drove him to a restaurant a few blocks from the Soviet Embassy compound. At this point, his handler indicated to Yurchenko that he was free to go, and watched as he put on his new coat and hat and walked out the door. After he was gone, his CIA companion called neither the FBI nor the Washington police, who could have intercepted him at the gates of the embassy compound. It was the ultimate test: If Yurchenko had betrayed the KGB, he would not be expected to make a beeline for the KGB; if, on the other hand, he had acted under its control, he would.[9]

Yurchenko later telephoned a CIA phone number he had been given, and advised his handlers that he had safely arrived at his destination—the Soviet Embassy. Whatever else it was, it could hardly be called an escape.

The affair might have ended then and there if Yurchenko had quietly returned to Moscow on his diplomatic passport. Even if anyone asked about him, the CIA was under no obligation to respond to queries about double agents. And this may have been what his CIA handlers expected.

But the KGB had yet another surprise in store for the CIA, and its Deputy Director, who had already bet his reputation on Yurchenko. On Monday, November 4, reporters received an invitation to a televised news conference that afternoon. The speaker was Yurchenko (who, as far as was publicly known, was still the CIA's prize defector).

Mocking the Agency at every opportunity, Yurchenko egregiously claimed that he had been kidnapped from Rome, drugged, and held a prisoner for three months by the CIA. He insisted that, rather than divulging intelligence to the CIA, he had been using the debriefing sessions to learn from it its major areas of interest and its interrogation techniques. He even described his meeting with Casey.

The KGB teased the CIA with lightly disguised clues as to their control over Yurchenko. For example, earlier that week, the State Department had lodged a protest with the Soviet Foreign Ministry charging that eight years earlier an American intelligence agent, Nicholas Shadrin, had been paralyzed with drugs by the KGB in Vienna and transported across international borders to Hungary. The source for this assertion the State Department gave was Yurchenko. Now, the Soviet Embassy filed an almost identical protest with the State Department, charging that Yurchenko had been paralyzed with drugs by the CIA and taken across international borders. The source for this story was also Yurchenko. A single KGB officer thus had the distinction, in a five-day period, of being the source for both American and Soviet protests, both of which were also denied.

The next day Yurchenko went to the State Department to demonstrate that he was acting without Soviet coercion. He met there with a half-dozen CIA and State Department officials as well as a psychologist—who agreed, after nearly a half-hour session, that Yurchenko was returning voluntarily to the Soviet Union. As he left, he jauntily clasped his hands over his head as a victory sign. By Wednesday, the Soviet dangle was on an Aeroflot plane heading home, his mission completed.

As this amazing case unraveled before his eyes, Senator Patrick J. Leahy, the vice chairman of the intelligence committee, concluded that Yurchenko was a double agent whom the KGB "foisted" on the CIA.[10] "This whole thing was very good theater," National Security Adviser Robert McFarlane told *The New York Times*. "And, to me, theater is something that is staged."[11] McFarlane had no doubt read the CIA report that Yurchenko had not furnished any important information not previously available to U.S. intelligence. The assessment that he was "staged" proceeded from two separate considerations. The first was that Yurchenko had evidently trusted the KGB sufficiently to return to its fold.

The Soviet Union has no history of granting amnesty to, or otherwise forgiving, intelligence officers who betray state secrets. Pointedly, the acronym for its counterespionage arm, SMERSH, stood for its slogan, "Death to All Spies." As a twenty-five-year veteran of KGB counterespionage, Yurchenko certainly knew the fate that would have awaited a traitor—or any KGB officer who had, without proper authority, divulged secret data to the CIA. While there are many cases of ordinary Soviet citizens— and even ballet dancers, intellectuals, journalists, and soldiers—

who did not have access to state secrets returning to the Soviet Union without facing punishment, KGB officers who commit treason fall into a different category. For that reason, any Soviet intelligence officer who returned to Russia without being punished for his treason was assumed by the CIA to have been acting under KGB orders in feigning disloyalty. (Over the past quarter century, there is only one known case of a Soviet intelligence officer redefecting—Anatoli Tchebotarev in 1971—and he was judged by CIA counterintelligence to be "a definite plant," who had been sent over for three months to test CIA debriefing procedures.)

Yurchenko's voluntary return could be explained in two ways. Either he had been a KGB officer sent on a mission, or he had been a traitor. In the first case, he could safely return; in the second, he was acting completely irrationally in putting himself in the hands of the KGB, because it meant risking death or imprisonment.

The second consideration was that the KGB evidently trusted Yurchenko enough to permit him to return two days later to the State Department. This voluntary Soviet action was telling because it meant that the KGB did not consider him to be irrational. If Yurchenko had been crazed, unstable, or even emotionally overwrought, it could not have taken a chance on allowing him to go for an interview to the State Department building where he would be examined by CIA representatives, psychologists, and State Department officials. At any point during this interview, he could again offer—or be persuaded—to defect. This possibility could not be excluded by the Soviet Union if he had been a traitor a day before. If he had been upset at the handling of this case by the CIA, or disturbed by the threat of unanticipated Soviet reprisals against himself or his family, the CIA could conceivably find some way of reassuring him. If he had indeed been a traitor who had changed his mind he could, at least from the Soviet perspective, change it again under American persuasion.

The Soviet Embassy was under no obligation to place Yurchenko back into American hands and give him another opportunity to save his life by defecting again. If Yurchenko had actually been a traitor, Soviet intelligence would need to exhaustively determine from him in precise detail every iota of information he had revealed to the CIA. This kind of damage assessment would require intense interrogation of Yurchenko by experts themselves familiar with the cases in which he had been involved for a quarter of a century. This meant that the KGB would now have to keep tight control over him—until he was squeezed of every drop of information.

Under these circumstances, Yurchenko would not have been returned to American officials (especially if he was unstable, deranged, or untrustworthy). The KGB could hardly be expected to trust a traitor who changed sides irrationally. It could only be fully confident that he would return from the State Department if it knew Yurchenko was a well-disciplined KGB officer who had already proven himself loyal by carrying out his provocative assignment. This would also explain his being allowed to give a press conference.

When both these developments—Yurchenko trusting the KGB and the KGB trusting Yurchenko—were taken together, they afforded little doubt that the KGB was controlling his actions. But admitting this sting had shattering implications for the CIA. If Yurchenko had been merely one of the scores of Soviet intelligence officers who approach their U.S. counterparts overseas every year, hold out a few misleading morsels, and then return to the fold, it would have been accepted as part and parcel of the dangle game. But Yurchenko had been taken public by the CIA and presented to critical senators as evidence that the CIA was both penetration-proof and deception-proof. It even took his word as final proof of the convenient "operating rules" it had hypothesized. Now he had returned to the fold—an active KGB officer in Moscow, which suggested that the messages he had passed to the CIA during his ninety days in the United States were part of his mission. If so, the CIA could not be certain how the other agents rounded up by the KGB had been compromised. Rather than yellow spy dust, it might have been through one or more penetrations in Western intelligence. Nor could the CIA accept as credible Yurchenko's claim that the KGB had made no recruits in North America in the past five years, or that there were no moles in the CIA. The Yurchenko mission had, moreover, violated the doctrine of not handing over KGB secrets that the CIA had imputed to the KGB. He himself had told the CIA about Edward Howard and Pelton—both KGB secrets (even if they would have been found out eventually), which meant that dangles could use cleared secrets for deception purposes.

This put the CIA in a bind. If it acknowledged that Yurchenko had been a KGB double agent all along, it would have to abandon its thesis about the "operating rules" of the KGB, which would in turn cut the heart out of the CIA's claim that it had an unambiguous means of evaluating its Soviet sources. Thus the CIA had no basis for denying the deception hypothesis, and all the data from hostile territory—including the multi-billion-dollar product of satellite "National Technical Means"—would have to be reevaluated.

But the CIA leadership, some of whom had staked their careers on Yurchenko prior to his return to the KGB, decided instead to maintain steadfastly that Yurchenko had neither lied nor misled the CIA during his short stay in the United States. It began issuing this version after he returned to Moscow, even though the President's national security adviser already had declared him a fake based on the findings of the CIA's own Soviet Division, which handled the case and allowed him to return to his KGB base; and President Reagan himself, based on this briefing, publicly stated:"The information [Yurchenko] provided was not anything new or sensational."[12]

CIA Director Casey asserted to senators and journalists that the CIA was convinced Yurchenko had told it the truth—though he was now lying in his press conferences and State Department interview. In other words, he had been a total truth teller from August 1 to November 3, when his story served the CIA's interest, and a total liar afterwards. The CIA thus declared Yurchenko, after he was back at KGB headquarters, a bona fide defector—which meant that he had proven himself loyal to the United States. Yet, Yurchenko had demonstrably betrayed U.S. intelligence, first by returning to the KGB; second, at the State Department, by pledging his allegiance to the Soviet Union; and third, by divulging secret details of his CIA debriefing to the KGB. Never before had a defector earned his "bona fides" in such a perverse manner. To come to this conclusion, Casey and other CIA executives had to override, in a single coup, virtually all the criteria that the CIA had developed for establishing the bona fides of double agents.

This denial also involved circulating stories among the media suggesting Yurchenko's instability, irrationality, and romantic liaisons (although both Casey and McMahon had endorsed his soundness less than a week before his redefection). One such story even cited the suicide of a Soviet woman in Toronto whom, in reality, Yurchenko had not known or had any connection with whatsoever. The campaign was capped in February 1986, when intelligence sources fed *Time, Life,* National Public Radio, and other media the false story that Yurchenko had been executed and added, for spice, that Yurchenko's family had been charged with the cost of the ammunition. No sooner did this "intelligence community" story appear on national television than Yurchenko appeared on European television announcing that he was preparing a book about the CIA.

The Yurchenko case demonstrates, if nothing else, that once an intelligence service adopts a policy of denying deception, it can be perpetuated indefinitely. Evidence of deception—even as gross as a redefection—can be discounted, held in abeyance, or ignored—even where it has become public.

214

The Denial of Deception

• • •

The final element in the state of mind that facilitates deception is denial of even the possibility of organized deception. Denial is, to be sure, sometimes a useful limit on the imagination. In the natural sciences, where the deception hypothesis would be ludicrous, denial amounts to placing an outer boundary on what explanations will be tolerated. Intelligence services could similarly benefit, at least organizationally, by excluding considerations of deception which could lead, as they did in the days of Angleton in the CIA, to dissension, demoralization, and even paralysis. After all, by applying the deception hypothesis, values can be continually reversed, with intelligence successes—such as the acquisition of a mole—transformed into failures; and whatever secrets spy masters, electronic wizards, and satellite technicians extract from Soviet bloc territories with great ingenuity and at great expense can be instantly impeached as disinformation by armchair counterintelligence experts.

The difference between intelligence services and the natural sciences is the subject being observed. Enemy nations, unlike microbes, do conspire at times to dupe those studying them. This is particularly true of the Soviet Union, which has even subtly but systematically falsified its maps since the 1930s to mislead foreign observers.[13] And, as we have seen from the telemetry double cross, Soviet intelligence has the means to affect the data being intercepted by even high-tech satellites.

The adoption of full-scale denial, as appears to have occurred in the Yurchenko case, is the element in the state of mind that allows the deceived to be a partner in its own deception.

CHAPTER FOURTEEN

The Confidence Game

What keeps a deception going, after the initial messages are accepted as genuine, is the gradual development of a tacit relationship between the deceiver and the deceived, based on a powerful coincidence of interest both parties have. As the KGB demonstrated in foisting Yurchenko on the CIA, the deceiver needs to retain his mark's confidence. He also has a direct interest in helping the mark enhance his own stature in the eyes of his superiors—and his allied intelligence services—since that will improve the chances of the deception's succeeding. The deceived, in turn, benefits from his access to the apparently valuable information that his source is providing him—if it does not become suspect. He has therefore a direct interest in protecting the reputation of his deceiver, as the CIA had with Yurchenko. The more money he pays his deceiver, and the more information he vouches for to his superiors as genuine, the commensurately greater stake the mark has in protecting the bona fides of his deceiver.

Moreover, the deceived and deceiver often must work closely together to protect the secrecy of this relationship. They must arrange secret meeting places, code words, recognition signals, and other conspiratorial exchanges. As in an illicit love affair, the very act of collaborating to arrange these liaisons tends to further heighten their mutual involvement. The more the mark becomes enmeshed in the conspiracy, the greater is his need to trust his deceiver.

This collaboration may even reach the point where the mark is forced to become the defender of his own deceiver—lest he open himself up to the charge of being a dupe. In many instances, the deceived tells the deceiver which elements of his story are suspect, and what further evidence he must supply to convince others of his legitimacy. This sort of tacit partnership developed in the Anglo-German Treaty of 1935, which limited the size of battleships. The Germans, who were systematically violating the treaty by building larger ships, were the deceivers; the British, who were adhering to it, the deceived.

As the Germans constructed two super dreadnoughts, the *Bismarck* and *Tirpitz*, British field intelligence determined through aerial reconnaissance that both ships would, when completed, exceed the treaty limits. The Plans Division of the Royal Navy, which had negotiated the treaty and verified German compliance, had a strong interest in maintaining that it had not been duped. As a subsequent British investigation found, there was a notable "tendency of Naval officers and others who have taken part in negotiations to become advocates of the integrity of the persons of whom they secured the agreement."[1] They consistently decided to ignore this early evidence of deception on the grounds it was ambiguous. The British thus gradually became active allies of their German deceivers. Even when the evidence became manifestly clear, they found ad hoc reasons for ignoring almost every violation. The result was that despite the evidence of aerial photography, the deception worked.

The Iranian manipulation of the President's staff, made public by the President's Special Review Board in February 1987, provides a more recent example of how this collaboration between deceiver and deceived works. The Iranian government needed the cooperation of the White House to get American-made spare parts for its anti-aircraft missiles, other military equipment, and American satellite intelligence that could prove crucial in its war against Iraq. Since the Reagan Administration publicly had taken an implacably hostile stance against it, and had gone to great lengths to organize an allied embargo against arms and technology shipments, this cooperation could only be achieved through Byzantine means.

In the summer of 1984, a number of agents of the Iranian government approached international arms dealers with connections to the CIA, and offered to supply them with intelligence about Iran in return for American weapons on the prohibited list. Like the double agents of Lenin's Trust, they explained that the Khomeini regime was about to collapse, and they wanted to be on the pro-Western side. The arms dealers immediately passed these offers over to the CIA, which noted, "We have . . . probably 30 to 40 requests per year from Iranians and Iranian exiles to provide us with very fancy intelligence, very important political insights, if we in return can arrange for the sale of a dozen Bell helicopter gun ships or 1,000 TOW missiles or something else."[2]

The CIA—assuming correctly, as it turned out, that these offers were all part of a deception—rejected them out of hand. With such negative responses, the Iranian officers responsible for getting these arms had to go back and at least refine the "come on" message to appeal to the preconceptions of the Reagan administration.

In November 1984, Manucher Ghorbanifar, an ex-Iranian intelligence officer who had represented the Khomeini regime in purchasing arms, approached Theodore Shackley, who had just retired from the CIA as one of its top executives, with a more appealing line.[3] Ghorbanifar said he "feared" Iran would become a "Soviet satellite," possibly by 1987, unless the more "moderate" elements in the Iranian government could "get a meaningful dialogue with Washington." Since the CIA had proved skeptical, Ghorbanifar tried to direct the new message to the White House; "We know the CIA . . . they want to tear us like Kleenex—use us for their purposes and then throw us out the window."[4] The message, as Ghorbanifar put it, was: "It is President Reagan who has the destiny of the Iranian people in his hands."

As specific proof of his bona fides, Ghorbanifar offered to arrange to ransom William Buckley—the CIA officer in Beirut who had been captured by terrorists and whose release, as the Iranians knew, had become a top objective of the CIA and its Director William Casey. Ghorbanifar also offered to trade secret Soviet equipment captured by Iran in Iraq for TOW missiles—which would appeal to the Pentagon.

This revised approach fit in more closely with the White House's picture of a struggle for succession in Iran. It consequently received serious consideration by the National Security Council. The State Department and Pentagon objected, however, saying that it would undermine the American-sponsored boycott, and the overture was rejected.

But in another respect Ghorbanifar and his principals in Teheran succeeded. The NSC accepted the idea that Khomeini was on his deathbed and that the United States should covertly intervene to block any Soviet move, which justified finding and making contact with the "moderate" faction. When the Iranians learned from feedback through third parties—notably Israeli arms dealers—that the United States was looking for representatives of the "moderate" faction, they merely had to modify Ghorbanifar's story so it fit the job description. For the deceiver, the tailoring of the "bait" is much like breaking an access code to a telephone answering machine: one keeps trying different digits until they produce the play-back tone.

The Iranians finally succeeded in July 1985 after Ghorbanifar, approaching the NSC staff through Israeli arms dealers, claimed to represent "high individuals inside the Iranian government."[5] Ghorbanifar claimed that this faction had both the will and the means to install an anti-Soviet government in Iran after Khomeini died. Since Khomeini was suffering from terminal cancer, according to Ghorbanifar, this event was imminent. Ghorbanifar explained that this faction, which included the Prime Minister, Mir Hosein Musavi-Khamenei, the Minister of Oil, Gholam Reza Aqazadeh, and most of the Iranian General Staff, feared that the Soviets were poised to take over Iran, through the Tudeh Party, which is the Communist Party in Iran. And that they had approached the President, Ali Khameini, and leaders in Parliament, with their plan to block the Communist coup. But they needed credibility and support—especially with the military. If they could demonstrate they had American backing, their chances of succeeding would improve immeasurably.

Ghorbanifar thus provided the White House with the exact geopolitical rationale it was looking for—to do what it wanted to do. The NSC could now open up secret negotiations with the Iranians.

Ghorbanifar suggested that the first step in the "dialogue" was for each side to show its good faith. He proposed that the United States deliver arms, spare parts, and satellite intelligence to the Iranian army—not the revolutionary guards. The Iranians would, in turn, arrange the release of American hostages, call off terrorist attacks against Americans, and avoid incidents in the Persian Gulf.

The situation was not very different from that of the FBI and Fedora. If the NSC accepted Ghorbanifar as its agent, it had to make him more credible with his principals—the "moderate" faction—by delivering some signs of American support. And the more they provided, the more they were committed to continuing the cooperation.

In August 1985, at the urging of the National Security Adviser, Robert C. McFarlane, President Reagan authorized Israel, which served as a "cover" in case things went wrong, to secretly ship 508 TOW missiles to Iran.

Initially, the exchange went well. After the arrival of the final installment of the weapons on September 14, Reverend Benjamin Weir, one of the Americans kidnapped in Lebanon, was immediately released—demonstrating that Ghorbanifar had the connections he claimed. Both sides thus got a payoff: Iran got U.S. arms, President Reagan got a hostage back.

Ghorbanifar then undertook another demonstration of his bona fides. He predicted that in their upcoming speeches in Teheran, Iranian leaders would conspicuously avoid attacking America. When the CIA checked the speeches, it found that he was right (the Iranian leaders had gone out of their way to denounce the Soviet Union instead). This confirmed, as far as the NSC was concerned, that they were dealing with the right man.[6] They apparently didn't consider the other possibility: Ghorbanifar was acting as an agent of the Iranian government, not a "moderate faction," in a deception aimed at causing the White House to break its own embargo.

As the clandestine collaboration deepened throughout 1986, with HAWK ground-to-air missiles being supplied through Turkey and the NSC staff taking over operational responsibility for the deliveries, the White House became increasingly committed to the idea it was dealing with a "faction," not the Khomeini regime. With each shipment and every clandestine meeting, the NSC staff's interest in maintaining the bona fides of Ghorbanifar increased.

Meanwhile, given his leverage, Ghorbanifar pressed for more deliveries of U.S. arms and intelligence to keep him in good stead with his principals.[7] At one point, after there was a delay in the shipment of HAWK missiles, Ghorbanifar intensified the pressure by claiming his principals in Iran—the Prime Minister and Oil Minister—had promised the President that the missiles would arrive, and any further delays might completely discredit them and the moderate faction. He thus confronted Colonel Oliver North, who was supervising the deliveries for the White House, with a dilemma. Stopping the deliveries would bring about the very result the White House most feared: the likely takeover by the Soviet-backed faction. Moreover, Ghorbanifar hinted that the operation might be exposed by hostile factions in Iran, thus severely embarrassing President Reagan. As in all tacit partnerships, there was the ultimate threat of blackmail.

North, to avoid this breakdown in the partnership, had to advocate Ghorbanifar's case. In a note to McFarlane, he pointed out: "Ghorbanifar's earlier game plan delivered Weir. He has proposed we 'deliver something' so that he can retain credibility with the regime in Teheran." North also drew up a somewhat disingenuous list of options designed to show that the NSC had no real option but to play ball with Ghorbanifar. He concluded, "Whether we trust Ghorbanifar or not, he is irrefutably the deepest penetration we have achieved into the current Iranian Government."[8]

The problem was that to outsiders not entrapped in this partnership, Ghorbanifar appeared to be far less candid and, as the CIA reported, "a fabricator . . . who had undertaken activities prejudicial to U.S. interests." In the lie detector test the CIA administered, of the 15 relevant questions Ghorbanifar was asked, "Deception [was] indicated in thirteen" and the other two answers were "inconclusive." Specifically, the report accompanying the test noted that Ghorbanifar "lied/fabricated his information on terrorist activities"; "tried to mislead us concerning his relationship with the rightist line inside Iran"; and, most importantly "showed deception on the question of whether he was in control of the Iranian Government." The test also indicated that Ghorbanifar knew ahead of time that hostages would not be released, as promised.[9] If this test was accurate, as collateral events proved it to be, Ghorbanifar was part of a major deception intended to make President Reagan believe he was advancing an anti-Soviet cabal in Iran—when, in fact, he was helping the Iranian government prosecute its war against Iraq.

Nevertheless, Colonel North and his superiors continued to advance Ghorbanifar's plan as if no doubts existed. In a memorandum he prepared for the President's signature, North asserted, "moderate elements in Iran can come to power if these factions demonstrate their credibility in aiding Iran against Iraq and in deterring Soviet intervention."[10] By delivering Iran the wherewithal for this defense, he further suggested that the United States could attain "a heretofore unobtainable penetration of the Iranian governing hierarchy." In addition, he ironically pointed out, as the deliveries accelerated, "a dependency would be established . . . thus allowing the providers to influence near term events." What he failed to point out was that the dependency was a two-way street.

With the President's approval of the memorandum, the CIA was brought in to acquire weapons for the Iranians, set up Swiss bank accounts, arrange for air transport, and forge documents. It also was called in, over the protest of its deputy director, to provide the Iranians with U.S. satellite photographs of Iraqi positions, and clandestinely obtained manuals of the equipment Iraq was using. The CIA also furnished secret data about Soviet deployments in Afghanistan and elsewhere—even though it had determined that Iranian methods of communication were "insecure," and the data could reveal highly prized CIA "sources and methods" if intercepted by the Soviets. This intelligence nonetheless was turned over to the Iranian "faction" in the spring of 1986 by the NSC staff.

As the NSC staff travelled to Iran for meetings that summer, the evidence became clear that they were not dealing with a conspiratorial cabal in Teheran but the Khomeini regime itself. No other explanation could account for how the missiles and spare parts were landed, paid for, test fired, and, as U.S. intelligence intercepts showed, widely discussed throughout the government. It seemed almost inconceivable that this was known only to Ghorbanifar's moderate faction, since the negotiations had been exposed in some detail by Jack Anderson's story in *The Washington Post* on June 29, 1986. In any case, one month earlier, the CIA Middle East analyst, Charles Allen, had learned that Khomeini himself was well aware of the "state of play" of the Iranian initiative. Allen concluded in a memorandum that the Khomeini regime had three objectives: it "needed weapons," it wanted to favorably conclude the war with Iraq, and it wanted to re-establish Iran's "rightful place."[11]

It was clear that Ghorbanifar had presented all the parts of a well-orchestrated deception. And the hostages had not been released because the Iranian government evidently assumed it needed them for bargaining chips to get further weaponry.

Even in the light of all this evidence, the NSC staff was not able to acknowledge the "faction" was a deception. North, McFarlane, Poindexter, and the other key participants had a definite interest in not discrediting their deceivers. Not only would their arms-hostage transaction be discredited, it might also raise questions about money transferred to other causes, such as the Contras. Instead, they held steadfastly in their memos to the illusion that they were dealing with an independent "faction." When Ghorbanifar himself became impossible to believe because of demonstrable lies he told about collateral matters—such as terrorists' hit teams—and the Iranian government appeared to collude with him in these fabrications, the NSC staff shifted to one of Ghorbanifar's contact's "relatives," whom they termed a "second channel," to the moderate faction. Final proof of the deception came in November 1986 when, after a Shiite newspaper fatally exposed the negotiations, the putative "cabal," instead of being arrested, continued in their jobs—and Khomeini's favor.

What Khomeini had gained through this extensive deception went beyond TOW missiles, HAWK missiles, spare parts, and satellite intelligence. By exposing it to the world, he had undermined the entire American embargo. If the United States would sell missiles to Iran, why shouldn't our allies in Europe and Asia do the same?

Despite the exposure, the NSC staff found it difficult to extricate itself from the tangled web it had been enmeshed in by its tacit partner. When the President discussed the matter in a televised news conference two weeks later, he still clung to the idea, presumably based on a briefing, that his staff had been in contact with "moderates." He said, testifying to the strength of the bond of trust that this collaboration had produced, "We still have those contacts . . . and we're going to continue on this path."[12]

As I studied these well-documented cases, it became clear to me that deception is the product of the actions of both the deceiver and the deceived. It ultimately depends for its success on the "mark" not only believing the messages he receives from the deceiver but being confident enough of his own judgment about them to reject suspicions that would interfere with the deception working. This trust blends deception and self-deception into one state of mind.

PART THREE

Winning Without Fighting

CHAPTER FIFTEEN

The Millennium War

"The prince should never attempt to win by force what he
might otherwise win by fraud."
—Machiavelli

There is no reason to assume, if there is to be a war between the
superpowers, that it is going to be either a nuclear or a conventional conflict. There are other forms of nonmilitary adversary
relations. Machiavelli argued: why expend resources fighting,
when the same objective could be more cheaply obtained by
peaceful deception? The same logic applies with even greater
force in an age when weapons can destroy an entire society. Lenin
adopted this Machiavellian strategy of winning without fighting
in the early days of Soviet power. Lenin's slogan "Peace is a
weapon" provided the context for his concept of peaceful coexistence. A state of peace was envisioned not as any agreement
to maintain the status quo but the continuation of class warfare
by other means. The objective remained the same, the destruction of capitalist societies; the means changed. Lenin thus reversed Clausewitz's dictum that war is the extension of policy by
other means. Peace, or at least what Soviet tacticians would call
by that name, would become the extension of warfare.

Nuclear weapons reinforced this logic. The United States
maintained a near monopoly over delivery systems up until the

early 1960s, and the Soviet strategy since at least Hiroshima has been to avoid any direct military engagement with the United States. For the past forty-four years, the Soviet Union, following Lenin's dictate, has found "other means" for continuing its expansion. It annexed Estonia, Latvia, and Lithuania as well as slices of Poland, Germany, Rumania, Finland, and Japan with the approval of the United States and its allies; it seized control of Czechoslovakia—and later a large part of Afghanistan—through coups d'état; and it acquired client states, such as Libya and Cuba, by supplying military, economic, and intelligence assistance.

The conflict between the United States and the Soviet Union, whether called a "cold war" or "peaceful competition," has been in effect at least since 1945. At times, through proxies such as North Korea and North Vietnam, American military forces have been engaged; but no Soviet troops have ever directly been involved in warfare against American troops. The premise of this book is that this current low-level conflict will continue through the millennium without turning into either a nuclear war or even a conventional one. It will be, as Lenin envisioned it, a deception war.

In such a conflict, adversaries can be expected to constantly attempt through peaceful means to disrupt each other's economic and military alliances, misdirect each other's energy on chimerical projects, and undermine each other's political and moral authority. Victory will come not from any single decisive battle but from the accumulation of gradual changes in the global balance of power. At one point in this scenario, one superpower—either the United States or the Soviet Union—might find it lacks the allies, resources, or will to compete with the other. This assessment itself might be tantamount to losing—without fighting.

The tactics for winning such a deception war are fairly straightforward. One side distorts the intelligence of the other. Specifically, it alters its rival's perceived reality in such a way that the rival neglects its true interests and pursues bogus ones. For example, it may mislead it to treat allies like foes and foes like allies.

Ever since the inception of the Soviet Union in 1917, when it was vastly outnumbered militarily by hostile nations while having access to virtually no modern technology, the nation has depended on fraud rather than force. Soviet strategy, at the height of the Cold War, as it was pieced together by U.S. intelligence, appeared to revolve around three main objectives: breaking up Western alliances; obtaining financial credits from Western nations to buy technology; and nullifying U.S. nuclear superiority by self-limiting treaties and other restrictions. The assumption is that if the Soviet Union could strip the United States of its alliances, technological edge, and nuclear superiority, it would become, if only by dint of its size and the deployment of its conventional military forces, the superior power.

The Soviets, to be sure, did not have an exclusive monopoly over the tactics of winning without fighting. In the late 1940s, the United States sought to bring about a political implosion within the Soviet bloc through what loosely went under the rubric of "containment policy." It involved, among many other things, a wide range of coordinated covert actions designed to create ruptures between the Soviet Union and its allies in Eastern Europe. An Anglo-American task force parachuted arms and émigré agents into Soviet-occupied territories to challenge the legitimacy of Soviet rule; U.S. intelligence passed disinformation through its double agents to provoke and discredit selected Soviet bloc leaders; the Office of Policy Coordination (which later merged with the CIA) attempted to create real and illusionary enemies for Stalin by planting forgeries, spoofing radio broadcasts from phantom traitors, and other such tricks. Meanwhile, radio stations in West Germany attempted to stir up popular dissension and play on nationalist and anti-Soviet sympathies. The idea was to mislead Stalin into taking actions that would further build up anti-Soviet pressure in Eastern Europe. As it turned out, these deception initiatives failed—as we have seen—

because, unknown to U.S. planners, Soviet intelligence had penetrated these exile movements as well as the Anglo-American coordinating unit through Kim Philby and other moles.

The scope of detailed planning in such operations is evident in the deception scenario that the State Department, CIA, and National Security Council developed in 1986 to overthrow the Qaddafi regime in Libya. It was predicated on the stated strategy that "any alternative leadership to Qaddafi would be better for U.S. interests." The plan aimed at playing on Qaddafi's own "paranoia" through a series of covert, diplomatic, military, and public actions to increase Qaddafi's distrust of his military command—and vice versa. The "key element," as a memo spelled it out, involved combining "real and illusionary events—through a disinformation program . . . with the basic goal of making Qaddafi think there is a high degree of internal opposition to him within Libya, that his key trusted aides are disloyal, that the U.S. is about to move against him militarily." The memo, classified TOP SECRET/VECTOR, proposed such illusions as having American submarines land rubber rafts, money, and communications equipment, which would make it seem to Qaddafi's security police that "a coup is planned or underway." Meanwhile, to fuel his paranoia, U.S. deception experts would fake radio and other signals that would make it appear American planes were flying over Libya. When his air force launched interceptors, they of course would fail to find the phantoms. Simultaneously, disinformation would be planted that America and France were preparing to launch an offensive from Chad, spooking Libya's army. And articles would be planted through background briefings in the press reporting "infighting among groups jockeying for [the] post-Qaddafi era." The rumors would be fanned by local diplomats. The idea was to keep adding "events" until Qaddafi's intelligence system (which was organized by East Germans), unable to find the nonexistent conspirators, either became discredited or focused suspicion on innocent parties, such as the General Staff. The plan then anticipated Qaddafi becoming paranoid and making wrong moves that would possibly bring about a real coup d'état by his military.

This deception plan was never put into effect because of a breakdown in security. A member of the National Security Council staff leaked the memorandum to *The Washington Post*. Once the plan was compromised, it was obviously useless against Qaddafi.[1]

It must be assumed that both sides have ample intellectual resources, and deception experts, to prepare similar plans that could be used to destabilize a hostile leader, disrupt an alliance, or mislead adversaries in other ways. The issue is how effective they will be. The real problem is not the ingenuity of their initial design—since such scenarios can usually be modified—but whether the other side will detect them before they can be fully played out (as was the case in Libya). Defense, not offense, is therefore paramount in the deception war.

The order of battle for the deception war cannot be assessed merely in conventional terms—i.e., divisions, tanks, ships, planes, or missiles—but in this effectiveness of each side's intelligence system. The success of deception for one side depends on the failure of the other side's intelligence system. The issue is: are the superpowers balanced in their ability to detect deception? If not, does one side have the wherewithal to blind, dazzle, beguile, incapacitate, confuse, and mislead the other side's intelligence apparatus? Can it penetrate the other side's operations, and thereby render them transparent? Finally, can it use these advantages to influence or control its evaluation of information? It comes down to which of the superpowers has the ability, inclination, and "mind" to detect fraudulent information that is put in its path.

From what I learned at the deception conferences, the United States may be at a distinct disadvantage in this type of warfare. The growing commitment of its intelligence establishment to the multi-billion dollar satellites and other forms of technology has, as we have seen in the case of the telemetry double cross, left it with little tolerance for the proposition that the data it collects through these devices may be part of, rather than proof against, an orchestrated deception. In keeping with the focus on information, rather than on its provenance, counterintelligence has been systematically downgraded, a process that Admiral Turner took pride in accomplishing in his autobiography. The resulting state of mind at the CIA even at times rejects the concept of deception when one of its prize sources openly returns to his KGB command in Moscow, as we have seen in the case of Yurchenko. The unwillingness to confront the possibility of deception creates a serious gap in America's defenses.

CHAPTER SIXTEEN

The Weak Look

"Pretend to be weak, so that an opponent will grow
arrogant."
—Sun-tzu, *The Art of War*

In June 1988, writing in the journal of the Communist Party,
Kommunist, Georgi Arbatov, a member of Gorbachev's Politburo,
laid out a Soviet strategy for winning without fighting. He noted:
"The 'image of the enemy' that is being eroded has
been . . . absolutely vital for the foreign and military policy of
the U.S. and its allies. The destruction of this stereotype . . . is
Gorbachev's weapon." He reasoned, "neither the arms race, nor
power politics in the Third World, nor the military blocs, are
thinkable without the 'enemy,' and without the 'Soviet threat.'"
He also suggested that the United States would acquiesce in this
erosion of the threatening image of the Soviet Union by confidently pointing out, "Of course, this weapon is not secret but it
does have tremendous power."[1] This strategy is predicated on
three assumptions.

1. The cement that held together the Atlantic alliance was
    the perception, whether or not it was grounded in reality,
    that the Soviet Union was a potential enemy. European
    nations pictured, in other words, the Soviet Union as
    physically capable of either directly attacking them with

tanks and bombers, cutting off their lines of communication, or subverting their political systems through stratagems. The result was the NATO Alliance, in which they militarily banded together with the United States and Canada. It allowed the United States to operate 278 military bases on their territory. It arranged intelligence service protocols, in which they, along with Australia, Japan, Israel, coordinated their counterintelligence efforts with that of the CIA to keep Soviet bloc agents under close surveillance and cooperated in a global network for intercepting and processing Soviet signals. It mandated economic arrangements in which they, together with Japan, worked to deny the Soviet bloc the war materials, technology, financial credit, and industrial wherewithal it needed to strengthen itself. And it negotiated political accords, both formally and informally part of the "containment policy," which aimed to prevent the Soviet Union from expanding its influence outside of its own bloc.

2. If this threatening image is erased, or even sufficiently vitiated, in the West, this alliance system would fall apart. Why should these European countries who are, after all, economic competitors with the United States pay a large part of their wealth to defend themselves against a nation that is no threat? Why should they maintain domestically unpopular military bases on their territory if there is no enemy? Why should they allow American war planes to land on their territory or practice maneuvers in their air space? Why should they risk turning themselves into nuclear battlefields for tactical weapons? Why should they embargo technology and restrict their domestic manufacturers from getting a privileged position in the Soviet bloc market? Why continue an anachronistic containment policy when there is no reason to contain Soviet influence?

3. Without this alliance system, the United States would be incapable of intervening in many areas of the world, or engaging in "power politics," as Arbatov terms it. If the United States did not have its refueling and weapon storage bases in NATO countries, and lacked the right to

overfly them, its aircraft could not reach or resupply such allied countries as Israel, Turkey, Saudi Arabia, or Pakistan on any dependable basis. Nor could the United States guarantee their safety in a crisis. Under these circumstances, its allies would have little alternative but to reach an accommodation with the Soviet Union.

These objectives could be realized through a single deception: misrepresenting economic weakness in the Soviet economy to the extent that the United States, its NATO allies, and Japan will no longer consider the Soviet Union to be a serious threat. By projecting an image of such weakness abroad, the Soviet Union could hope to undercut the rationale for maintaining the NATO alliance, as well as to weaken public support for the stationing of U.S. forces in Japan, West Germany, Korea, the Philippines, and other countries. The idea that the Soviet economy is in such dire straits, if not a total basket case, also provides a basis in the West for believing that the Soviet Union will make concessions in negotiations in order to get Western help in restructuring it. It is a tactic no different from a retail store feigning an "out of business sale" to make customers believe they are getting bargains or airlines pretending to be on the verge of bankruptcy to win concessions in their labor negotiations.

In 1985, Gorbachev himself helped launch this specter in his book *Perestroika* (published in Russian and sixteen foreign languages) which, describing the Soviet economy as "ossified," proposed sweeping reforms of the administrative structure of the government in the name of efficiency. The main evidence of this collapsing economy consisted of the statements of Soviet officials; Soviet economic reports furnished to the CIA and European intelligence by Soviet controlled sources; a drumbeat of stories in the Soviet press supporting this theme; and private briefings to Western journalists, academics, and VIPs by Arbatov's Institute for the Study of the United States and a handful of Gorbachev's top staff. The key briefer for the West here was Abel

Aganbegyan, Gorbachev's personal economic adviser, who supplied impressive sounding data at the beginning of the campaign in 1985 to Western economic authorities, foreign opinion leaders, and U.S. news media owners that economic growth in the Soviet Union since 1980 had been close to zero.[2] The resulting image of an ossified, faltering, and hapless Soviet economy had great appeal in the West.

On the right, it tended to confirm to die-hard anti-Communists that they were correct in claiming that communism did not work. On the left, it tended to support the view of those advocating disarmament that, whatever its past policy, the Soviet Union now needed peace. To pragmatists in the center, it suggested that ideology no longer mattered since both superpowers were converging in their political systems to solve economic and ecological problems. To those in business, it promised a bonanza of trade. To those in the administration, it justified their negotiations.

American national security policy accordingly adjusted to this new image, as The Wall Street Journal reported in a front-page story on August 11, 1988, entitled "Strategic Shift." It stated, based on an impressive number of interviews with present and former officials: "For the first time since the start of the Cold War, the U.S. is redefining its concept of national security." It further explained that the revision of policy, though "still in its infancy," proceeded directly from the change in the image that American leaders had of their Cold War enemy. Specifically, American officials cited "Russia's domestic problems," and they further assumed that "Gorbachev's current drive to reform his economy highlights the failings of communism."

As these officials now believed that both the Soviet economy and communism had failed, they also could logically find that the past U.S. policy of containing the Soviet Union was outdated. In the new consensus, as summed up by The Wall Street Journal, the policy of containment no longer "fit an era in which the Soviet Union is struggling to restructure its ossified economy, communism is in decline as an ideology, and the American public worries more about economic competition from Japan or terrorist attacks against the United States than superpower confrontation." What emerged from these interviews was that the Reagan administration, denied its image of an enemy threat, was turning its attention from the activities of the Soviet Union to those of America's principal allies.[3] The image of an ossified economy thus provided an acceptable rationale for doing what was politically convenient—replacing Cold War containment policies with more popular trade and anti-drug policies.

But is this alternative image, which has been projected on the West so skillfully, consistent with the realities of the Soviet economy? Even if the Soviet economy does not produce enough consumer goods for a Western standard of living, is it no longer capable of sustaining a military or political threat? There are many measures of the output of an economy. By using gross national product—the sum of the value of all the goods and services with which inhabitants are provided—the United States measures the extent to which its economy services its people. It counts, in other words, entertainment, car repair, weddings, funerals, and personal commuting as part of its product. And here the United States has far exceeded the Soviet Union. If everyone in America, for example, decided to dent and then repair their cars, the GNP would increase by the national repair bill (though no one necessarily would be better off). If, on the other hand, the yardstick of industrial production is used—which measures the capacity of an economy to produce the energy, materials, weapons, and wherewithal necessary for a nation to expand, to fight a war, and to dominate and intimidate other nations—the Soviet economy is not stagnating but gaining against the United States.

In 1948, Soviet industrial production was one fifth that of the United States; in 1988, it was three quarters that of the United States. In other words, it had closed most of the gap.

Consider the key components in this race for industrial superiority. Energy, which is the basis of all industry, is an example of the Soviet surge. In 1948, the Soviet Union produced only 500,000 barrels a day, one tenth as much oil as the United States. In 1988, it produced 12 million barrels a day, or 50 percent more oil than the United States. In 1948, the Soviet Union produced less than 8 million cubic meters of natural gas, which was only 2 percent of what the United States produced (and not enough feedstock for manufacturing petrochemicals). By 1988, the Soviet Union produced almost 800 billion cubic meters of natural gas, which was nearly twice U.S. production. Its gas pipelines network will deliver 48 billion cubic meters a year to Europe in the 1990s, making the Soviet Union the main supplier of heating and industrial fuel to most European nations.

The Soviet economy has also surpassed the United States in producing the basic structural materials. In 1948, for example, the Soviet Union produced only 25 million tons of steel, which was only one quarter as much as the United States produced. In 1988, it produced 162 million tons, which was twice as much steel as the United States produced. In 1948, it produced only 700,000 tons of aluminum, one tenth as much as the United States. In 1988, it produced over 3 million tons, about equal to U.S. production. It produced more cement, copper wiring, and titanium.

The Soviet economy has also benefited from the accelerating transfer of technology from the West, especially after the 1971 détente, in which it received machine tools, dry docks, and computers. This modernization allowed the Soviet Union to move ahead of the United States in such categories as shipbuilding, tractor assembly, space launches, and factory construction. It also provided the Soviet Union with the largest truck production facility in the world, the Kama River industrial complex.

In 1948, the Soviet non-agricultural labor force was 20 percent smaller than that of the United States. By 1988, it was 10 percent larger. And, whatever other inefficiencies it had, production was not lost because of strikes, work stoppages, or acts of industrial sabotage. (In the United States in 1988, over 10 million man days were lost because of strikes.)[4]

In 1988, the CIA belatedly determined that the data supplied the Western media and academic sovietologists in private briefing two years earlier by Abel Aganbegyan was wrong. The CIA found that the zero growth claimed to have occurred in the pre-Gorbachev years of the Soviet economy had been "unrealistically low." But why would Gorbachev's briefer purposely understate the expansion of the Soviet economy? The tentative explanation the CIA offered for this distortion was that it had been intended to help Gorbachev in his "domestic politics." This was not the first time that the Soviets had led the United States to underestimate Soviet production. Earlier the CIA had been similarly misled by Soviet assessments of its future petroleum production. It had obtained these technical reports through its own and West German sources. They suggested that Soviet oil fields were rapidly deteriorating and would run dry in the early 1980s. The CIA report based on this data, which predicted the Soviet Union would be an importer of oil, proved to be wrong. The Soviet Union in 1988 was the second largest exporter of oil, after Saudi Arabia.

Moreover, the Soviets have been able to dedicate an ever larger portion of the product of their economy to military and state purposes compared to the United States—despite the rhetoric of Glasnost, which suggests that the Soviet Union needs to give its people more consumer goods, and consequently is less of a threat. In reality, according to the best CIA estimates, the Soviet Union has increased the proportion it spends on guns and decreased the proportion it spends on butter, even under Gorbachev in the 1980s, from 10 to about 12 percent of its GNP, which is more than twice the proportion spent by the United States.[5] And even these conventional comparisons tend to underestimate Soviet military capacity, since many civilian categories, such as merchant ships and airlines, contain equipment designed for and fully integrated into the Soviet military forces.

Even when confronted with a catastrophic earthquake in Armenia in December 1988, the Soviet air force continued to fly an average of 200 to 300 bombing missions a day in Afghanistan. The result is that the Soviet military has dramatically increased its power since the onset of the Cold War.[6]

Take air defense, for example. In 1948, the Soviet Union was completely vulnerable to attack. It had no nuclear forces or intercontinental bombers to retaliate against or deter such attacks. It was literally encircled by U.S. bomber bases in Africa, Europe, and Asia, and U.S. spy planes overflew its territory at will.

By 1988, the situation had drastically changed. The United States no longer had a nuclear monopoly, a tactical air defense, a string of air bases, civil defense bunkers, or even safely deployed land missiles.[7] The Soviet Union, on the other hand, had a sophisticated tactical air defense system that could be used against bombers, reconnaissance planes, or even submarine-launched missile warheads. It also had deployed around Moscow an antiballistic missile defense system, and, in other locations, giant phased-array radars capable, with the proper software, of coordinating mobile rocket launchers and smaller truck-mounted radar trackers into a more extensive antiballistic missile system. And it had built underground bunkers, serviced by private railroads, large enough to accommodate the entire policy-making apparatus of the Soviet Union.

The Soviet Union has similarly moved ahead of the United States in the space race—at least in its capacity to lift tons of equipment into orbit. It presently has in orbit radars, powered by nuclear reactors, which appear capable of spotting the signatures of U.S. submarines.

Nor is there any reason to assume that the Soviet decision to use its economy to increase its military capacity rather than its standard of living has weakened its hold over its own people. A 1988 econometric study by the RAND Corporation suggests that the Soviet Union, and its allies, have instead organized their societies so that they require that fewer goods be channeled to

consumers than in non-Communist nations. And the higher proportion of national income spent on police and military is in-
herently part of the system through which Communist parties
maintain control.[8]

While the Soviet leadership may well want to increase the
future efficiency of its industry and develop new technological
capacities, by virtually any present empirical measure—economic, military, or political—the Soviet Union is a greater threat
today than it was in 1948. The erasure of the image of a Soviet
threat is therefore based not on how many barrels of oil the
Soviet produces, nor on the size of its armed forces, nor on its
capacity to lift nuclear reactors into space, nor on the increasing
number of foreign bases to which it has access, but rather on the
claims of its own leadership that it is no longer a threat. These
claims may be sincere, of course. They might also be part of a
strategy for winning without fighting.

To look ahead in the deception war, it is useful to look back-
ward.

CHAPTER SEVENTEEN

The Sixth Glasnost

Glasnost—a Russian concept that originally meant publicity or notoriety—has been an effective instrument of Soviet policy since the early days of the Bolshevik Revolution. It was first used by Lenin, who realized that power proceeded from denying others a veil of privacy for their decision making. Hence, Glasnost, or "public airing," became a weapon for the Communist Party.[1] By forcing local officials to engage in a process of "criticism and self-criticism" in which they had to confess to their own mistakes or point to those of others, Lenin made all government officials and lower-ranking Party members increasingly vulnerable to Party discipline and purges. In so doing, he strengthened the hold of the Party hierarchy while at the same time increasing the appearance of free speech. As he noted, "Glasnost is a sword which itself heals the wound it inflicts."[2]

This miraculous sword could also be used as a powerful instrument of deception. To the extent that these controlled bouts of self-criticism were seen by foreign eyes as unrestricted freedom of criticism, it created the illusion of a budding democracy. As in all deceptions, a single indicator of a phenomenon—in this case, criticism—is represented as the phenomenon itself, an open society. The logic went: Democracies allow public criticism of officials; the Soviet Union allows public criticism of officials; therefore the Soviet Union is a democracy.

Glasnost served a further, more practical purpose. In order for the press in the Soviet Union, which is entirely controlled by the Communist Party, to serve as an effective means of delivering messages to foreign audiences, the illusion had to be created that it was independent. By fostering the impression of a free speech and a free press, Glasnost lent credibility to government-controlled newspapers that otherwise would be regarded by foreign newsmen, and their audiences, as mouthpieces for the straight Party line. It provided the Soviet government with the means of altering its image abroad. It could be used to establish a set of convenient peepholes for journalists, academics, and other Kremlin-watchers through which they could see selected pictures of Soviet society.

From its inception, the Soviet leadership was justifiably concerned with its image abroad. Lenin, to get his revolution accepted by both capitalist governments and socialist parties abroad, had to represent it as something it was not: a constitutional union of democratic states. Its very name, the Union of Soviet Socialist Republics, was a fiction designed to make it appear that the Soviet Union was not a state, run by the Kremlin, but a grouping of autonomous "Republics" governed by elected "Soviets" of workers.

The Soviet Constitution was similarly a fiction. It described a government, complete with a Presidium, Supreme Soviet, and court system; but they existed in name only. Even the ministries were merely fronts for the agencies of the Communist Party. Lenin also fabricated entire activities of the notional "Republics" to impress foreign audiences. At one point, he even staged a breakdown in relations between one of these "Republics," the Far Eastern Republic, and Moscow, in order to encourage the American and Japanese governments to believe it was a dissident republic, and to provide it with munitions and equipment.

These early deceptions had little staying power, however. What modest credibility staged press releases about Soviet democracies had was quickly undermined by Communist spokesmen crudely stating that news releases should be used for agitation and propaganda, or "agitprop." This crisis of credibility came at a time when the Soviet Union faced a desperate economic situation.

By 1921, industrial production had fallen to about one fifth of the level it had been in 1913, and total national income, even in inflated rubles, was only one third the prewar level.[3] Factories were shut for lack of spare parts; the railroads were paralyzed by lack of fuel, oil fields had stopped production because of lack of drilling bits, trucks and tractors had run out of tires, and farmers lacked the fertilizer and equipment to produce food to export to the cities. Moreover, the Soviet revolutionists could not import the equipment they needed. The United States, Britain, France, and Japan not only had intervened in the civil war on the side of the anti-Communists, but now embargoed the export of these desperately needed items from the Soviet Union. And even if they could buy them from other countries, the Soviets had no way of paying for them. The Western Allies had frozen Russia's foreign gold reserves, and denied them credits.

Lenin recognized that the survival of the Soviet Revolution now depended on changing this situation. The Soviet Union had to get nations that perceived it as an intractable enemy to ship it the necessary equipment and materials to revive its economy. To do this, Lenin had to alter their image of the Soviet Union from a hostile to potentially friendly nation. The instrument was Glasnost.

THE FIRST GLASNOST: THE NEP

In the spring of 1921, Lenin proclaimed to the world a 180-degree reversal from the policies that had alienated the Western powers. He explained this change as the evolution of communism. He announced that "war communism," in which Soviet citizens had no freedom, rights, property, or even money, had come to an end. It would be succeeded by the second phase of communism, called the New Economic Policy, or NEP, in which there would now be a gradual return to a free market economy. Individuals would be allowed to own property; peasants would be allowed to own their land; small and medium businesses could be owned by workers and entrepreneurs in the form of cooperatives; and large industries would be reconstituted as publicly owned "trusts." Money would again become legal tender, debts would be recognized, and, wherever possible, the profit motive would be reinstituted.

Moreover, this economic "restructuring" would be accompanied by political liberalization. Individuals would be allowed to travel within Russia without permission, to emigrate, and to participate in local politics. Even émigrés abroad would be offered amnesty. Taken together, these measures suggested that the Soviet Union, despite its rhetoric about revolution, was slowly but irreversibly moving toward an accommodation with capitalism.

The message implicit in NEP was: The desired reversal of communism would be accelerated by trade with the West. It was thus in the interest of the Western Allies to supply, rather than deny, trade credits to the Soviet Union.

Feliks Dzierzhinski, as head of the OGPU, the security service of the Communist Party, was charged with getting this message convincingly through to the West. Dzierzhinski had already established the Trust deception which, it will be recalled, allowed him to send messages through the medium of putative dissidents to eleven Western intelligence services. Lenin also appointed him head of the NEP's Supreme Economic Council. From this dual vantage point, Dzierzhinski could control the covert as well as the open channels to the West. While the former was used to convince the West that the Revolution was faltering, the latter was used to show how democracy was surfacing.

Here Dzierzhinski activated a number of underground "opposition" newspapers, such as *New Russia*, which were read by, and cultivated working relations with, Western journalists in

Moscow. They echoed the theme that the Soviet Union was in a period of exciting change. At the same time, Dzierzhinski had his OGPU agents arrange tours of the "underground" for Russian émigré writers who had fled to the West. They were allowed to return to the Soviet Union, to interview recently released political prisoners, and to witness dissident meetings. They then reported back to their readers in first-hand accounts on how censorship on books, art, plays, and cultural criticism had been suspended under the NEP.

The Soviet leadership was even willing to manipulate its institutions to further this effect. For example, in 1922, the Commissar for Foreign Affairs enthusiastically proposed to Lenin: "In case the Americans would insist on representative institutions . . . we can deceive them by making a small ideological concession which would not have any practical meaning."[4] Lenin had no problem with falsifying institutions in the Soviet Union that were fictions to begin with. As he privately explained to the Communist leadership, the new policy "did not mean peace with capitalism but war on a new plane."

Within this Glasnost atmosphere, the Soviet Union also opened a "path," as Lenin called it, to the corporate business community in the United States that helped facilitate the Soviet Union's acquisition of credit, commodities, and technology, and also gave American lobbyists, public relations firms, and politically influential contacts a powerful incentive to support Soviet objectives.

Lenin pointed to the potential of this path during an acrimonious debate he had with other Bolsheviks soon after the Revolution. After he had hyperbolically asserted the Communists would triumph by hanging the capitalist nations, one skeptical colleague interrupted, and, referring to the critical shortages of war material in Russia, asked where the Communists would get enough "rope" for such a massive hanging. Lenin answered: "The capitalists will sell it to us." Moreover, they would sell it on credit.[5]

Underlying Lenin's quick reply was a powerful insight. Although foreign capitalists were the ultimate target of communism, they were also, in the short run, its most promising allies. The explanation to this paradox was simple enough: Western corporations had a concrete interest in helping Lenin break the diplomatic and economic isolation that the Western governments had imposed on the Soviet Union—because they wanted the Soviet Union's business. Lenin dangled in front of capitalists the sort of opportunity they could not easily find in their own free markets: a government-guaranteed monopoly. It would take the form of "concessions" in which foreigners would invest the capital in Russian ventures—and reap a large share of the profits.

The immediate problem for Soviet strategists was to convince Western businessmen, who had seen the Bolsheviks seize their property without compensation in 1917, that now, four years later, it was safe to accept these "concessions." The problem was compounded by the fact that the Soviet Union was virtually bankrupt—and Soviet ideology eventually required nationalizing private property.

To get around such formidable obstacles, Lenin suggested a program of misdirection that would focus the attention of the audience on the future promise of a Soviet Golconda—while distracting it from the inherent risks. Specifically, Lenin ordered his staff to find an American businessman who could be awarded the first concession under the NEP and, by parading before other American corporations, convince them that it was prudent and safe. It was much the same strategy as slaughterhouses using Judas goats to lead the cattle in. Lenin noted: "What we want to show and have in print . . . is that the Americans have gone in for concessions." He added, showing his appreciation of the lobbying role corporations play in the United States, "This is important politically."[6]

The American chosen for this role was Armand Hammer.[7] Although he was then only a twenty-one-year-old medical student visiting Moscow, his father, Julius Hammer, was well known

to Lenin. Julius Hammer had been a founder of a radical wing
of the American Communist Party, and, in this capacity, had met
Lenin and other Soviet leaders before the Revolution. After
Lenin seized power in 1917, Julius Hammer, who became the
exclusive agent for Soviet trade with America, helped supply the
Soviet government with embargoed goods by laundering them
through a third country—the short-lived Republic of Estonia.
He also made the Soviet government a silent partner in his Allied-
American Corporation, through which this business was funneled. Although an American citizen, Hammer was appointed
the Soviet commercial attaché in New York, and worked closely
with a Soviet official named Ludwig Martens in organizing trade
arrangements, and evasions of the American embargo.

By late 1921, these relationships between Hammer and the
Soviet government were investigated by the Department of Justice, and Martens was unceremoniously deported. Shortly there-
after, Julius Hammer himself was jailed on supposedly unrelated
charges stemming from an illegal abortion he had performed,
and he was sent to Sing Sing for three years. This prison sentence
left his son Armand with the task of sorting out the tangled
strands of the Allied-American Corporation.

Armand Hammer had little problem making contact with the
Soviet strategists. As soon as he arrived in Moscow, he called
Ludwig Martens, his father's former associate, who was now
working directly for Lenin's intelligence chief, Feliks Dzierzhinski, on the Supreme Economic Council, and, even more to the
point, was directly in charge of the effort to open the path to
Western business. Martens brought Hammer to Boris Reinstein,
who was in charge of organizing "International Propaganda" for
Lenin. Then, with Reinstein's endorsement, Hammer was allowed to meet Lenin, who approved awarding him the show
concession to "advertise" Soviet opportunities.

Since the purpose of this exercise was not to mine ore from
the concession but to use it as bait for other potential conces-

sionaires, Lenin instructed Martens in October 1921 to immediately give Hammer's corporation a contract for a concession, "even if it is a fictitious one." He suggested it could be "asbestos or any other Ural valuable or whatever you will."[8]

Lenin then wrote to Joseph Stalin, the newly appointed General Secretary to the Communist Party, asking that he and other Politburo members fully "support" this notional venture with Armand Hammer. He explained, "This is a small path to the American business world and this path should be made use of in every way." The emphasis was added by Lenin, who used "in every way" as a term of art suggesting this path could be used for covert action, influence agents, and intelligence. A copy of the letter was sent to Dzierzhinski as well as Stalin.[9]

After receiving this concession in 1922, Hammer set out to publicize it in America (as did Boris Reinstein's propaganda bureau). Hammer went from industrialist to industrialist in America, extolling the virtues—and potential profit—of investing in the Soviet Union. Hammer told these businessmen that Lenin had openly admitted to him that "Communism does not work," and that now the Soviet Union needed capitalists to repair the system. By 1925, Hammer had succeeded in recruiting no fewer than thirty-eight prestigious corporations, including the Ford Motor Company, into investing in Soviet enterprises. As the "path" gradually expanded to a superhighway for doing business with the Soviet Union, another three hundred foreign companies signed up for concessions. There followed a vast infusion of machinery, trucks, spare parts, ships, planes, and even whole factories—all financed by Western credit.[10]

In supporting this path, Dzierzhinski demonstrated that the Soviet Secret Service was capable of using covert channels to Western intelligence, such as double agents, false defectors, and sham communications, to reinforce and give credibility to the government's overt channels. As Lenin had accurately predicted, as long as the capitalists were told what they wanted to hear, they would tacitly accept rather than expose the deception. The message they wanted to hear was that the USSR was a potential gold mine.

The Soviet government also used diplomatic channels to reinforce the Glasnost message that the Soviet Union was evolving into a moderate government. Instead of calling for world revolution, as they had done prior to 1921, Soviet diplomats and trade delegations now stressed peaceful coexistence. The Soviet Foreign Ministry, using codes it knew were being deciphered by England, instructed its overseas agents to cease support for anti-West subversion. It also claimed that the Communist International, or Comintern, which Lenin headed, was a separate entity, not under its control.

This Glasnost message was accepted partly because it coincided with what Western governments wanted to believe. It was convenient to assume that the Soviet Revolution was a failure if only because it ended the pressures to take military action against Moscow. And it was in the interest of Western governments to believe that trade with the Soviet Union would weaken, rather than strengthen, the revolutionary elements in the government.

In any case, the NEP succeeded in breaking the effort to isolate the Soviet Union. Every major country except the United States normalized its diplomatic relations with Moscow, the trade embargo was abandoned, Germany helped rearm the Red Army, and no fewer than twelve foreign Communist parties joined the Comintern during this period. The Soviet Union also got the credits it needed to refurbish its industry.

Finally, in 1929, having accomplished its purposes, the NEP was abruptly ended. All private enterprises were nationalized; foreign concessions were canceled (and most foreign investment was expropriated without compensation); agriculture holdings were seized and farms collectivized. ("Perestroika" meant in this context the forced merger of private farms into state collectives.)[11] Censorship was reimposed; dissident movements were quashed; non-Party newspapers were shut down; and, within weeks, all traces of NEP disappeared.

THE SECOND GLASNOST: THE SOVIET CONSTITUTION, 1936–37

The next Glasnost offensive was more short-lived. Stalin suggested in the mid-1930s that the Soviet Union should move in the direction of restructuring its economy along capitalist lines, if necessary. He called these radical reforms "reconstructions," or *Perestroika*. They included profit incentives that were determined not by any Marxian need but by individual efficiency in increasing production. He explained: "There was no point in overthrowing Capitalism in 1917 . . . if we do not succeed in enabling people to live in a state of prosperity." To support this picture of a rapidly changing Soviet state, he proclaimed that the Soviet Union was returning to a Western-style constitutional government.

The new 1936 Constitution had all the trappings that suggested a democracy in Western eyes.[12] It guaranteed, on paper at least, that there would be freedom of speech, freedom of the press, and freedom of assembly. There would also be elections where citizens would be able to use secret ballots.

While the foreign press, which was the immediate target of these announcements, expressed some skepticism that this constitution would turn the Soviet Union into a democracy overnight, it accepted that Stalin was moving in the right direction. Even *Time*, which had been an avowed opponent of communism, grudgingly reported: "Last week Russia, having come of age, allowed her people all the fun and trapping of a real national election . . . to vote not in public by a show of hands but in private in a red-curtained booth, by secret ballot, according to their own convictions." It raised questions about "How capable Russia's ignorant masses are of assimilating democratic doctrine . . . and how capable Joseph Stalin is of permitting them to do so," but concluded that these constitutional changes, despite their limitations, suggested Stalin "had evidently revised his theory" about communism.[13]

The liberal constitution was only the opening shot in this campaign to make the Soviet Union appear similar to European states. It gave credibility to Soviet journalists, trade officials, diplomats, and other spokesmen who could claim to their foreign counterparts that they now could speak candidly, and critically, about the Soviet system because they were protected by the new guaranteed freedom of speech, press, and so forth.

Stalin, meanwhile, used embassies in neutral countries and diplomatic chatter at the League of Nations to further reinforce this theme. Agents of influence such as President Edvard Beneš of Czechoslovakia—who was secretly in the debt of Soviet intelligence, if not the pay—were mobilized to pass discreet messages, disguised as diplomatic insights, to British, French, and Polish diplomats. At a more subterranean level, messages that dovetailed with these were put directly into the hands of Western intelligence services by a supposedly anti-Soviet émigré organization, based in Bulgaria, called "the Inner Line." Although this group originally had worked against the Soviet agents in Europe, and served as a security service for other anti-Communist groups, it had been taken over by Soviet intelligence officers by the thirties. Like its immediate predecessor, the Trust, the Inner Line now was a controlled channel for disinformation.

The thrust of these messages was that Stalin was a pragmatist, not an ideologue; a nationalist, not an internationalist; an administrator, not a revolutionist; a manager, not an exporter of terrorism. It was therefore possible for the West to do business with him.

Through Beneš and other diplomatic channels, it was reported that Stalin's actual foreign policy, as distinct from his Communist rhetoric, involved developing alliances with capitalist countries opposing Hitler. Stalin's celebrated call for "socialism in one country" was seen as a face-saving rationalization for ending the Leninist policy of intervention and subversion abroad.

To further advance this idea, Stalin made a number of concrete demonstrations to foreign leaders that he was willing to make changes. For example, he openly pledged not to support the American Communist Party or any other group that advocated the overthrow of the American government, even though such a promise backed away from the principles of a Communist International. But it made it easier for President Roosevelt, who finally had recognized the Soviet Union in 1933, to extend credits and trade preferences in Moscow. Moreover, Communist parties abroad were even allowed to criticize the decisions of Moscow, which added to the appearance that they were becoming independent.

Previously, Communist parties had been considered to be Stalin's agents in foreign countries. Now they could claim to be independent and patriotic institutions. This made more plausible their demands to participate with non-Communist parties in "popular front" governments. Stalin also benefited: by advancing the legitimacy of local Communist parties, he laid the conceptual groundwork for Euro-Communism.

This Glasnost offensive came to an end with Stalin's purge of the Communist Party in 1937–38. All the constitutional guarantees, electoral demonstrations, foreign policy pledges, and diplomatic promises were revealed to be shams. The promised Perestroika turned into the "Great Terror." Then, in 1939, Stalin's alliance with Hitler, which was supported by the Euro-Communist parties, wrecked the illusion that these parties were independent entities.

THE THIRD GLASNOST: THE UNCLE JOE PARTNERSHIP, 1941–45

After Hitler invaded Russia in June 1941, Stalin revived Glasnost in the form of a Soviet partnership with the United States and

Britain that would bring democracy and peaceful cooperation to the postwar world. He again sent out the message that the militant phase of communism had now ended.

As a further demonstration of good faith in 1943, he dissolved the Comintern, which had been one of the famous Soviet organs dedicated to promoting Marxist-Leninist revolution abroad. By then, however, it had only symbolic significance; the coordination of Communist parties was now done by the International Department of the Communist Party. In an equally symbolic gesture, Stalin expunged from the national anthem references to international revolution. He also restored the rights of the Russian Orthodox Church, proposed the liberalization of censorship and other controls, and permitted Russians to own private plots to grow food. And he agreed to joining the United Nations after the war ended.

Even though these were only token gestures, they were accepted as evidence of change by Anglo-American leaders who wanted the alliance with Stalin to be more palatable to the public. Churchill, for example, responded by drafting a letter to Stalin, noting: "We feel we were right in interpreting your dissolution of the Comintern as a decision by the Soviet Government not to interfere in the internal political affairs of other countries."

These messages were delivered by diplomats and intelligence officers stationed in neutral countries in the form of "slips" or planted stories. For example, one British intelligence report in 1944, which it later turned out was assembled by a Soviet agent, stated that Russia had based its postwar recovery on "a structure of trade that would allow a slower pace of re-industrialization and the import of consumer goods—and, through political collaboration with a view to establish real security in the West."[14]

Again, this was what the Allies wanted to believe: the Soviet Union would be buying goods from the West—not threatening it with subversion. This justified massive economic and military aid through the Lend-Lease program, which the Red Army needed to remain in the war against Hitler. Harry Hopkins, President Roosevelt's adviser, wrote after the meeting with Stalin at Yalta in 1945: "We really believed in our hearts that this was the dawn of the new day we had been praying for. . . . The Russians had proved that they could be reasonable and far seeing, and there wasn't any doubt in the mind of the President, or any of us that we could live and get along with them peacefully for as far into the future as any of us could imagine."[15] The British Foreign Office similarly concluded: "The old idea of world revolution is dead."[16]

Encouraged by such optimistic assessments of a Soviet partnership, the United States and Britain sanctioned de facto Stalin's earlier annexation of the three Baltic states—Latvia, Lithuania, and Estonia—as well as his postwar plan to annex parts of Poland, Prussia, Rumania, Finland, and Japan. They also accepted in this spirit of goodwill the concept of a Soviet sphere of influence over much of Eastern Europe.

The euphoria hardly outlasted the end of the war. The Soviet takeover of Czechoslovakia, sponsorship of the civil war in Greece, and occupation of part of Iran, among other things, brought this entente to an abrupt end. The Iron Curtain, as a metaphor, replaced the spirit of Glasnost.

THE FOURTH GLASNOST: DESTALINIZATION, 1956–59

On February 24, 1956, at the XXth Party Congress in Moscow, Nikita Khrushchev launched yet another Glasnost offensive based on economic and political reforms. He blamed Stalin, who was dead, for the present problems. He argued that the "cult of the personality" that Stalin created had perverted the Communist Revolution and led to the loss of individual freedom.

Khrushchev thus equated ending Stalin's "cult of the personality" with the restoration of democracy in the Soviet Union. Although the publication of this speech was portrayed as an intelligence coup in the United States by the CIA, its message was hardly secret.[17] Khrushchev had copies of the speech distributed to over 2 million Communists in the Soviet Union and Eastern bloc, and according to Angleton, no fewer than six different Communist diplomats, under Soviet control, offered it to the CIA as well as to other Western intelligence services. The "leaking" of this secret speech set the basis in the West for the most sweeping Glasnost offensive since the NEP.

Then Khrushchev announced, with great fanfare, reforms that appeared to constitute what approached another Russian Revolution—equivalent, as *The New York Times* reported, to "the spring break up of ice on a Siberian River."[18] He proclaimed that competition would play a major role in restructuring agriculture and industry. And, in a well-publicized experiment, economically autonomous teams would be allowed to act like private businesses. This return to capitalism was then made the subject of a film, released abroad under the title *Man of the Soil*.

The Soviet press, amplifying the return-to-capitalism theme, published numerous stories about private millionaires, underground businesses, and the thriving black market.[19] In addition, there were drives to eradicate alcoholism, nepotism, and corruption.

The economic reforms were accompanied by political reforms. Russian Church leaders were allowed to travel abroad; Moscow artists were permitted to hold exhibitions of abstract paintings; poets like Yevtushenko were allowed to give readings in the United States; and Solzhenitsyn was allowed to publish works critical of the Soviet Union under Stalin, such as *One Day in the Life of Ivan Denisovich*. Soviet dissidents were allowed to have contact with the Western press. Academic enterprises, such as the Institute for the Study of the United States and Canada, were similarly given a new role as sources of "news" for American journalists.[20]

Khrushchev also decided to again make use of the business

path to build support for his Glasnost. He turned to Lenin's original choice, Armand Hammer, who had in 1957 taken control of Occidental Petroleum, a minuscule company in Los Angeles with no real assets.

By 1961, Occidental, which was listed on the Stock Exchange, had become a sufficiently large energy company for Hammer to return to the Soviet Union under the imprimatur of the U.S. Commerce Department to, as he put it in a press conference, "inquire into opportunities for increased peaceful trade."[21]

In Moscow, Khrushchev warmly applauded Hammer, in a speech to Communist leaders, for the role he had played under Lenin's New Economic Policy in the twenties, and further, while reminiscing about him, justified the policy of luring capitalists to Russia as a means of advancing the revolutionary cause. He stated, in terms that left little room for doubt: "The measure our government took under Lenin's initiative yielded good results; it contributed to the success of socialism in our country." He asked rhetorically, "Was the New Economic Policy a retreat?" He then answered the question, No—it had only appeared to be a retreat. "Now it is clear to all that it was an attack by socialism on capitalism."[22] In other words, the NEP was a successful deception.

In a private conversation with Hammer, in which there was not even a translator present, Hammer reported that Khrushchev complained about inefficiencies in the Soviet economy, and then stated, in an almost word for word repeat of Stalin's earlier message to the West, "If we cannot give our people the same standard of living that you give your people under the Capitalist system, we know that Communism cannot succeed."[23] Again, as he did with Lenin, Hammer was given the message to repeat that the Soviet leadership was admitting the failure of communism, and making internal economic reform its highest priority.

When Hammer returned to the United States, he sought an audience with President Kennedy to report on what Khrushchev had told him. The message, as he also announced to the press, was that the Soviet Union could provide a bonanza of profits and jobs for American business. "If you give us credit. . . . you will keep your plants busy," he quoted Khrushchev as saying.[24] Hammer explained that Khrushchev had confided in him that "Communism was sure to fail" unless it could provide its people with more food and consumer products. The Soviet Union thus had to change from a wartime to peacetime economy to save the Revolution.

Although it was the same message that had been sounded in the NEP (and by the same American capitalist), it was a message American business—and labor—still wanted to hear. The Soviet Union could, in Khrushchev's estimate, furnish America with a million new jobs.

Whatever success it had in projecting the image of a more moderate and non-threatening state, this Glasnost did not prevent the Soviet leadership from carrying out its other strategic goals. In 1959, as Golitsyn later revealed, it radically reorganized the KGB, so that it would be capable of securely carrying out long-term deceptions (a reorganization confirmed in the late 1960s by U.S. Communications Intelligence). At the same time, it also created the special strategic deception staff, GUSM, under military command. Soon afterwards, as we have seen in the telemetry double cross, the Soviets began projecting an image of missile incompetency through biased electronic signals and double-agents' disinformation while perfecting highly accurate missiles. These missiles gave the Soviet Union the ability to destroy America's land-based missiles in a surprise attack, although U.S. intelligence did not realize it for almost a decade. And then, in Cuba in 1962, Khrushchev attempted to change, if not the balance of power, U.S. confidence in its ability to defend itself by covertly deploying intermediate-range missiles in Cuba. But by this time such events as the shooting down of an American U-2, the mass arrest of Soviet dissidents, and the erection of the Berlin Wall had ended this Glasnost.

THE FIFTH GLASNOST: DETENTE, 1970–75

The fifth Glasnost, initiated by Leonid Brezhnev, supplied the context and goodwill atmosphere for the Soviet policy of Detente. If the Soviet offer to restrict strategic arms, negotiate mutually beneficial accords, and relax internal tensions was to be made credible, Brezhnev had first to establish that the Soviet Union no longer seriously aspired to change the East-West status quo.

The "public airings" of issues helped explain to relevant audiences in the West why the Soviets had abandoned its prior aim of world revolution. The central theme was that the Soviet government was now run not by ideologues but by technocrats who had no interest in adhering to the Leninist doctrine of class warfare. Instead, like technocrats in the West, they wanted to expand and rationalize their industrial base. They wanted, in short, to substitute butter for guns.[25]

Soviet scientists sent to international conferences, such as Pugwash, told their Western counterparts about how they were coming into increasing conflict with Communist ideologues. These dovetailing reports, elicited and analyzed by CIA debriefers, advanced the idea that, under Brezhnev's leadership, the scientific-technical elite was winning the battle.

During this same period, Georgi Arbatov's Institute intensified its program of briefing Western academics, journalists, media executives, and congressmen on the effect of technocratic changes in Soviet society. These backgrounders directed attention to differences purportedly developing between the outdated but still mandatory rhetoric of the Revolution and the actual policies of the new Soviet leaders. Briefers at the Institute told their subjects that Brezhnev's real agenda, whatever he said for internal consumption, was getting the Soviet economy working. To make progress, he recognized the need to relax the controls on Soviet scientists, engineers, and other members of the Soviet meritocracy, and to import Western methods and ideas. Dissidents in Moscow who were scientists and engineers were permitted to speak to foreign correspondents. Even if they had no mandated brief and merely spoke their mind, their complaints about inefficiency and bureaucratic restrictions would support the justification for a technocratic revolution.

As this Glasnost progressed in the mid-1970s, Brezhnev, like Stalin before him, promulgated a new constitution for the Soviet Union. It too granted freedom of speech, press, assembly, meeting, and public demonstration—as well as the right to education, medical treatment, and employment. The Soviet Union even signed the Helsinki Accords in 1975, which appeared to legitimize an opposition to Communist rule.

This technocratic revolution line was also fed by Soviet diplomats into intelligence channels. At the UN, the double agents code-named Top Hat and Fedora suggested to the FBI that Brezhnev's qualifications as an engineer were being given prominence to placate Soviet engineers and scientists who were fed up with ideological red tape. In 1969, both Soviet diplomats reported that they had received new "priority" questionnaires from their Soviet controllers demanding they find out about the American Chemical-Biological Weapon (CBW) program.

Fedora, after being recalled to Moscow for a briefing, then told the FBI that Soviet intelligence was being put under this pressure because the Soviet military had determined that the United States had an almost unbeatable lead in chemical-biological weapons. It was thus demanding the budget for a crash program to catch up. But the Politburo did not believe that the Soviet economy could afford to spend the money. Fedora claimed to be caught in the battle between doves, who demanded further intelligence, and hawks, who wanted to build chemical and biological weaponry.[26] (This message that the United States had won the race gave Nixon a further reason for making a dramatic decision that had been under consideration. He unilaterally ended U.S. production of CBW weapons.)

But the Soviets did not have to rely on chancy public or intelligence channels to get the main message of détente through to the White House. They had at their disposal a superb vehicle for laser-beaming messages to strategic planners in the Office of the Secretary of Defense, the Joint Chiefs of Staff, the State Department, and the National Security Council without the intermediation and scrutiny of the counterintelligence staffs in the CIA and Pentagon that test the more ordinary communications sent from the enemy camp. This channel was the arms control process.

Whatever else they might accomplish in terms of actually limiting or reducing the strategic weapons of either the United States or the Soviet Union, arms control negotiations have provided the Soviets with a means of educating an elite American audience about Soviet defense policies, which, up until then, it had learned about mainly through espionage, satellite images, signals interceptions, and military displays paraded by the drag strips in Moscow. In these negotiations, the Soviets could tell this audience the meaning of the jigsaw pieces that they had collected in years past through conventional intelligence gathering. They could also use this channel to test the technological abilities of American intelligence by staging treaty violations to see if they could be detected. They could learn what could and could not be seen. And they could then use this channel to direct the attention of U.S. satellites to events and developments in Soviet territory that Soviet deception planners wanted seen. If, for example, Soviet negotiators suggest that mobile missiles are being confined to a base in Eastern Europe, they can be reasonably sure that U.S. intelligence will point its cameras there, and that the resulting photographs will be closely scrutinized. The Soviet negotiators, in other words, could steer U.S. satellites to peepholes that would reinforce a message sent through any other channel. And the messages need not be limited to weapons. They could concern the nature of the Soviet regime, the new leadership, and its desire for change.

The Soviet version of arms control was developed in the early

1960s under the direct supervision of N. R. Mironov, a close associate of Brezhnev's.[27] As head of the Administrative Organs Department of the Communist Party, Mironov had the responsibility for coordinating military, diplomatic, covert, and intelligence actions aimed at furthering state policy. He was also, according to Golitsyn, Brezhnev's chief deception strategist and had personally led to the successful drive in the late 1950s to reorganize the KGB and International Department of the Communist Party so that they could securely execute long-term disinformation programs modeled on Lenin's NEP deception. General John Sejna, who acted as a liaison with the Administrative Organs Department and Czechoslovakian military planners in the 1960s, and who defected to the United States in 1968, explained in his debriefings that Mironov initially envisioned using the arms control process to delay U.S. military programs, disrupt the relations between the United States and its NATO allies, and gain some indication of how the West perceived of Soviet policies.

As the arms control channel developed, Mironov brought in another top deception planner. He was N. I. Savinkin, who subsequently, as deputy head of the Administrative Organs Department, took over the job of making sure that the negotiations not only dovetailed with but advanced Soviet objectives. Since this task required coordinating what military and ballistic equipment was seen by U.S. satellites and military attachés, he made General (later Marshal) N. V. Ogarkov—who had been in charge of GUSM, the Soviet General Staff's Directorate for Strategic Deception—the chief military representative to the SALT arms control negotiations.[28] This put Ogarkov in a perfect position to ensure that what the United States was told through the negotiations would be confirmed by what it "saw" and "heard" through its photographic and electronic surveillance of the Soviet Union.

Arms control also was an effective two-way channel. From it, Soviet strategists could learn what the prevailing American preconceptions of Soviet strategies were. Soviet negotiators were in fact told by the Americans precisely what they assumed Soviet weaponry, strategy, and objectives consisted of—and asked, after consultations with Moscow, to correct them if they were wrong. This technique, described by SALT negotiators, was meant to foster a common language about such issues as deterrence, mutual assured destruction, first-strike capabilities, mobile missiles, and so on. But it also helped Soviet deception planners to make information more credible by keying it in to the preconceptions of the American negotiators.

The more extended arms control negotiations become, the more dependent the Americans have been on the Soviets for public signs of support—such as official statements indicating progress or even the scheduling of summit conferences. And as the talks progress, the incentive has commensurately increased for American negotiators to assume that their Soviet counterparts are acting in good faith. Otherwise, they would have to conclude that their own efforts have been, at best, a waste of time. Further, they have depended on the Soviets to provide them, by both words and deeds (which could be conveniently photographed by satellites), some corroboration of this presumed good faith. The Soviets, in turn, needed to know precisely what words and acts would be taken as evidence of their credibility. In other words, it was in both the American and Soviet negotiators' interests to tacitly cooperate on verifying hypotheses that the United States was relying on. Not uncommonly, according to participants, the Americans would suggest to the Soviets what further evidence had to be displayed—or withdrawn—to make the Soviet position credible to the White House, Congress, and the American media. By doing so, they would also provide Moscow with feedback.[29]

The Soviets have encouraged this tacit cooperation by reinforcing the notion that there is an internal struggle between "doves" in the Foreign Ministry and "hawks" in the Soviet military. As Soviet Ambassador Anatoli Dobrynin told Henry Kissinger in 1971, the Americans could intervene on the side of the doves by taking certain actions in the SALT talks. To his credit, Kissinger realized that the Soviet suggestion did not coincide with reality. As he notes in his autobiography, "the proposition that elements of the Soviet government would squabble while dealing with foreigners was cleverly geared to American pre-conceptions of the 'doves' in the Kremlin fighting a valiant battle against 'hard-liners.' "[30]

The assumptions about Soviet intentions advanced through the arms control channel have affected much more than the deployment of missiles. Nixon explained in his 1972 report to Congress that the Soviet willingness to enter into arms accords "indicates constructive intentions in political as well as strategic areas," and that "progress in controlling arms can reinforce progress in a much wider area of international relations."[31] What this linkage led to was the reversal of America's postwar policy of containing the Soviet Union. Instead of maintaining political, military, and economic pressure on the Soviet Union, the new détente now strove to relax this tension. Instead of questioning the legitimacy of the Soviet rule over Eastern Europe, it recognized the "organic unity" of the Communist bloc—Kissinger's deputy, Helmet Sonnenfeldt, suggested that Communist bloc unity, rather than dissonance, was in the long-term interest of the United States. Instead of confronting the Soviet bloc, American forces were withdrawn from areas of conflict, including Vietnam. And instead of attempting to isolate the Soviet bloc, it was granted access to Western credit, technology, and markets— at times on "most favored nation" terms. Whereas earlier the United States had attempted to intensify economic disaffection within the Soviet Union, it now shipped out its own wheat to help the Soviet government satisfy the populace.

As Brezhnev held out the carrot to American business of a ten-fold increase in trade by 1980, Hammer recruited the support of some of the largest capitalist enterprises in the world to détente. Through Occidental, he announced deals amounting to over 28 billion dollars. (Most of these projects either did not materialize or proved largely unprofitable for Occidental.)

The Soviet Union also appeared willing to allow Communist countries in Eastern Europe to pursue independent relations with the West and engage in their own versions of Glasnost. Rumania, for example, advertised itself as a Communist nation that the West "could do business with," according to Ion Pacepa who, up until his defection in 1978, served as acting director of Rumanian intelligence and a personal adviser to President Nicolae Ceausescu. "To convince the West that Rumania was becoming a Western-oriented country, independent of Moscow," Pacepa said, "Ceausescu himself publicly attacked the Soviets, unmasked many of his predecessor's abuses, allowed the press to criticize the party bureaucracy, simulated a decentralization of the economy, instituted dual candidates for local elections, and launched a campaign against alcoholism, corruption, and nepotism." By 1975 the U.S. granted Rumania "most favored nation" status, and within three years, the West extended Rumania credits of $20 billion (or nearly $1,000 per capita). Then, in 1978, after he defected, Pacepa revealed that the "independent line" was largely a sham staged by the Rumanian intelligence service under his direction. He explained in a post-defection interview "Ceausescu's Glasnost was an . . . influence operation."[32]

Brezhnev also announced with great fanfare a unilateral troop cut in Soviet forces in Europe. Accordingly, the Russian Sixth Tank Guard Division, with its 10,000 troops and armor, moved out of its base in Wittenberg, East Germany, presumably reducing Soviet offensive power in Europe. In fact, as Western intelligence determined only in 1981, the withdrawn division had distributed its tanks and other equipment to other Soviet front line divisions in Germany and then, although officially taken out of the Soviet order of battle, it was re-established under a different name just across the Polish border, where it received all new equipment. The "withdrawal" thus actually added to rather than reduced Soviet offensive capabilities in Europe.[33]

The test of this "linkage" concept came in Vietnam in 1973. Kissinger believed that he could count on Soviet cooperation to prevent North Vietnam from breaking the Paris Accords, which would permit America to withdraw the last of its troops without losing face. As Kissinger reports, Brezhnev told Nixon that he had stopped "military deliveries to North Vietnam."[34] If so, the North Vietnamese Army would not be able to invade the South. Suggesting a deal had been struck, Brezhnev added: "There may be rifles but nothing of considerable significance. We will urge [the North Vietnamese] to adhere to the Paris Agreement." Kissinger concluded "we . . . had used detente to isolate Hanoi and extricate ourselves from Vietnam."[35]

The judgment turned out to be wrong. Despite the negotiated peace, the North Vietnamese Army—with tanks, ammunition, and electronic intelligence supplied by the Soviet Union—blitzkrieged through South Vietnam in the spring of 1975. North Vietnam took over South Vietnam, and its army occupies most of Laos and Cambodia. The Soviet Union, for its part, obtained the huge air and naval base at Cam ranh Bay that the United States had evacuated, which greatly extended the effective range of the Soviet Navy.

Brezhnev's Glasnost, and the assumptions that Soviet activities could be taken at face value, were called into question by a secret reassessment of Soviet strategy in 1976. What occasioned this reassessment was a glaring discrepancy between CIA predictions of the number of intercontinental missiles that the Soviets would aim at the United States—and the reality. Rather than the few hundred missiles the CIA projected, the Soviets deployed by 1973 well over a thousand warheads aimed at targets in the United States. In 1974, Albert Wohlstetter argued in a series of highly influential articles that the CIA's persistent underestimation of Soviet missile deployments came, not from a lack of contrary photographic intelligence of silo construction, but from a mind-set among CIA analysts that began with the premise that the Soviets had the same deterrent strategy as the United States.[36]

This "mirror-image" view of deterrence came from the arms control channel. It held that the only rational use of nuclear weapons was to deter, rather than win, a war. Consequently, the Soviet Union, like the United States, would build, and deploy, only the minimal number of missiles it needed to threaten—in the event it was attacked—the assured destruction of the attacker. If this logic of "mutually assured destruction," or MAD, was valid, the Soviet Union could be expected to build no more than the number of city-destroying missiles it needed to assure that the United States would not start a nuclear war. Since the Soviet Union would not need either numerical superiority, or highly accurate missiles that could attack U.S. missile silos, the CIA had assumed that it would not waste resources on them. The observed facts were interpreted accordingly, which led to the underestimates in the late 1960s.

This error caused such unease at the President's Foreign Intelligence Advisory Board (PFIAB), which included some of the most distinguished experts on military technology, that its chairman, Admiral George W. Anderson, suggested to President Nixon that he appoint an independent group of experts to reexamine the intelligence data. The idea, however, was strongly opposed by the CIA, and Nixon, under tremendous pressure to resign because of Watergate, rejected it. But when Gerald Ford replaced him in 1974, he ordered the CIA to produce a review of how well it had fared in estimating Soviet capacity in the past decade. According to Lionel Olmer, the executive secretary of PFIAB, the consequent review was "so condemnatory of the performance of the [intelligence] community over ten years on those issues that it left no room for argument that something ought to be done."[37]

Admiral Anderson, at this point, revived his earlier proposal, suggesting that two teams reanalyze the evidence. Team A would be drawn from the CIA's own experts; Team B would be outsiders selected by PFIAB, with the approval of CIA Director George Bush. The experiment would test whether two different sets of experts, analyzing the same data, would come to different conclusions—and, if so, why? By July 1976, President Ford approved that competitive analyses would provide the basis for a new intelligence estimate of Soviet strategy, and Richard Pipes, a Harvard professor of Russian history, was selected to head the strategic review of Team B.[38]

The Pipes panel, which included a top group of experts on military weaponry and strategy, then began, as Pipes put it, "a broad and in depth survey of Soviet strategic policies, and programs." The point of the exercise was to test the validity of the prevailing assumption that Soviet nuclear strategy was identical to America's own "MAD" strategy. It considered in this regard such factors as Soviet missile accuracy, aiming points, deployment patterns, and reload capacity. And it closely analyzed assertions of military doctrine in Soviet military journals. It concluded that the MAD theory did not fit the observed facts about the development of the Soviet rocket force. This was supported by the two other Team B technical panels, which demonstrated that the CIA had underestimated the accuracy of the newer generation Soviet missiles and that, once this error was corrected, these Soviet missiles could be seen not as part of a MAD deterrent but as weapons designed to destroy U.S. silos, with the least amount of collateral damage. They were, in other words, war-fighting rather than war-deterring weapons. In addition, it was calculated from the positioning of the land-based Soviet missiles that they were aimed not at American cities, which would have been consistent with a MAD philosophy, but at U.S. military targets. Further, these panels interpreted data indicating that the Soviets were developing or deploying no fewer than eleven new systems of missiles as inconsistent with the notion that Soviet strategy was based on maintaining the status quo.

The Pipes panel concluded that this evidence was completely

in keeping with stated Soviet doctrine that "military missions are driven by political missions, not the other way round." It asserted that, if U.S. analysts avoided "mirror-imaging," or the assumption that Russians and Americans had the same strategy, the available evidence led to only one conclusion: The Soviet leadership, rather than subscribing to MAD, was deploying nuclear weapons, like any other military force, to achieve its national goals. As Pipes noted, "Soviet nuclear strategy had to be seen in context of grand strategy."[39]

This was a radical departure from what the CIA's Team A had concluded. Team A held that the Soviet leadership, believing victory was unobtainable, had developed its nuclear force to deter the United States from attacking the Soviet Union. It held that Soviet nuclear weapons were based on MAD and therefore future Soviet deployments were reactive to U.S. deployments.

The confrontation between these two different views of the same evidence, which was not unlike the religious disputations in medieval Europe, took place at CIA headquarters in Langley, Virginia, on November 5, 1976. The audience included the fourteen members of PFIAB and the Director of the CIA. After considerable debate, Team A, unable to explain more recent Soviet missile deployments in terms of MAD, more or less gave up the battle. It then revised its report, and in agreement with Team B, concluded that the observed facts of Soviet missile deployments did not support the theory that they were a deterrent—or even defensive in nature. This revised assessment, accepted by PFIAB and CIA Director George Bush, thus became, at least briefly, the official American view of Soviet strategy. It was encapsulated in the 1977 National Intelligence Estimate (NIE-11 3/8). This new view completely contradicted the most fundamental assumption of détente—that both sides sought only to maintain the status quo.

The conflict was resolved in the Carter administration by discrediting not only Team B itself but the entire process of outside review. The new CIA leadership, under Admiral Turner, made what amounted to an ad hominem attack on the B team. Rather than dealing with the fact that the report had been accepted by Team A and the PFIAB, it called into question the personal integrity of its members, suggesting that they had used the "competitive review" merely as camouflage to assert their own biased view of Soviet intentions. The main source for this charge was a CIA officer, John Paisley, who had been assigned to the B team as a "liaison"—though actually, as it turned out, his job, according to Pipes, was to monitor and control its work for the CIA. Paisley himself was found shot to death in 1978, chained and weighted, in Chesapeake Bay.*

By 1979, with the widespread arrests of Soviet dissidents, including members of the Helsinki Watch Committee, the closing of the underground newspapers, the resumption of Soviet covert actions abroad, and the invasion of Afghanistan, the discrediting of this Glasnost was complete.

THE SIXTH GLASNOST: THE GORBACHEV REVOLUTION, 1983–?

After the XXVIth Congress of the Communist Party decided to sanction a peace initiative in 1981, there was a false start. Yuri Andropov, the new General Secretary, who was presented to the media as a liberal in the Western mold—tall, athletic, Scotch-drinking, jazz-loving, English-speaking, and intellectual—became terminally ill soon after assuming office, and died in February 1984.[40] The Glasnost offensive thus had to wait for his heir

---

*Angleton was intrigued by the circumstances surrounding this mysterious death. He suggested that if it had not been for some of the weights slipping off the body and consequently its surfacing, Paisley's disappearance would have been written off as a presumed suicide. Because Paisley had obtained a crucial overview of the credence given by the CIA to the different methods of assessing Soviet developments, Angleton speculated that Paisley's knowledge would have been of "great value" to the KGB, and that if they had obtained it they might also have had an incentive to hide this success by disposing of Paisley.

apparent, Mikhail Gorbachev, to assume the mantle in 1985.

Gorbachev wasted little time in announcing reforms reminiscent of the NEP. Like his predecessors, he advanced the thesis that the Soviet system had to be radically restructured to meet the pragmatic needs of the modern world. It needed to produce more consumer goods to satisfy its citizens, import more technology to modernize its industry, use free market incentives to increase the output of farms and factories, and reform government to make it less bureaucratically intrusive.

Gorbachev held that this massive Perestroika would require a shift in Soviet industry from military to civilian priorities, cooperation from the West in the form of credits and liberalizing trade, and better motivation for workers in the form of profit incentives and more personal freedom. To further rationalize the economy, individuals would be permitted to join together to form cooperative businesses, and farmers could lease for periods of up to fifty years small plots of land.

In focusing world attention on these promised reforms, all the past Glasnosts became prologue to this design. Censorship was partly lifted—and the works of authors, artists, and musicians with followings in the West became prominent. High-profile dissidents, such as Andrei Sakharov, who had become symbols of Soviet repression, were released from internal exile or prison. Refuseniks were allowed to emigrate to Israel. Newspapers published criticism of government inefficiency. At the same time, the Soviets permitted the publication of some twenty-five non-official journals. Even though these publications remained largely dependent on the government for access to printing plants, paper, financing, and distribution, they claimed to be editorially independent. One of them, *Ekspress-Khronica*, supplied to Western news media a compilation of government declarations, policy implementations, and public demonstrations that appeared to measure the accelerating progress of Soviet reforms.[41]

While Gorbachev's Glasnost did not immediately afford Soviet citizens more civil liberties than had previous Glasnosts, nor bring about more substantial changes in ownership, incentives, and economic relationships than had these earlier "Perestroikas," it succeeded far more effectively in changing the image of the Soviet state. This success proceeded in large part from the linkages it forged to foreign media and academia. Unlike any previous Glasnost, it persuaded foreign specialists that government-controlled organs were independent sources.

Consider, for example, how even the usually conservative *Wall Street Journal* accepted this notion in a front-page story on the "Glasnost's impact."[42] The report, focusing on *Izvestia*, the national newspaper of the Soviet government, stated that "the Communist Party Central Committee apparently no longer gives orders about everything that can and can't be published." This remarkable assessment of *Izvestia*'s independence could not be based on its organizational structure. *Izvestia* is a government-owned and -operated publication. Its editors are members of the Communist Party, under Party discipline and, as such, required by the principles of "Partynost" to support the Party line. Even if they wanted to publicly deviate, they could not without the approval of the special committee of the Politburo, which scrutinizes their work on a daily basis and on which they are dependent for their continued tenure at the newspaper. The conclusion of *The Wall Street Journal* that *Izvestia* has editorial freedom was drawn from the paper's content, or more specifically, from the letters it carries complaining about government services. Again, the very controlled self-criticism that is the cutting edge of the Glasnost sword is taken as evidence of a free press.

Before Gorbachev's offensive, foreign news media treated the Soviet government-owned media as a propaganda arm of the government. They further assumed that government spokesmen who permitted interviews furnished them with nothing more than pre-packaged briefs, and that private citizens who would talk to them were restricted by secrecy laws from revealing any newsworthy data. Now, under Glasnost, the assumption became that they could get reliable data from these formerly suspect sources.

This development not only made the job of American journalists in Moscow much easier but it enhanced their status as Soviet experts. They could rewrite stories they found in the Soviet press (as was commonly done in countries with free presses). They even could get Glasnost stories delivered to their hotels in English in the form of a daily newsletter published by unofficial newspapers. They could also interview Soviet spokesmen who were fluent in English and presumably free to tell them on a background basis their views about Soviet policy. These assumptions also raised the credibility of Soviet universities, think tanks, and quasi-academic research institutes and, in so doing, gave both journalists and visiting academics other resources to shape their picture of Soviet policy.

Even the word *Glasnost* was retranslated in 1986 by the Soviet press agency Novosti to mean "transparency" rather than merely publicity.[43] This semantic change helped support the idea that the new Glasnost news and academic media were not just publicizing government-sanctioned releases but, like their counterparts in the West, rendering government institutions transparent.

To determine the right kind of "spin control" to put on the messages about sensitive subjects, such as the environment and nuclear safety, the Soviets hired American public relations firms which specialized in planting stories in the American media in the form of news releases. They also provided feedback on the response to different test balloons sent up through Glasnost.

Glasnost also benefited heavily from the cooperation of the Reagan administration, which had its own reason for not questioning messages sent through these channels to the American media. President Reagan had begun his administration by describing the Soviet Union as an "evil empire," Soviet arms negotiations as systematic "cheating," and Soviet summits as

275

"propaganda exercises." Subsequently, in his second term, when he described the Soviet Union as a promising "partner," signed arms control agreements, and made summits a regular event on his calendar, he could only justify this radical change in policy by asserting that the Soviet Union itself was changing into an open society—which was the precise message of Glasnost.

The U.S. government thus not only accepted the Glasnost line but provided funds to support cultural, academic, and journalistic exchanges that offered photo opportunities—and television pictures—reinforcing the idea that the Soviet Union had radically changed. Tours were organized for famous American rock singers, like Billy Joel, who were then photographed in concert in Russia. When the films were shown on Western television, they relayed the predictable, if clichéd impression of freedom, abandon, and permissiveness. The State Department officially encouraged American television networks to exchange programs and presentations with Soviet networks which gave the Soviets the opportunity to further the illusion that their system of government was roughly the same as the American system. The ABC program Nightline, for example, broadcast a three-hour exchange between the American Congress and Supreme Soviet, suggesting an equivalence between the two, even though, in reality, the latter is nothing more than a ceremonial body that meets only twice a year and has no legislative powers.

Moreover, the business path that Hammer had been assiduously paving for 65 years developed into a bipartisan lobby for extending Western credit and trade preferences to the Soviet bloc called the U.S.-Soviet Trade and Economic Council. One measure of this lobby's access to the Reagan White House was the appointment in 1987 of its former chairman, C. William Verity, as Secretary of Commerce.

By 1988, the United States Trade and Economic Council (USTEC), with the assistance of Armand Hammer, had arranged for over four hundred American corporate leaders to attend conferences in Moscow, where they were invited to banquets with

Soviet leaders, driven around with motorcycle escorts, and given other kinds of red-carpet treatment they could not so easily get in a capitalist country.[44]

Aside from such prestigious junkets, these American businesses also received the opportunity to participate in a series of NEP-type concessions. Just as he had in the NEP, Hammer took the lead in organizing consortiums to invest in Russian chemicals, industries, and mining. USTEC also encouraged the American corporate establishment to trade with Soviet cooperatives, projecting that the Soviet market could absorb 25 percent of American exports—even though, in 1988, it actually accounted for only about 1 percent of American exports. In exchange, USTEC arranged for hundreds of Soviet executives to visit the United States and receive training at American corporations in the art of management.

The business channel, even by the fact it existed, reinforced the central message of the arms control and Glasnost channels—that the Soviet Union was rapidly changing. The announcement by Hammer that Occidental was entering a six billion dollar joint venture with the Soviets to build a petrochemical complex near the Caspian Sea, followed by a rush of announced "joint ventures" by other American corporations appeared to confirm that the Soviet Union was in the process of abandoning part or all of the Communist dogma. Why else would American corporations seek to invest there? Each announcement also whetted the appetite of other capitalists in Europe and Asia, as well as the United States, who were anxious to find a new and protected market for their product. And this competition for concessions gives governments—especially if they are responsive to corporate pressure—an additional reason to normalize their relations with the Soviet Union. The business channel makes it progressively more difficult for the United States and other Western governments to block the admission of the Soviet bloc to the main international economic organizations—such as the International Monetary Fund, GATT, and the Bank of International

Settlements. These positions would further enhance the image of the Soviet Union as a partner of capitalism, rather than a foe.

This sixth Glasnost was all the more impressive because the underlying control structure of the Soviet Union had not substantially changed. Soviet secrecy laws still prohibited discussions of state policies with foreigners. The Soviet press was still owned by the state, or, in the case of the underground newspapers, totally depended on it for newsprint and permits. Soviet research institutions, like Arbatov's Institute, were still supervised by units of the Communist Party. Soviet government bodies were still national fronts for units of the Communist Party. Dissident groups were still under the KGB's electronic surveillance, which, if anything, was made more effective by advances in intelligence-gathering technology such as computers, which could search out key words, numbers, and images, and listening devices that could eavesdrop from a remote distance.

Nor, despite the images of permissiveness and democratization, did individuals have any more freedom of action. Soviet citizens still required permits to travel to other cities in the Soviet Union. They also could not change residences or jobs, or even obtain a telephone without permission. And, as a deterrent and ultimate control mechanism, there were still concentration camps and psychiatric confinement for political prisoners.

Moreover, other measures the United States employs to evaluate developments in the Soviet bloc, such as photographic reconnaissance from space and signals interception, sharply contradict the picture painted by the stream of anecdotal stories, briefings, and other data released under Glasnost. They show, for example, that the Soviet Union has not decreased the size of its prison camp establishment or the extent of the systematic electronic surveillance of its own citizens and telephone system.

But such data showing that the control structure of the Communist Party had been tightened, not loosened, from 1983 to 1988 were either put in abeyance as anomalies to be explained later or dismissed as merely technical restrictions.

The sixth Glasnost has thus succeeded in creating a cooperative atmosphere in which American conventional intelligence-gathering can be overridden by Soviet self-reporting delivered through quasi-official media and academic sources. The CIA's reporting could be interpreted on the basis of a context that has been supplied by briefings from experts at Georgi Arbatov's research institute and other newly accredited sources. It has also succeeded in switching the sources for the Western media from its own diplomatic and intelligence services to Soviet-based sources, which are represented as independent media.

The very independence that the Soviets have called attention to in order to give Glasnost the requisite credibility has also served to project a more favorable image for the Soviet Union—one of an open society. Glasnost thus sets the stage for Soviet leaders to offer Europe and Japan an economically-appealing and militarily non-threatening alternative to their security arrangements with the United States.

By 1989, at virtually no cost to Soviet power, the sixth Glasnost had provided the Soviet leadership with not only the tens of billions of dollars in credits it required to further expand its industrial (and military) capacity but, if public opinion polls in West Germany are any measure, an image in which the Soviet Union, with its weak look, was perceived of as less of a threat to Western Europe than the United States.

Epilogue: Angleton's Questions

In November 1983, I received a message on my telephone answering machine from James Angleton suggesting that I call him when I was next in Washington, D.C. I went the following week to see him.

It had been nearly eight years since Angleton was forced out of the CIA, but his interest in intrigue had not waned. His eyes sharpened like those of a hawk when he fastened on the details of the event he was describing. It was the recent assassination of seventeen South Korean officials during a state visit to Burma.

On October 9, 1983, while the President of South Korea, Chun Doo Hwan, and members of his cabinet and staff were attending a wreath-laying ceremony at the Martyrs Mausoleum outside Rangoon, four powerful bombs were detonated by remote control. They had been concealed in the roof of the shrine in such a way that they had not been detected by either South Korean or Burmese security.

Although President Chun escaped injury because of a momentary delay in his schedule, the explosion killed thirteen of his top aides and four of his cabinet ministers. In a single well-planned coup, a major part of the South Korean government had been obliterated.

The assassins were caught the next day as they attempted to leave the country. When Burmese police challenged them, the three men tried to kill themselves with explosives. One died and two survived badly wounded. Under interrogation, the survivors admitted that they were captains in an elite unit of North Korean military intelligence that specialized in covert actions. They further explained that they had entered Burma September 22 on forged diplomatic passports issued to them in North Korea. They said that their orders included detailed instructions on how to carry out the assassination, that they received the plastic explosives through the embassy pouch, and, during the two weeks it took them to plant the explosives, they had stayed at the residence of the North Korean Embassy counselor. The police investigation confirmed their story. Their personal documents, which had been expertly fabricated, were vouched for by the embassy. They had access to secret communications between the South Korean and Burmese governments that could only be intercepted by a sophisticated intelligence service. The plastic explosives had been manufactured in Eastern Europe, and designed especially to fit into the roof of the shrine. The remote-control detonators used state-of-the-art electronics. And a reexamination of the surveillance of the North Korean Embassy showed that they were aided and sheltered by North Korean Embassy officials in Rangoon.

The evidence left little doubt that this assassination had been sponsored by North Korea and carried out by its intelligence service. "It is rare to find such a clear example of an act of state," Angleton delicately said. He suggested that a political assassination involved not only the murder of an incumbent officeholder but the intimidation of his successors. It did this latter task by demonstrating to them that they too were vulnerable to the reach of the assassin. He pointed out that in this case the North Koreans had shown the South Koreans that they could obtain their leader's travel schedule weeks in advance, penetrate his personal security, and plant lethal bombs in his path that could not be detected. It demonstrated "pure power." As in Mario Puzo's book *The Godfather,* when the Mafia chief put a horse's head in the bed of a recalcitrant film producer, the point of the exercise was not punishing the Koreans who were blown up by the bombs but inducing future cooperation from their successors.

It quickly became clear that Angleton's real concern was not what had happened in Burma or even what would happen in Korea but the nature of the statecraft practiced by Soviet bloc nations. For him, there was still the nagging problem of what he called "the relationship."

"It may be politically convenient to assume that Soviet bloc intelligence services act independently of the Soviet Union, especially when it concerns an assassination, but what we don't really know, or perhaps want to know, is what is the nature of the relationship between the KGB and other Communist intelligence services." He pointed out that the issue could not be peremptorily disposed of. Golitsyn and other defectors had described an extraordinary degree of coordination between these services, guaranteed by a systematic Soviet penetration of the top ranks of satellite services by the KGB's Second Chief Directorate. One role assigned to the satellite services, according to these defectors, was to afford the Soviet Union cover, distance, and deniability in potentially embarrassing operations. In the case of North Korea, Soviet intelligence had established, staffed, trained, and supplied its service. Moreover, using a kind of a "barium test" in which intelligence was especially concocted so that it could be traced as it was passed from one intelligence service to another, the CIA had been able to determine that the Soviets passed messages they intercepted through their Pacific signals satellite concerning the location of American ships in Korean waters to North Korean intelligence. This sort of cooperation had continued, according to Angleton's sources, up until the shrine bombing. "Remember, the North Koreans needed, and got, very exact communication intelligence."

Angleton then abruptly changed the subject to Edwin Wilson, the former CIA officer who had been arrested for diverting

American technology to Libya. It was less of a digression from the subject at hand than it initially seemed.

Wilson, lured by the prospect of making tens of millions of dollars, had gone to work for the Libyans in the early 1970s. Among other matters, he undertook to help organize covert activities for the Libyan intelligence service. To this end, he used his CIA contacts to buy the instruments of assassination, including a special CIA mixture of plastic explosives called "C-4", miniaturized timers used by the CIA, and unregistered weapons stolen from special forces arsenals, and then smuggle them into Libya. He even imported an entire sophisticated bomb factory, which had previously been used exclusively by the CIA to manufacture booby-trapped ashtrays that could innocently sit on a table for months until the target arrived and then be detonated from a remote location. He also recruited ex-CIA assassins, explosive experts, and couriers to work for him in Libya, leading them to believe that they were still working for the CIA when in fact they were working for the Libyan intelligence service. The first three targets of Wilson's assassins were Libyan exiles living in Egypt and France.

"It was a clever enough false flag recruitment," Angleton continued, with a glint of admiration for the opposition. Behind Wilson's bogus CIA flag was the Libyan intelligence service, which was paying Wilson; and behind this Libyan flag of convenience, whether or not Wilson entirely realized it, was an old KGB hand, Karl Hanesch, whose career Angleton had closely followed. Hanesch had been working for the KGB on deception projects for over a quarter of a century and had specialized in arranging politically embarrassing false flag assassinations in Germany. When Qaddafi came to power in 1966, Hanesch was transferred from the East German intelligence service to the Libyan intelligence service, where he became their key security adviser. It was, according to communication intercepts, a part of the Soviet bloc arrangement to provide intelligence aid to Libya.

Hanesch wasted little time in developing Wilson as a plausible "flag" for compromising others in American intelligence. One of his first recruits was Waldo H. Dubberstein, a top-level CIA analyst who transferred to the Defense Intelligence Agency, where he prepared the daily intelligence briefing for the Secretary of Defense. Dubberstein, who sold Wilson documents that were of interest to Soviet as well as Libyan intelligence—and who committed suicide in 1980 after being exposed—further demonstrated the coordination between the KGB and the Libyan service. Then, through Wilson's CIA connections, Hanesch was able to assemble all the necessary components for assassinating targets with CIA personnel and materials.

But why go to the expense and risk of smuggling them in from the United States? These tools of terrorism were readily available in East Germany, Czechoslovakia, or the Soviet Union at a fraction of the price, and they were just as effective. Angleton's answer was that there could be only one plausible purpose for assembling this extraordinary American-equipped apparatus: "To ghost murder trails leading to the doorstep of the CIA." The unique value of Wilson's C-4 explosives, timers, detonators, and ashtrays was their "signatures." They would indicate to investigators that the assassinations carried out with these devices were the work of the CIA. In addition, in the event that Wilson's ex-CIA operatives were apprehended, they would further implicate the CIA (especially since they believed that they were still employed by the CIA). It would be a no-win situation for the Agency if the investigation became public. Even if the CIA could successfully exonerate itself from the assassination charges by showing it had been framed, it would have to explain manufacturing exploding ashtrays and employing free-lance assassins, which could prove almost as embarrassing.

Angleton's fascination with this complex case, and his point, was that the Wilson Affair was not exclusively the work of the Libyans. It was the product of well-orchestrated and solid coordination between the KGB, the East German security services, and Qaddafi's intelligence services. The purpose of this coordination, in his view, was for the Soviets to use the Libyans, who were perceived as fanatic and wild, as a front in case the assassinations went wrong.

It was now clear what he was driving at. Had there been the same sort of coordination at the shrine in Burma? Had his counterintelligence staff been able to establish through barium tests, marked cards, double agents, or other means the extent of this relationship?

He did not answer directly. Instead, he said elliptically, "It's too complicated to get into," which was his way of saying he did not want to discuss a subject. Then, to my surprise, he added, with some weariness in his voice: "It is a shame you never got those questions answered." It took a few minutes before I realized that he was referring to the questions he had dictated in 1976 for me to ask Nosenko.

When I returned to New York the next day, I searched for and found his thirteen questions. They were scrawled on 3 by 5 cards in my Nosenko file. I recalled that Angleton had reeled them off after many brandies and, at the time, they seemed to make little sense. Now, as I rearranged them, I could see the thread running through them.

ANGLETON'S QUESTIONS FOR NOSENKO

1. What happened to Rumyanstev when he tried to defect to the U.S. in 1959? Why did you omit this in your debriefing in 1964?

2. Is there rivalry between the KGB's First and Second Chief Directorates?

3. To what extent did the Second Chief Directorate know the operations of the Thirteenth Department of the First Chief Directorate?

4. What would Department Thirteen have known regarding Oswald's defection? Would General Rodin have known?

5. What happens when the Second Chief Directorate recruits an agent who returned to the West? Is he jointly handled?

6. Is an agent recruited by the Second Chief Directorate who is of value prepared to be handled by a stranger? Would this be true of an ideological agent as well as a mercenary agent?

7. To what extent do the First and Second Directorates coordinate the activities of foreign services?

8. Why was a KGB officer named Shitov sent to Cuba as the first Soviet Ambassador, under the pseudonym Alexiev?

9. What was his role, if any, in coordinating Soviet and Cuban intelligence operations?

10. Oswald was issued an entrance visa to Cuba from Havana after he returned to the United States. Would this require the prior approval of the Second Chief Directorate?

11. If so, would it be arranged in Moscow or Havana? If the latter, would a Second Chief Directorate officer be called on to participate in the decision?

12. Agee went to Cuba under aliases four times while writing his book. Would he have seen Soviet intelligence in Moscow? Would these meetings be coordinated with the KGB? Why was Colonel Semenov, who knew Agee in Uruguay, there during Agee's trips?

13. What was Korovin doing in London in 1961?

The first question was no more than a trap question. Rumyanstev had been a KGB officer in the Second Chief Directorate in 1959 who attempted to defect to the CIA at the American Exhibition in Moscow but was caught because he approached a KGB officer at the exhibition who spoke fluent English and was masquerading as an American official. He was executed in 1960 (although the CIA only learned about the aborted defection from another defector in 1963). Since Nosenko claimed to have worked on the Oswald case in the same small unit of the KGB's Second Chief Directorate as Rumyanstev in 1959, he would have been well aware of what had happened. Yet he had not mentioned the incident to the CIA when he was debriefed in either 1962 or 1964. Angleton wanted to know how Nosenko explained this gap.

The purpose of the next question had been explained to me by Golitsyn. It would have been standard procedure in the KGB for the First Chief Directorate's Department Thirteen to consult with Nosenko's Second Chief Directorate Department if Oswald had approached one of its officers. Nosenko claimed, after all, that his department had originally handled the Oswald case in Moscow, and, two months before the assassination of President Kennedy, the CIA had intercepted a telephone call in Mexico City in which Oswald was making contact with Sergei Kostikov, an officer in Department Thirteen. Angleton's questions were thus designed to force Nosenko to acknowledge that he and his department would have to have been aware of any relationship between Oswald that had developed, since Oswald would have been jointly handled.

The next three questions appeared aimed at focusing Nosenko on Department Thirteen, and specifically on assassinations. As Stephen de Mowbray had explained to me in London, a defector from Department Thirteen had told British intelligence that its job was conducting "wet affairs," which was a euphemism for assassinations and sabotage. Angleton had been interested in the KGB's capacity for organizing assassinations since the explosion experts in the CIA's Scientific and Technical Division traced the explosive used to destroy the airplane that flew UN Secretary General Dag Hammarskjold from Africa to East Germany in 1961.

The sixth question was Angleton's key to the relationship he sought. Before and after Oswald had contacted the Soviet Embassy, he had contacted Cuban Embassy officials in Mexico, who would have been considered "strangers." Golitsyn had insisted that if Oswald had been recruited by the Second Chief Directorate, especially as an ideological agent, it would not turn him over to be handled by Cuban "strangers"—unless it had a role in the activity.

Angleton evidently believed Oswald's shuttling between the Cubans and Soviets in Mexico City required cooperation, especially since Oswald was eventually telegraphed a visa by the Cuban Foreign Ministry in Havana. His next five questions aimed at further exploring the coordination that would be necessary between the KGB and the Cuban intelligence service for this to happen.

His twelfth question apparently was meant to prod Nosenko into talking about Soviet coordination of Communist intelligence services. Angleton believed that Philip Agee was a case in point, as he told me on another occasion. According to Angleton's view, Agee had been initially recruited by the KGB while he was serving with the CIA in Montevideo, Uruguay. His recruiter was Colonel Semenov, the Soviet military attaché in Uruguay. After Agee was forced out of the CIA, the KGB used him to embarrass the CIA by publishing exposés. But so as to afford itself "a modicum of distance," as Angleton put it, the KGB worked through the DGI, the Cuban intelligence service. Even so, whenever Agee made his visits to the DGI in Havana, Semenov was sent to Havana to oversee the joint operation.

Angleton's final question about the 1961 activities of "Korovin" addressed the same pattern. "Korovin" was the pseudonym General Rodin used on his diplomatic passport during his tour of duty in Britain in the early 1960s. Rodin, as head of the London station of the Thirteenth Department of the First Chief Directorate, was directly responsible for the operations of Kostikov in Mexico, and therefore would have had to authorize any contacts Kostikov had with Oswald. And Nosenko had claimed to have examined the relevant file after Oswald had contacted Kostikov in 1963. Rodin's London station was apparently of great interest to Angleton. According to a 1971 defector, Rodin insulated the Soviet Union from blame in Britain and Germany by employing the Bulgarian intelligence service or other cooperative intelligence services to carry out the actual murders. Angleton no doubt wanted through this line of questioning to lead Nosenko to describe how Department Thirteen arranged these joint operations.

After reviewing these curious questions for nearly a week, and the bits and pieces that seemed to fill in the gaps, I telephoned Angleton. As he had done many times in the past, he refused to talk about Oswald. When I began to tell him my interpretation of the questions, he abruptly cut me off, saying they were "water over the dam" and that I should "forget them"—as if I could. I never understood whether his questions were really intended for Nosenko or me, or whether they were merely an inebriated outburst.

Almost a year passed before I spoke to Angleton again. When we lunched together at the Hay-Adams Hotel, I initially avoided bringing up the subject of the Soviet bloc "relationship." But, to my surprise, he began discussing it as if there had been no hiatus in our conversation. This time he spoke about it in a scholarly, almost detached way, as if he were discussing the pollination of orchids. "Sun-tzu explained this strategy as succinctly two thousand years ago as anyone can today: Hide order behind a cloak of disorder." He pointed out that just as monolithic corporations often set up subsidiaries with different names in different countries to accomplish their purposes, so intelligence services, which closely coordinate their work, often find it advantageous to appear to the outside world to be divided into independent, and even competing, entities. He reasoned that at times the U.S. government finds the fiction that the Eastern bloc services are independent of the KGB "convenient" because it allows it to blame the Cubans, Libyans, Afghans, Bulgarians, or East Germans instead of directly confronting the Soviet Union.

But how do we know they are really united, I asked.

"The business of intelligence services is establishing precisely what the relationship of their opposition is," he answered. He then pointed out that since 1948 the CIA, and its allied services in Britain, France, and West Germany, had been following Soviet, Bulgarian, East German, Libyan, Cuban, Hungarian, Rumanian, and Polish intelligence officers posted to embassies in NATO countries, as well as reading their mail, intercepting their coded traffic, and tracing their flow of money and equipment. "We found sufficient evidence of coordination over extended periods to satisfy even the skeptics."

It was when Angleton attempted to apply this concept to governments rather than intelligence services that he got into trouble. He advanced the theory that the Soviet Union and China had faked the disunity between them to dupe the West, which proved to be wrong. Nevertheless, he clung to it, and stubbornly warned that it would be the Soviets who would trump the American China card by announcing a Sino-Soviet rapprochement. Those with knives out for him used this mistaken analysis to discredit and ridicule him.

The final irony, which became clear only after his death, was that Angleton was far less wrong in his prediction that the split would be transitory than his premise that it had been fabricated. In 1988, as cadres of Soviet technicians returned to China, and Sino-Soviet military cooperation resumed, Gorbachev announced his plans for a summit meeting in 1989 to end the split, leaving in the lurch much of America's strategy that had been predicated on an irreconcilable split between China and the Soviet Union.

Source Notes

PART ONE

CHAPTERS 1–7

There are no secret sources for this book. I do not believe it is either necessary or fair to conceal from the reader where the information for an assertion comes from. The identity of the source is part of the context. Without it, the reader has only part of the story.

The way in which sources are treated distinguishes different forms of knowledge. Historical research requires every source be made explicit so that assertions can be assessed by outside observers. Science makes similar demands. A scientist conducting an experiment must disclose all the relevant data about its circumstances so another scientist in another laboratory can replicate and thereby test the experiment. Judicial knowledge is even more strict in this respect. A lawyer must expose the names of all his sources, and allow them to be cross-examined; otherwise their testimony will not be accepted. It is even a requirement of espionage assessment. Intelligence officers must subject their spies to counterintelligence scrutiny, or their reports are not accepted.

Only two forms of knowledge cross this principle: gossip and journalism. The gossip purposely obscures his sources, saying in effect, "Don't ask who I heard it from," to make the story more titillating. The journalist obscures his sources out of self-interest, claiming that unless he hides their identities, they will not provide him with further information. This claim assumes the sources are acting out of altruistic motives. If, however, they are providing the information out of self-interest—and much information comes from publicists and other paid agents—then their motive is part of the story.

I've never understood the journalistic argument for concealing sources except that it is self-serving. While a source might talk more freely if he need take no responsibility for what he says, he also has far less incentive to be completely truthful. The only check on the source's license to commit hyperbole, if not slander, under these rules is the journalist himself. But the very premise of concealing sources is that the journalist needs the cooperation of the source in the future. This makes the journalist himself an interested party.

Much of the writing about the CIA, FBI, and other intelligence services which has depended on cooperation from these agencies has been particularly blurred by source concealment. The common practice of authors, magazines, and publishers of making it appear that defectors have approached them by serendipity, when in fact they have come at the behest of the CIA or FBI, with which they have binding contracts restricting what they can say to a prepared brief, has made it more difficult to understand the job that intelligence services actually do. But rather than cultivating sources for future writing through the gift of anonymity, there is also the need to clarify the material provided by past sources especially as the author's client is his readers, not his sources.

The Angleton quotes come from interviews and conversations I had with him from 1977 to 1987. Whatever inhibitions I had about publishing this material while he was alive were lifted when he died in April 1987.

I have also spoken to many of the men who worked under him on his counterintelligence staff. Ray Rocca provided me with the staff's perspective on the Trust and other prewar Soviet deceptions. Scotty Miler, whom I saw in New Mexico six times over a five-year period, provided me with case histories of Golitsyn and Nosenko. I also spoke to Donovan Pratt, William Johnson, and William Hood about Angleton himself. Only one former staff member I spoke to provided a negative picture of Angleton, Claire Edward Petty. He had made the case in 1975 that Angleton himself would have been a prime candidate for recruitment by the KGB.

Aside from those on Angleton's staff, I learned a considerable amount on the cases, especially Nosenko and Golitsyn, from the foreign and American liaisons with whom Angleton dealt. The former category, which includes Stephen de Mowbray (MI6), Philippe de Vosjoli (SDECE), and Amos Manor (Mossad), were particularly helpful. The FBI liaison, Sam Papich, although he had been badly mistreated by Hoover, remained circumspect. Thomas Fox of the Defense Intelligence Agency, who had recently retired, was more open with me.

William Sullivan, who had his own ax to grind, believing that Hoover had made him into a scapegoat, told me about Fedora and Top Hat, which opened many other doors.

My chief source on Nosenko was Pete Bagley. We met together in Belgium, France, England, and the United States. At one point, we considered writing a book together on moles which never materialized. Jack Maury, a former chief of the Soviet Bloc Division, described the anti-Bagley "sick think" view. The Soviet Bloc division was called the Soviet Russia Division prior to 1965. As it involved the same personnel and tasks, I have referred to it throughout the text as the Soviet Division. I also discussed the Nosenko conflict within the CIA with Richard Helms, who described his role in the case, as did Admiral Rufus Taylor, whom Helms ordered to clear it up.

Other CIA executives with whom I spoke about the Nosenko

case were Vincent Marchetti, a former Deputy Director, Gordon Stewart, the Inspector General who investigated it, David Slawson, who investigated Nosenko for the Warren Commission, and Stanley Pottinger, the Justice Department attorney who investigated the legality of Nosenko's confinement.

There were also supporters of Nosenko's, including Donald K. Jameson, whom I interviewed five times; John Barron, the Washington editor of the *Reader's Digest*, who had become a friend of Nosenko's and even attended his wedding; William Gunn, who did public relations work for the FBI; Richard Heuer, CIA analyst, who developed the view that the KGB had rules that would preclude it from sending a Nosenko-type defector; and John Hart, who unfortunately spoke to me only briefly over the telephone.

I did further research into Nosenko as a consultant on a BBC television docudrama in 1985–86 called "Nosenko, KGB Agent." When Richard Helms expressed surprise that one of the CIA's most esoteric cases could be turned into popular fare, William Hood joked, "The only thing left is a Nosenko ballet."

The most valuable public source on Nosenko is the published Appendix to the Hearings of the Select Committee on Assassination, U.S. House of Representatives, 95th Congress, 2nd Session, March 1979. The quotes about confining Nosenko come from the February 17, 1964, memorandum, "Nosenko: Current Status and Immediate Plans," Vol. IV, p. 87. Nosenko's contract with the CIA is revealed in pp. 67–70. Helms's testimony is in the same volume, see pp. 1–250. The testimony of Bagley (under the title "Deputy Chief") is in Vol. XII, pp. 573–644. Volume XII also has testimony from Nosenko, John Hart, and Bruce Solie, which provides important perspectives on the case.

The transcripts of my interviews with Nosenko are available at Boston University Library, as are Angleton's questions and Golitsyn's answers to my queries.

I discussed the issue of the CIA using defectors as surreptitious authors in "The Spy Who Came in to Be Sold," *New Republic,*

July 15, 1985, p. 35. The defector who told me a book had been prepared for him by the CIA which he rejected was John Sejna.

The Trust has been the subject of a number of books and studies. See Geoffrey Bailey, *The Conspirators* (New York: Harper & Row, 1960); V. I. Brunovsky, *The Methods of the OGPU* (London: Harper, 1931); and Anatoly Golitsyn, *New Lies for Old* (New York: Dodd Mead, 1983).

The version published under Kim Philby's name after he defected to Moscow, which has to be assumed to be a product of the KGB, is *My Silent War* (New York: Ballantine Books, 1983). This version has outcroppings in other books that relied on either Philby's book or Philby himself as a source. See, for example, Bruce Page, David Leitch, and Philip Knightley, *The Philby Conspiracy* (Garden City, N.Y.: Doubleday, 1968).

The Polish side of the WINS deception was described to me by Michael Goleniewski, the former Deputy Director of Polish Military Intelligence, who defected to the United States in 1961. My interviews with him are in the Boston University Archives.

The conflict within the CIA, which did not emerge publicly until the mid-1970s, can be found in my "The War Within the CIA," *Commentary* (August 1978); William Colby's *Honorable Men: My Life in the CIA* (New York: Simon & Schuster, 1978); Seymour Hersh's "Angleton," *The New York Times Magazine*, June 25, 1978; and David Martin's *Wilderness of Mirrors* (New York: Harper & Row, 1982).

For the "Chinese strategist Sun-tzu," see Sun-tzu, *The Art of War* (London: Hodder & Stoughton, 1981), p. 17. The book, which is the bible of deception, was written by Sun-tzu, a general for the King of Wu in China in about 500 B.C., along with commentaries handed from one generation to another of Chinese leaders. The Giles translation was made in 1905. For "When able to attack," see *ibid.*, pp. 15–18. For "categories of spies," see pp. 95ff. The intelligence system of Sun-tzu also included two other categories of spies: the "return" spy, who served as courier and paymaster for inward spies; and the "local spy," who was a clandestine observer sent behind enemy lines to glean specific facts. In *The Chinese Machiavelli: 3,000 Years of Chinese Statecraft* (New York: Farrar, Straus, 1976), Dennis and Ching Ping Bloodworth demonstrate that Sun-tzu provided much of the continuity in Chinese military doctrine.

PART TWO

8. THE DECEPTION CONFERENCES

1. The first conference I went to was called officially "Intelligence: Deception and Surprise." It was held April 24–26, 1979, in Cambridge, Massachusetts, under the auspices of the International Security Studies Program of Tufts University. At that conference I met Roy C. Godson, an energetic professor from Georgetown, who invited me to participate in his Consortium for the Study of Intelligence. The first meeting took place on November 1, 1979, at the International Club in Washington, D.C. I presented a brief paper there on deception that was later published in a book edited by Godson, *Intelligence Requirements for the 1980s: Analysis and Estimates* (New Brunswick, N.J.: Transaction Books, 1980). I continued to attend these meetings over the course of the next two years.

2. R. V. Jones had written of his work as a deception planner in *Most Secret War* (London: Coronet Books, 1979), as well as in "The Theory of Practical Joking," *Bulletin of the Institute of Physics* (June 1957), pp. 193–201. Barton Whaley wrote, among other things, *Stratagem: Deception and Surprise in War* (Cambridge, Mass.: Center for International Studies, MIT, 1969). In a 600-page appendix, he lists both the tactical and strategic deceptions and shows that in the vast preponderance of cases, they worked. Only 150 copies of this work were made available. Michael I. Handel had written "Perception, Deception and Surprise," *Jerusalem Papers on Peace Problems,* no. 19, The Hebrew University (Jerusalem: Jerusalem Post Press, 1976).

3. For narcotics stings, see my book *Agency of Fear* (New York: Putnam, 1976). For the Navy scandal, see *The New York Times,* October 30, 1984, p. A21. The IRS undercover operations are described

in "Stinging Success," *Barron's,* October 8, 1984, p. 16. The undercover operations of no less than three hundred Fish and Wildlife Service employees in Operation Falcon were reported in *The New York Times,* August 30, 1984, p. A15. A similar deception was used in 1984 to trap car owners in New York City who falsely reported their cars stolen after they had sold them, to collect the insurance money. Here the FBI set up a fake business called G&N Storage and Towing, which offered to discreetly buy cars for scrap. After the owners reported them stolen, they were confronted with the actual car and charged with fraud. *The New York Times,* "Car Insurance Fraud 'Sting' Nets 122 in City," December 18, 1984, p. 1.

4. For the czarist agent provocateur system, see A. T. Vasilyev, *The Okhrana: The Russian Secret Police* (Westport, Conn.: Hyperion Press, 1930). The Grand Duke was assassinated on the orders of the Okhrana-controlled agent Yevno Azev. In 1893, Azev began his career as an agent provocateur, and by 1901 had become the head of the "Combat Section," which undertook assassination and sabotage, for the Social Revolutionaries—perhaps the most radical of all the anti-czarist groups. Through his activities, the Okhrana not only had foreknowledge of the group's terrorism but it was able to use it to discredit the entire dissident movement. For a description of Azev's career, see Boris I. Nikolaevskii, *Azeff: The Russian Judas* (London: Hurst & Blackett, 1934).

5. For the FBI's undercover operations, see Select Committee to Study Government Operations with Respect to Intelligence Activities, *Final Report,* U.S. Senate, 94th Congress, 1st Session, 1976, Book 2. Aside from the FBI, the hearings it is based on provide a detailed picture of the use of deception by the military and CIA to control domestic dissidence. James Q. Wilson, Henry Lee Shattuck Professor of Government at Harvard, received unique access to study the central files of both the FBI and the Drug Enforcement Agencies in the late 1970s, and his book *The Investigators* (New York: Basic Books, 1978) illuminates the logic and strategy of employing agents provocateurs. William Sullivan, who was Assistant Director of the FBI, explained to me Hoover's rationale for maintaining the Communist Party in interviews I had with him in 1977.

6. For the British deception plan, see Anthony Cave Brown, *Body-*

guard of Lies (New York: Harper & Row, 1976). Also, the remedial review of it by Michael Howard, *Times Literary Supplement,* May 28, 1976.

7. See Frederick Winterbotham, *The Ultra Secret* (London: Weidenfeld & Nicolson, 1974), and Ronald Lewin, *Ultra Goes to War* (London: Hutchinson, 1978).

8. On the German deception of Stalin, see Barton Whaley, *Codeword Barbarossa* (Cambridge, Mass.: MIT Press, 1968).

9. On Stalin's deception of the Germans, see Frederick S. Feer, "Incorporating Analysis of Foreign Governments' Deception into U.S. Systems," in Godson, ed., *Intelligence Requirements for the 1980s: Analysis and Estimates.* Feer, who attended some of the conferences, was a former CIA officer.

10. For the Japanese deception, see Masatake Okumiya and Jiro Horikoshi, *Zero: The Story of the Japanese Naval Air Force, 1937–1945* (London: Cassell, 1957), p. 37. Also, Gordon W. Prange, *At Dawn We Slept* (New York: McGraw-Hill, 1983). Roberta Wohlstetter provides the classic study about the transmission of intelligence during the attack itself in her *Pearl Harbor: Warning and Decision* (Stanford, Calif.: Stanford University Press, 1962).

11. On the British "double cross system," see John Masterman, *The Double-Cross System* (New Haven: Yale University Press, 1972). The subject was updated and expanded in 1981 by Nigel West in *MI5* (London: Bodley Head, 1981).

12. For the German double cross, see the account of H. J. Giskes, who organized it, in *London Calling North Pole* (New York: Bantam Books, 1982), pp. 2–89. See also Lauren Paine, *The Abwehr* (London: Hale, 1984), p. 134ff. For other German double-cross systems in Europe, see West, *op. cit.,* pp. 143–153, and Paine, *op. cit.,* pp. 145–147.

13. For the Soviet double cross, see Chapman Pincher, *Their Trade Is Treachery* (New York: Bantam Books, 1982), p. 125. On the Soviet use of military disinformation, see Frederick S. Feer, *The Impact of Soviet Misinformation on Military Operations: 1920–1979* (Marina del Rey, Calif.: Analytical Assessment Corp., 1979), pp. 12–13.

9. THE GOLDHAMER INVENTORY

1. Herbert Goldhamer's unfinished work is contained in Herbert Goldhamer, *Reality and Belief in Military Affairs: A First Draft* (Santa Monica, Calif.: RAND, 1977), and Joan Goldhamer, *Reality and Belief in Military Affairs: An Inventory of Additional Material in the file of Herbert Goldhamer* (Santa Monica, Calif.: RAND, 1981).

2. For "little offensive capability," see William Manchester, *The Arms of Krupp* (New York: Bantam Books, 1970).

3. See Michael Mihalka, *German Strategic Deception in the 1930s* (Santa Monica, Calif.: RAND, 1980).

4. For "legacy of fear," see George H. Quester, *Deterrence Before Hiroshima* (New York: Wiley, 1966), p. 90. In France, see Ladŏslas Mysyrowicz, *Autopsie d'une défaite* (Lausanne: Editions l'Age d'Homme, 1973), pp. 184–185.

5. See William R. Harris, "Counterintelligence Jurisdiction and the Double Cross System by National Technical Means," mimeo (Washington, D.C., Consortium on Intelligence, April 24, 1980), p. 2.

6. See Geoffrey Bailey, *The Conspirators* (New York: Harper & Row, 1960), pp. 194–198.

7. For "Winterbotham himself had feigned sympathy for Hitler," and the curious relationship between Winterbotham, De Ropp, and German intelligence, see Ladislav Farrago, *The Game of the Foxes* (New York: David McKay, 1971), pp. 91ff.

8. The quote "Naturally we were aware . . . of all the major powers" is from Heinz Riechoff, cited in Mihalka, *op. cit.*, p. 61.

9. For General Joseph Vuillemen's exposure to a "vastly inflated figure of German air strength," see Paul Stehlin, *Témoignage pour l'histoire* (Paris: Editions Robert Laffont, 1964), pp. 82–92.

10. "Convinced that war would mean the ruin of Paris": see Donald Cameron Watt, *Too Serious a Business* (Berkeley: University of California Press, 1975), pp. 86–93. Also Herbert Malloy Mason, Jr., *The Rise of the Luftwaffe* (New York: Dial Press, 1973), pp. 244–245.

11. On Goering's use of Lindbergh, see Leonard Mosley, *Reichs Marshall: A Biography of Hermann Goering* (Garden City, N.Y.: Doubleday, 1974). See also the review of Mosley's book by J. D. Miller, *Times Literary Supplement*, November 12, 1976, p. 1432.

12. On the "flying pencil" deception, see Mason, *op. cit.*, p. 240.

13. On the "Amerika-Bomber" deception, see *ibid.*, p. 372n.

14. The quote "In addition to the systematic bluff organized at [the] top level . . . also willing self-deception" is from Heinz Riechoff, cited in Mihalka, *op. cit.*, p. 61.

15. Mason, *op. cit.*, pp. 344–346. Mason points out that after the German bombing of Rotterdam it was reported 30,000 people had been killed. In fact, according to a body count, there were only 814 fatalities.

16. For British press coverage, see John Wood's Ph.D. dissertation, "The 'Luftwaffe' as a Factor in British Policy, 1935–1939," (Tulane University, New Orleans, 1965). See also Mihalka, *op. cit.*, p. 71.

17. The quote by Hitler on "bombs or ammunition" is cited by David Irving, *The War Path* (London: Papermac, 1983), p. 74.

18. A. J. P. Taylor, *The Origins of the Second World War* (London: Penguin Books, 1964), p. 18.

19. For Hitler's quote about "our tail between our legs," see Irving, *op. cit.*, p. 46.

20. Mason, *op. cit.*, p. 210ff.

21. On French liaison officers and British attachés in Paris, see George H. Questor, *Nuclear Diplomacy* (New York: Dunellen, 1970), pp. 97–98.

22. On the Munich negotiations, see Telford Taylor, *Munich: The Price of Peace* (London: Hodder & Stoughton, 1979).

23. On Hitler's gain at Berlin, see Mason, *op. cit.*, p. 244.

24. "Hitler himself made no secret": His speech is quoted by Z. A. B. Zeman, *Nazi Propaganda* (New York: Oxford University Press, 1973).

25. "What only the Luftwaffe High Command knew": Mason, *op. cit.*, p. 244.

26. The account of the purge, and the quote "a blow could be struck at the leadership of the Red Army," comes from Walter Schellenberg, *The Labyrinth* (New York: Harper & Row, 1956), p. 25.

27. On Stalin's purge, see Bailey, *op. cit.*, pp. 133ff.

28. For "staging a fake attack on a German outpost," see Schellenberg, *op. cit.*, pp. 48–54.

29. On the Ellis affair, see Chapman Pincher, *Too Secret Too Long* (New York: St. Martin's Press, 1984), pp. 440–456.

30. For the Venlo Incident, see Nigel West, *MI6* (London: Weidenfeld & Nicolson, 1983), pp. 70–75. Also, for a first-hand account, Sigismund Payne Best, *The Venlo Incident* (London: 1950). The latter was based on his 1945 debriefing.

31. For "the British still clung to the hope," see West, *MI6*, pp. 75–76.

32. "Hitler launched surprise attacks": Klaus Knorr and Patrick Morgan, *Strategic Military Surprise* (New Brunswick, N.J.: Transaction Books, 1983), pp. 17–23.

10. THE NEW MAGINOT LINE

1. Bobby Ray Inman view of Soviet deception and "Potemkin villages," Bob Woodward, *Veil: The Secret Wars of the CIA* (New York: Simon & Schuster, 1987), pp. 474–475. For the NSA and the CIA assumed Soviet data "came in relatively pure," *ibid.*, p. 202.

2. Stansfield Turner, *Secrecy and Democracy* (Boston: Houghton Mifflin, 1985), p. 92.

3. The panel discussion on the allocation of funds at the Air Force Academy at Boulder, Colorado, on June 6, 1984, Panel B-4.

4. The Krasnoyarsk delay, p. 65. For the failure to photograph Soviet fourth-generation missiles, see Angelo Codevilla, "Ignorance vs. Intelligence," *Commentary* (May 1987), p. 77.

5. William Kampiles: See Henry Hurt, "CIA in Crisis: The Kampiles Case," *Reader's Digest* (June 1979), pp. 65–72.

6. See William R. Harris, "Soviet Maskirovka and Arms Control Verification," mimeo (September 16, 1986), pp. 21–25.

7. The Satellite Warning System used "to prepare and carry out . . . special measures for disinformation of the enemy": Aleksei Myagkov, *Inside the KGB* (New Rochelle, N.Y.: Arlington House, 1976), p. 121. For fake military equipment, see William J. Broad, "US Designs Spy Satellites to Be More Secret Than Ever," *The New York Times*, November 3, 1987, p. 1.

8. For the special staff, GUSM: Victor Suvorov, "GUSM: The Soviet Service of Strategic Deception," *International Defense Review*, vol. 18, no. 8 (August 1985), pp. 1235ff.

9. World War II photographic capacity: My interviews with Amrom Katz, 1979.

10. On signals intelligence satellites, see Jeffrey Richelson, *American Espionage and the Soviet Target* (New York: Morrow, 1987), pp. 222ff.

11. For the Christopher Boyce betrayal, see Robert Lindsey, *The Falcon and the Snowman* (New York: Simon & Schuster, 1979).

12. Angelo M. Codevilla, "Space, Intelligence and Deception," mimeo (September 26, 1985), p. 8.

13. The quote is from Malcolm Wallop and Angelo Codevilla, *The Arms Control Delusion* (San Francisco: ICS Press, 1987), p. 65.

11. THE TELEMETRY DOUBLE CROSS

1. For Amrom Katz's role, see Merton E. Davis and William R. Harris, "RAND's Role in the Evolution of Balloon and Satellite Observation Systems and Related U.S. Space Technology," paper (Santa Monica, Calif.: RAND, 1988).

2. For a fuller discussion of the logic of "National Technical Means," see Amrom H. Katz, *Verification and SALT* (Washington, D.C.: Heritage Foundation, 1979).

3. See William R. Harris, *Intelligence and National Security: A Bibliography with Selected Annotations* (Cambridge, Mass.: Center for International Affairs, 1968). His interests can be gleaned from such other of his writings as "Counter-deception Planning," paper (Cambridge, Mass.: Harvard University, 1972); "Soviet Maskirovka and Arms Control Verification," mimeo (Monterey, Calif.: U.S. Navy Postgraduate School, September 1985); "Breaches of Arms Control Obligations," mimeo (Stanford, Calif.: Stanford University, September 22, 1983); "A SALT Safeguard Program: Coping with Soviet Deception Under Strategic Arms Agreements," paper (Santa Monica, Calif.: RAND, 1979); and "Counterintelligence Jurisdiction and the Double Cross System by National Technical Means," in Roy C. Godson, ed., *Intelligence Requirements for the 1980s: Counterintelligence* (New Brunswick, N.J.: Transaction Press, 1980), pp. 53–91.

4. Harris provided me with a non-classified computer printout of Soviet scientific articles detailing the method the CIA assumed the Soviets were using. They described a system in which the three

accelerometers on each axis would "vote," with the least accurate dropping out and the measurement of the other two averaged together.

5. For greater detail on NSA defectors Mitchell and Martin, see James Bamford, *The Puzzle Palace* (Boston: Houghton Mifflin, 1983).

6. See West, *MI6*, pp. 28ff.

7. For a public account of crater deception, see "Soviet False Craters," *The Washington Times*, August 7, 1985, p. 1.

8. My book was *Agency of Fear* (New York: Putnam, 1977). Fox served in the Office of National Narcotics Intelligence in 1973.

9. Whalen was paroled in 1972. See my "Spy War," *The New York Times Magazine*, September 28, 1980, p. 102.

10. Fox also helped me to obtain under the Freedom of Information Act the investigative report by General Joseph P. Carroll that revealed the pilfering ring.

12. THE WAR OF THE MOLES

1. The Soviet bloc case officer was Pete Bagley. He told me about his novel in 1977. Angleton commented on it five years later.

2. False flag compromises: Frederick Forsyth's novel *The Odessa File* (New York: Bantam, 1974) is based on an actual case in which East German intelligence officers assumed the identities of die-hard Hitlerites, and even created a secret Nazi organization, to recruit West German intelligence officers who secretly harbored pro-Nazi sympathies.

3. I found the study "Motivations to Treason" in the Teheran Archive, Vol. 51, p. 30.

4. Bagley did the CIA's damage assessment report on Felfe. I later discussed the case with Angleton; the analysis of it in the text is Angleton's.

6. The conclusion that there had been over one hundred defectors comes from the study done by Richards J. Heuer, a former CIA case officer, and the discussion of it afterwards at the Conference at the U.S. Navy Postgraduate School in September 1984.

7. The best chronology on the Penkovsky case is by Joseph D. Douglass, Jr., "Colonel Oleg Penkovsky, Intelligence Coup—But Whose?", mimeo, privately circulated (November 1981).

8. For Moellering quote and "blow back," see Woodward, *op. cit.*, p. 473.

9. For Richard Craig Smith, see *The New York Times*, April 5, 1984, and April 10, 1984.

13. THE DENIAL OF DECEPTION

1. Richards J. Heuer, Jr.: "understand the KGB better than any agency of the U.S. government" and "If there is one thing more important to the Soviets . . . it is protecting their own security". These quotes are from discussions at the conference which I attended and Heuer's paper, "Soviet Organization and Doctrine for Strategic Deception," mimeo (1985), pp. 26–30.

2. The source for the CIA's conclusion that it had never been deceived by a Soviet double agent on any issue of strategic importance is David Sullivan, who drafted Senator Helms's questions and supplied me with their answers. Sullivan, a former CIA analyst and critic who was fired for making CIA data available to Senator Henry Jackson, attended this conference.

3. For Admiral Turner's assessment about the "paranoia of the CIA's counterintelligence staff," see his revealing autobiography *Secrecy and Democracy* (Boston: Houghton Mifflin, 1985), p. 72.

4. Vitaliy Yurchenko biography: CIA document (available in my archives, Boston University). The investigation I did of the Yurchenko case in 1985–86 was for *Life* and *The Observer* (London).

5. The original report on A. G. Tolkachev was by William Kucewicz, "KGB Defector Confirms U.S. Intelligence Fiasco," *Wall Street Journal*, October 17, 1985.

6. Defections of Igor Gheja, Sergei Bokhan: *Christian Science Monitor*, October 28, 1985, and *The New York Times*, October 1, 1985, and November 1, 1985. Oleg Antonovich Gordievsky: *Time*, September 23, 1985, p. 20, and *The Washington Post*, September 14, 1985. A number of false stories were put out by British intelligence MI5, including one in which he was whisked out of Moscow.

7. Secret 1973 CIA memorandum, entitled "Turning Around RED-TOP Walk-ins": Teheran Archive, Vol. 53, pp. 28–29.

8. Wallop and McMahon: My interviews with Senator Wallop on December 5, 1985.

9. "The information [Yurchenko] provided was not anything new or sensational" is by President Reagan: "President Sees a Soviet 'Ploy,' " *The New York Times*, November 7, 1985, p. 1.

10. Yurchenko's re-defection: "Washington Ponders Nosenko," *The New York Times*, November 9, 1985. For prohibition on contact, see my interview with Scotty Miler, 1985. Also, "How Yurchenko Bade Adieu to CIA," *The New York Times*, November 7, 1985.

11. *The New York Times*, November 6, 1985, p. A12.

12. "This whole thing was very good theater": "US Aides Split," *The New York Times*, November 8, 1985, p. A10.

13. For Soviet map falsification, see "Soviet Officials Admit Maps Were Faked," *The New York Times*, September 3, 1988, p. 1.

14. THE CONFIDENCE GAME

1. "Tendency of Naval officers and others who have taken part in negotiations, to become advocates of the integrity of the persons of whom they secured the agreement." Amrom Katz, *Verification and SALT* (Washington, D.C.: Heritage Foundation, 1979), pp. 12–14.

2. "We have . . . probably 30 to 40 requests per year from Iranians and Iranian exiles": President's Special Review Board, *The Tower Commission Report* (New York: Times Books/Bantam Books, 1987), p. 106.

3. Ghorbanifar and Theodore Shackley: *ibid.*, p. 106.

4. "We know the CIA . . . they want to tear us like Kleenex—use us for their purpose and then throw us out the window.": *ibid.*, p. 107.

5. "High individuals inside the Iranian government.": *ibid.*, pp. 210–213.

6. Ghorbanifar's bona fides: *ibid.*, pp. 205–207.

7. Ghorbanifar pressed for increased deliveries of U.S. Arms: *ibid.*, pp. 224–244.

8. "Whether we trust Ghorbanifar or not, he is irrefutably the deepest penetration we have achieved into the current Iranian Government.": *ibid.*, pp. 193–4.

9. CIA lie detector results: *ibid.*, p. 206–212.

10. "Moderate elements in Iran can come to power if these factions demonstrate their credibility in aiding Iran against Iraq and in deterring Soviet intervention.": *ibid.*, p. 215.

11. Charles Allen memo: *ibid.*, pp. 212–213.

12. "We still have those contacts . . . and we're going to continue on this path.": *ibid.*, pp. 502–505.

PART THREE

15. THE MILLENNIUM WAR

1. See Woodward, *op cit.*, pp. 473ff.

16. THE WEAK LOOK

1. "The 'image of the enemy' ": Georgi Arbatov, "Facing a Choice," *Kommunist,* no. 5 (June 1988), p. 18.

2. Aganbegyan distortion: "CIA Cites Doubts on Soviet Economy," *The New York Times,* November 2, 1988, p. A9.

3. Walter S. Mossberg and John Walcott, *The Wall Street Journal,* August 11, 1988, p. 1.

4. The data on Soviet industrial production comes from "Gorbachev's Economic Plans," *Study Papers,* Joint Economic Committee, U.S. Congress, 100th Congress, 1st Session (Washington, D.C.: Government Printing Office, November 23, 1987).

5. Soviet defense budget: Henry S. Rowen, "Gorbachev's Best Defense," *The Wall Street Journal,* September 29, 1988, p. 30.

6. Soviet military developments: *Soviet Military Power: An Assessment of the Threat, 1988* (Washington, D.C.: Government Printing Office, 1988). For NATO, see Harry F. Yopung and Colleen Sussman, *Atlas of NATO* (Washington, D.C.: Government Printing Office, 1985).

7. On decline in U.S. bases, see Thomas H. Moorer and Alvin J. Cottrell, "The World Environment and U.S. Policy," *Strategic Review,* no. 2 (Spring 1976), p. 64.

8. RAND study of Soviet economy: Benjamin Zycher and Tad Daley,

"Military Dimensions of Communist Systems," paper (Santa Monica, Calif.: RAND, June 1988), pp. 3–7.

17. THE SIXTH GLASNOST

1. Glasnost defined: Mikhail Heller, *The Formation of Soviet Man* (New York: Knopf, 1988), p. xiii.
2. "Glasnost is a sword": *ibid.* Heller points out that Lenin used the expression "Glasnost" no less than forty-six times in his writing.
3. For 1921 Soviet industrial production, see Alec Nove, *An Economic History of the Soviet Union* (London: Penguin Books, 1982).
4. Golitsyn, *op. cit.*, p. 42.
5. "They will sell it to us": Joseph Finder, *Red Carpet* (New York: New Republic/Holt Rinehart & Winston, 1983), p. 8.
6. The quotes from Lenin are from Vol. 45 of V. I. Lenin, *Collected Works* (Moscow: Progress Publishers, 1970). "What we want to show and have in print . . . is that the Americans have gone in for concessions": *ibid.*, p. 347.
7. Hammer: for a fuller account, see my "The Riddle of Armand Hammer," *The New York Times Magazine,* November 29, 1981, p. 69. The business records of Hammer's enterprise are from Department of Justice investigations: see my archives, Boston University. I discussed these matters with Hammer in 1981 in a series of interviews.
8. "Even if it is a fictitious one": Lenin, *op. cit.*, p. 347.
9. "This is a small path to the American business world and this path should be made use of in every way": *ibid.*, p. 559.
10. For the transfer of Western industry to the Soviet Union, see Anthony C. Sutton, *Western Technology and Soviet Economic Development* (Stanford, Calif.: Hoover Institution Press, 1968).
11. "Perestroika" as the "restructuring" of agriculture: *The New York Times,* Letter to Editor, February 28, 1988.
12. On the 1936 Constitution, see Heller and Nekrich, *op. cit.*, p. 319.
13. *Time,* vol. 30, December 20, 1937, pp. 17–18. "Socialism is one country": Isaac Deutscher, *Stalin* (New York: Oxford University Press, 1966), pp. 431ff.
14. "By technocrats and managers": Stephen de Mowbray, "Soviet Deception and the Onset of the Cold War," *Encounter* (July 1982), p. 8.

15. Alex de Jonge, *Stalin* (New York: Morrow, 1986), p. 434.

16. "The old idea of world revolution is dead": de Mowbray, *op. cit.*, p. 8.

17. The "secret" speech: Joseph D. Douglass, Jr., "Soviet Strategic Deception," mimeo (April 2, 1984), pp. 2–6. The defectors are John Sejna and Anatoly Golitsyn; interviews with the author, 1982.

18. Harrison Salisbury, *The New York Times*, March 25, 1956, p. 1.

19. On private millionaires, underground businesses, and the thriving black market, see Golitsyn, *op. cit.*, p. 120.

20. *Ibid.*, p. 125.

21. "Inquire into opportunities for increased peaceful trade": Finder, *op. cit.*, p. 142.

22. *Ibid.*, p. 146.

23. "If we cannot give our people the same standard of living": Armand Hammer, *Hammer* (New York: Putnam, 1987), p. 323.

24. "If you give us credit. . . . You will keep your plants busy": Finder, *op. cit.*, p. 146.

25. For the technocratic theme, see Albert Parry, *The New Class Divided: Russian Science and Technology Versus Communism* (New York: Macmillan, 1966).

26. Fedora's message was told to me by William Sullivan.

27. Soviet arms control and N. R. Mironov: see Joseph Douglass, Jr., *Why the Soviets Violate Arms Control Treaties*, Vol. I (Maclean, Va.: Falcon Associates, 1986), p. 67. General John Sejna was debriefed by Douglass and wrote an appendix to his book. Douglass also arranged for me to interview Sejna.

28. The Soviet General Staff's Directorate for Strategic Deception: William R. Harris, "Soviet Maskirovka and Arms Control Verification," mimeo (September 26, 1986), p. 24.

29. Soviet negotiations: see Roger F. Staar, "Deception at MBFR: A Case Study," presented at the U.S. Navy Postgraduate College, September 1985, Monterey, Calif.

30. "The proposition that elements . . . preconceptions of the 'doves' in the Kremlin fighting a valiant battle against 'hard-liners' ": Henry Kissinger, *Years of Upheaval* (Boston: Little, Brown, 1982), p. 269.

31. Quoted in Douglass, *Why the Soviets Violate Arms Control Treaties*, Vol. 1, p. 123.

32. Ion Pacepa interview by Michael A. Ledeen, *Politique International,* October 1988, p. 12. The draft was supplied to me by Michael Ledeen.

33. *Wall Street Journal,* December 12, 1988, p. A9.

34. "Military deliveries to North Vietnam": Kissinger, *op. cit.,* p. 295.

35. "We . . . had used detente to isolate Hanoi and extricate ourselves from Vietnam": *ibid.,* p. 1030.

36. Underestimating Soviet missiles: Albert Wohlstetter, *Legends of the Strategic Arms Race* (Washington, D.C.: U.S. Strategic Institute, 1975).

37. "So condemnatory of the performance . . . ought to be done," Lionel Olmer, "Watchdogging Intelligence," in *Seminar on Command Control Communications and Intelligence* (Cambridge, Mass.: Center for Information Policy Research, Harvard University, 1980), pp. 179–180.

38. Richard Pipes, "Team B: The Reality Behind the Myth," *Commentary* (October 1986), pp. 25ff.

39. "Soviet nuclear strategy had to be seen in context of grand strategy": *ibid.,* p. 33.

40. For Andropov, see my "The Andropov File," *New Republic,* February 7, 1983, p. 18.

41. Underground journals: *The New York Times,* January 12, 1988, p. 1.

42. *Izvestia: Wall Street Journal,* August 8, 1988, p. 1.

43. 1986 Glasnost translation: Heller, *op. cit.,* p. xiii.

44. United States Trade and Economic Council: see my "Hammerization of Reagan," *Manhattan, Inc.* (May 1988). Also, Peter Gumbel, "Soviet, U.S. Firms Agree," *Wall Street Journal,* June 2, 1988, p. 2.

APPENDIX A

James Jesus Angleton's proposed questions for KGB defector Yuri Nosenko.

1. What happened to Rumyanstev when he tried to defect to the U.S. in 1959? Why did you omit this in your debriefing in 1964?

2. Is there rivalry between the KGB's First and Second Chief Directorates?

3. To what extent did the Second Chief Directorate know the operations of the Thirteenth Department of the First Chief Directorate?

4. What would Department Thirteen have known regarding Oswald's defection? Would General Rodin have known?

5. What happens when the Second Chief Directorate recruits an agent who returned to the West? Is he jointly handled?

6. Is an agent recruited by the Second Chief Directorate who is of value prepared to be handled by a stranger? Would this be true of an ideological agent as well as a mercenary agent?

7. To what extent do the First and Second Directorates coordinate the activities of foreign services?

8. Why was a KGB officer named Shitov sent to Cuba as the first Soviet Ambassador, under the pseudonym Alexiev?

9. What was his role, if any, in coordinating Soviet and Cuban intelligence operations?

10. Oswald was issued an entrance visa to Cuba from Havana after he returned to the United States. Would this require the prior approval of the Second Chief Directorate?

11. If so, would it be arranged in Moscow or Havana? If the latter, would a Second Chief Directorate officer be called on to participate in the decision?

12. Agee went to Cuba under aliases four times while writing his book. Would he have seen Soviet intelligence in Moscow? Would these meetings be coordinated with the KGB? Why was Colonel Semenov, who knew Agee in Uruguay, there during Agee's trips?

13. What was Korovin doing in London in 1961?

APPENDIX B

Secret CIA memorandum on defectors captured from the files of the U.S. Embassy in Teheran.

[A transcript of this memorandum follows on pp. 316–322.]

DISPATCH	CLASSIFICATION	PROCESSING ACTION	
	SECRET RYBAT		MARKED FOR INDEXING
TO Chiefs of Station and Base		x	NO INDEXING REQUIRED
INFO			ONLY QUALIFIED DESK CAN JUDGE INDEXING
FROM Chief, SB Division			MICROFILM
SUBJECT RYBAT REDTOP — Turning Around REDTOP Walk-ins			
ACTION REQUIRED - REFERENCES			

ACTION: Read and Retain for Reference

    1. In recent months a number of REDTOP nationals have walked into LNBUZZ installations seeking political asylum. Most have eventually been processed as refugees or defectors and many of the latter have provided useful information. A substantial number have been persuaded to return to their homelands to work on our behalf and most of these are now of very great value as long-term in-place agents. In some cases, Stations have handled REDTOP walk-ins well; in others, extremely valuable opportunities have been lost. These losses have generally resulted from misunderstandings in field Stations about WOMACF goals, priorities and capabilities and from difficulty in communicating with the walk-in. This dispatch and its attachments are designed to clarify our aims, to acquaint field Stations with BKHERALD abilities to exploit REDTOP walk-ins, and to enable officers to obtain essential information from REDTOP nationals with whom they have no common language.

    2. Putting aside the question of LNBUZZ responsibilities for asylum seekers and for assistance to refugees, which have been covered elsewhere in dispatches and airgrams, we are here concerned only with individuals of intelligence interest. While defectors can and do provide critical information, there are very few cases in which the same individual would not have been of greater value if he had returned to his post and remained in place, at least for a reasonable period. A "turn-around" therefore should remain the first goal in handling a well-placed walk-in. In addition, normally with Headquarters guidance, an attempt should sometimes be made to turn around an individual who appears to be promising

E2 IMPDET
CL BY 054581

(Con't)

CROSS REFERENCE TO	DISPATCH SYMBOL AND NUMBER	DATE	
	Book Dispatch 8737	9 January 1973	
	CLASSIFICATION SECRET RYBAT	HQS FILE NUMBER	

28

CONTINUATION OF DISPATCH	CLASSIFICATION	PATCH SYMBOL AND NUMBER
	SECRET RYBAT	Book Dispatch 8737

Page

agent material even if, at the moment, he does not enjoy good
access. If a young and personable walk-in with strong motivation but without immediate apparent access should walk
in, we are prepared to guide and assist him in his career,
running him in place until he develops the access we need.
Most such walk-ins would qualify only as refugees, not
defectors, which fact can be used as an argument in favor
of turning around.

3. When we speak of turning the walk-in around to
"work in place," we usually mean working in place after
his return to his home country. Obviously, if a REDTOP
official stationed in your area can be turned around, we
would hope to exploit his position for intelligence purposes
as long as he remains stationed outside REDTOP. Other than
in exceptional cases, however, our ultimate objective is to
have the walk-in return to his home country and continue his
agent relationship while working inside.

4. BKHERALD can and does run many resident agents
inside the REDTOP countries. We have the capability to
mount and support such operations over an indefinite period,
and we are currently able to exfiltrate agents, in most cases
with their families, from the REDTOP countries when it is
time for them to leave. To enable us successfully to turn
walk-ins into resident REDTOP agents, however, it is essential
that all BKHERALD officers who are likely to interview such
persons should have some familiarity with our procedures;
and it is equally essential that all field Stations have on
hand the operational tools to obtain information necessary to
Headquarters to enable us to recommend courses of action. In
virtually all walk-in cases, the time available is extremely
limited; unless the case officer obtains at least the minimum
information necessary, unless Headquarters is notified immediately, and unless Headquarters can respond quickly with
guidance, we may find that time has robbed us of the opportunity
to turn the walk-in around. Field Stations must, therefore,
be prepared to handle walk-in cases in which there may be no
immediate opportunity of meeting again with the potential
agent, as well as those in which planning may be somewhat
more leisurely.

5. General procedures used in "turn-arounds" are perhaps
best illustrated by outlining how typical cases have been
handled recently when time available is relatively limited:

a. In the initial meeting the individual is
debriefed by the Station or Base as to his motives,
for biographic data and for necessary PRQ. If time
permits, additional questions relating to areas of
particular Station or Base interest could be included
in this or subsequent debriefings prior to his departure.

b. Headquarters is informed of the situation
and provided with all pertinent details by immediate
or Flash cable precedence. In this respect a series **NIACT**
of short cables will frequently be more efficient
than one, more lengthy, cable.

c. Headquarters responds with guidance for both
the Station or Base and the walk-in, including assignment
of a particular SW receiving system. The walk-in is
instructed in recovery of this SW system and an SW
indicator is established. The walk-in is then told
to return to his country and expect a letter (mailed

29

CONTINUATION OF DISPATCH	CLASSIFICATION	DISPATCH SYMBOL AND NUMBER
	SE RET RYBAT	Book Dispatch 8737

P. e 3

securely in his c n country by a BKHERALD officer)
containing an SW essage with instructions approximately two to th e months after his return.

d. Headqua rs then assembles a package
containing covert ommunications materials,
reporting require nts and other instructions,
which is deaddropped or otherwise securely
delivered to the a ent in his homeland.

e. An SW message is subsequently mailed
internally to the w lk-in giving him directions
on how to retrieve the ops package.

6. The precise operational planning will vary, of course,
with the situation; e.g. are the identity and access of the
walk-in established, or is he an unknown quantity? Is this
a crash operation in which our time with the walk-in is
severely limited, or is there sufficient time to evolve a
more sophisticated and efficient operational plan? The
answers to these questions will help determine such questions
as whether to handle him initially via indirect, non-personal
communications, or whether to move him immediately into a
communications plan involving more risky commitment of our
REDTOP area staffers. I: time permits and the replies to
our questions so indicate, some turn-arounds may even be
issued materials for preparing SW messages before they return
to their homeland.

7. The most important single requirement to keep in
mind in the crash situation is that we must have the walk-in's
mailing address in his homeland. By that we mean an address
at which he can securely receive internally posted mail; i.e.,
mail posted within his country. This might be his home address
or the address of a friend or relative who would not be made
suspicious by the arrival of mail for him. The most efficient
method of acquiring this information is to have him address
a sample envelope to himself in his own language, assuring
him that this is merely an exemplar which will not itself be
used. We also need to establish with the walk-in an SW
indicater, perhaps a name or a phrase within the body of the
open text, which will tell him that the letter contains SW.
In its initial response, Headquarters will normally indicate if
SW is authorized, and which of the SW receiving systems is to be
issued. If there is insufficient time for consultation with
Headquarters, do not hesitate to issue the soorch or water
developed system to any promising walk-in. Under such circumstances, should a walk-in not be willing to accept either
of these two systems, or if for any other reason they are not
suitable, the station may also issue the microdot receiving
system without prior approval from Headquarters.

8. In the case of the walk-in where circumstances give
Headquarters more time to provide guidance and expertise, the
handling will be somewhat different. If we have enough time
and the individual has sufficient promise, we will probably
dispatch a staff officer experienced in the communications
systems we use in the REDTOP area to train him directly for
these highly disciplined communications. In this case, we
might do away completely with the initial letter mailed inside
the REDTOP area to the agent and put him directly on personal
communications. Where we have enough time, but are dealing
with an unknown quantity, we would probably be inclined to
take that time to probe his motivations and his suitability
as agent material. This could be done through cabled communications with Headquarters, or might be handled through a
dispatch of a TDY officer from Headquarters.

CONTINUATION OF DISPATCH	CLASSIFICATION SECRET RYBAT	DISPATCH SYMBOL AND NUMBER Book Dispatch 8737

Page 4

9. To facilitate walk-in debriefing in both the crash and less hurried situations, Attachment "A" contains copies of a questionnaire in English and the various REDTOP languages. A walk-in should be asked to complete this questionnaire in his own handwriting, printing the answers in capital letters. A transliteration table to Latin letters is provided for the CKPOLAR, VSYOKI and YKBANE alphabets to allow accurate cabled reporting in his native language of an individual's responses. If desired, cables can be keyed to the attachment's numeration, by referring to this Dispatch. The questionnaire is divided into two Sections. Section I relates to the walk-in's current situation, status and biographic history. Section II requests basic of information which would assist in clandestine communications planning. If time is available, the walk-in should be asked to fill out Section II only after Section I had been completed and Headquarters has authorized the Station to proceed. In promising situations, however, where time is short, stations are authorized to proceed with Section II on their own initiatives. The value of these questionnaires is that all necessary information may be obtained by an officer not fluent in the walk-in's native language. Further, it assures that the most pertinent questions will be asked even if the available time is limited and that, by virtue of the walk-in providing written answers to the questions, ambiguities and inaccuracies are considerably reduced.

10. **Attachment "B"** contains forms in English and the REDTOP languages, to assist in the establishment of communication with the walk-in. Included are questions concerning the individual's mailing address in his homeland and the type of mail he receives there, the establishment of an SW indicator, sets of instructions for the development or reading of several different agent SW receiving systems (including microdot) which do not require a specific developer, and SW carbon writing instructions. The agent-receiving instructions are accompanied by exemplars of developed messages and prepared messages which will enable the walk-in to practice developing if time and circumstances permit. Microdot receiving instructions include bullet lenses and exemplars of buried microdots. Practice SW carbons are provided with the SW carbon writing instructions. The foreign language versions are provided in two forms: on standard stationery, and in reduced printing on water soluble paper. The latter may be given the walk-in for subsequent study at his leisure; however, in no instance should he attempt to return to his country with these instructions.

11. The Attachment "B" instructions are more detailed than the standard WOLOCK forms intended for use primarily in conjunction with actual training by an SW technician. These expanded versions presuppose situations in which the attending case officer can provide little or no instructional assistance to the walk-in. However, it should be clearly understood that while these instructions are as comprehensive as possible their use cannot approach the effectiveness of training by a qualified SW instructor. In most cases where time and circumstances permit, we would prefer that a WOLOCK technician be called in to train the individual. By the same token, Chiefs of Station or Base should avail themselves of the opportunity, when a WOLOCK/CCB technician visits, to have case officers thoroughly trained in the use of the systems provided so that they can competently perform training if the need arises. As a minimum, all officers who might handle a walk-in should experiment with exemplars provided in Attachment "B". Additional copies for this purpose will be provided on request. All field operations officers should be completely familiar with these basic techniques.

CONTINUATION OF DISPATCH	CLASSIFICATION	DISPATCH SYMBOL AND NUMBER
	CRET RYBAT	Book Dispatch 8737

Page 5

12. Analysis of REDTOP walk-ins in recent years clearly indicates that REDTOP services have not been using sophisticated and serious walk-ins as a provocation technique. However, fear of provocation has been more responsible for bad handling of walk-ins than any other cause. We have concluded that we do ourselves a real disservice if we shy away from promising cases because of fear of provocation. We are willing to run any apparently useful case for a reasonable period and can do so in such a way that little or no harm will be done if the case should turn out to be controlled. We are confident that we are capable of determining whether or not a producing agent is supplying bona fide information.

13. A legal matter involving "turn-around" inducement requires special comment. Many walk-ins and defectors appear to be adamant in their insistence on guaranteed resettlement in WODUAL; Stations are not authorized to make such promises on their own; and Headquarters is traditionally reluctant to grant such authority. In fact this problem is more apparent than real. An agent who serves us loyally "inside" for a reasonable period of time (normally several years) will obviously be well taken care of when he wishes to "retire" and competent field operations officers will normally be able to make this clear without specific promise of resettlement in WODUAL. "The West" or "a friendly country" are acceptable. As a last resort, however, Headquarters will consider making a commitment to WODUAL resettlement when a walk-in's value appears to justify it. However, Stations should make every possible effort to turn around all walk-ins without such a commitment.

14. One final problem which has caused some difficulty is the fact that traffic relating to a walk-in is not always received by interested Headquarters elements on a timely basis. To expedite handling, as well as to insure security, cable traffic should be slugged "RYBAT PLAERONAUT" and must by at least Immediate precedence. Use of a higher precedence may be dictated by time considerations. At least during the initial exchanges, the cable should not carry the EIRACTIVE indicator nor should there be any formal involvement with WONICK until approved by Headquarters. The PLAERONAUT slug will usually be used at least until all reasonable hope of turn-around is abandoned.

Robert P. TACEY

Attachments:
As stated

32

315

DECEPTION

CLASSIFICATION: SECRET RYBAT

DATE: 9 January 1973

TO: Chiefs of Station and Base

FROM: Chief, SB Division

SUBJECT: RYBAT REDTOP
Turning Around REDTOP Walk-ins

ACTION: Read and Retain for Reference

1. In recent months a number of REDTOP nationals have walked into LNBUZZ installations seeking political asylum. Most have eventually been processed as refugees or defectors and many of the latter have provided useful information. A substantial number have been persuaded to return to their homelands to work on our behalf and most of these are now of very great value as long-term in-place agents. In some cases, Stations have handled REDTOP walk-ins well; in others, extremely valuable opportunities have been lost. These losses have generally resulted from misunderstandings in field Stations about WOMACE goals, priorities and capabilities and from difficulty in communicating with the walk-in. This dispatch and its attachments are designed to clarify our aims, to acquaint field Stations with BKHERALD abilities to exploit REDTOP walk-ins, and to enable officers to obtain essential information from REDTOP nationals with whom they have no common language.

2. Putting aside the question of LNBUZZ responsibilities for asylum seekers and for assistance to refugees, which have been covered elsewhere in dispatches and airgrams, we are here concerned only with individuals of intelligence interest. While defectors can and do provide critical information, there are very few cases in which the same individual would not have been of greater value if he had returned to his post and remained in place, at least for a reasonable period. A "turn-around" therefore should remain the first goal in handling a well-placed walk-in. In addition, normally with Headquarters guidance, an attempt should sometimes be made to turn around an individual who appears to be promising agent material even if, at the moment, he does not enjoy good access. If a young and personable walk-in with strong motivation but without immediate apparent access should walk in, we are prepared to guide and assist him in his career, running him in place until he develops the

access we need. Most such walk-ins would qualify only as refugees, not defectors, which fact can be used as an argument in favor of turning around.

3. When we speak of turning the walk-in around to "work in place," we usually mean working in place *after* his return to his home country. Obviously, if a REDTOP official stationed in your area can be turned around, we would hope to exploit his position for intelligence purposes as long as he remains stationed outside REDTOP. Other than in exceptional cases, however, our ultimate objective is to have the walk-in return to his home country and continue his agent relationship while working inside.

4. BKHERALD can and does run many resident agents inside the REDTOP countries. We have the capability to mount and support such operations over an indefinite period and we are currently able to exfiltrate agents, in most cases with their families, from the RED-TOP countries when it is time for them to leave. To enable us successfully to turn walk-ins into resident REDTOP agents, however, it is essential that *all* BKHERALD officers who are likely to interview such persons should have some familiarity with our procedures; and it is equally essential that all field Stations have on hand the operational tools to obtain information necessary to Headquarters to enable us to recommend courses of action. In virtually all walk-in cases, the time available is extremely limited; unless the case officer obtains at least the minimum information necessary, unless Headquarters is notified immediately, and unless Headquarters can respond quickly with guidance, we may find that time has robbed us of the opportunity to turn the walk-in around. Field Stations must, therefore, be prepared to handle walk-in cases in which there may be no immediate opportunity of meeting again with the potential agent, as well as those in which planning may be somewhat more leisurely.

5. General procedures used in "turn-arounds" are perhaps best illustrated by outlining how typical cases have been handled recently when time available is relatively limited:

a. In the initial meeting the individual is debriefed by the Station or Base as to his motives, for biographic data and for necessary OI. If time permits, additional questions relating to areas of particular Station or Base interest could be included in this or subsequent debriefings prior to his departure.

b. Headquarters is informed of the situation and provided with all pertinent details by [*Immediate*] NIACT or *Flash* cable precedence. In this respect a series of short cables will frequently be more efficient than one, more lengthy, cable.

c. Headquarters responds with guidance for both the Station or Base and the walk-in, including assignment of a particular SW receiving system. The walk-in is instructed in recovery of this SW system and an SW indicator is established. The walk-in is then told to return to his country and expect a letter (mailed securely in his own country by a BKHERALD officer) containing an SW message with instructions approximately two to three months after his return.

d. Headquarters then assembles a package containing covert communications materials, reporting requirements and other instructions, which is deaddropped or otherwise secretly delivered to the agent in his homeland.

e. An SW message is subsequently mailed internally to the walk-in giving him directions on how to to retrieve the ops package.

6. The precise operational planning will vary, of course, with the situation; e.g., are the identity and access of the walk-in established, or is he an unknown quantity? Is this a crash operation in which our time with the walk-in is severely limited, or is there sufficient time to evolve a more sophisticated and efficient operational plan? The answers to these questions will help determine such questions as whether to handle him initially via indirect, non-personal communications, or whether to move him immediately into a communications plan involving more risky commitment of our REDTOP area staffers. If time permits and the replies to our questions so indicate, some turn-arounds may even be issued materials for preparing SW messages before they return to their homeland.

7. The most important single requirement to keep in mind in the crash situation is that we must have the walk-in's mailing address in his homeland. By that we mean an address at which he can securely receive internally posted mail; i.e., mail posted within his country. This might be his home address or the address of a friend or relative who would not be made suspicious by the arrival of mail for him. The most efficient method of acquiring this information is to have him address a sample envelope to himself in his own language,

assuring him that this is merely an exemplar which will not itself be used. We also need to establish with the walk-in an SW indicator, perhaps a name or a phrase within the body of the open text, which will tell him that the letter contains SW. In its initial response, Headquarters will normally indicate if SW is authorized, and which of the SW receiving systems is to be issued. If there is insufficient time for consultation with Headquarters, *do not hesitate to issue the scorch or water developed system to any promising walk-in.* Under such circumstances, should a walk-in not be willing to accept either of these two systems, or if for any other reason they are not suitable, the station may also issue the microdot receiving system without prior approval from Headquarters.

8. In the case of the walk-in where circumstances give Headquarters more time to provide guidance and expertise, the handling will be somewhat different. If we have enough time and the individual has sufficient promise, we will probably dispatch a staff officer experienced in the communications systems we use in the REDTOP area to train him directly for these highly disciplined communications. In this case, we might do away completely with the initial letter mailed inside the REDTOP area to the agent and put him directly on personal communications. Where we have enough time, but are dealing with an unknown quantity, we would probably be inclined to take that time to probe his motivations and his suitability as agent material. This could be done through cabled communications with Headquarters, or might be handled through a dispatch of a TDY officer from Headquarters.

9. To facilitate walk-in debriefing in both the crash and less hurried situations, attachment "A" contains copies of a questionnaire in English and the various REDTOP languages. A walk-in should be asked to complete this questionnaire in his own handwriting, printing the answers in capital letters. A transliteration table to [unreadable] letters is provided for the CKPOLAR, VSYOKE and YKBAND alphabets to allow accurate cabled reporting in his native language of an individual's responses. If desired, cables can be keyed to the attachment's numeration, by referring to this Dispatch. The questionnaire is divided into two Sections. Section I relates to the walk-in's current situation, status, and biographic history. Section II requests basic OI information which would assist in clandestine communications planning. If time is available, the walk-in should be asked to fill out Section II only after Section I has been completed and Head-

quarters has authorized the Station to proceed. In promising situations, however, where time is short, stations are authorized to proceed with Section II on their own initiatives. The value of these questionnaires is that all necessary information may be obtained by an officer not fluent in the walk-in's native language. Further, it assures that the most pertinent questions will be asked even if the available time is limited and that, by virtue of the walk-in providing written answers to the questions, ambiguities and inaccuracies are considerably reduced.

10. Attachment "B" contains forms in English and the REDTOP languages to assist in the establishment of communication with the walk-in. Included are questions concerning the individual's mailing address in his homeland and the type of mail he receives there, the establishment of an SW indicator, sets of instructions for the development or reading of several different agent SW receiving systems (including microdot) which do not require a specific developer, and SW carbon writing instructions. The agent-receiving instructions are accompanied by exemplars of developed messages and prepared messages which will enable the walk-in to practice developing if time and circumstances permit. Microdot receiving instructions include bullet lenses and exemplars of buried microdots. Practice SW carbons are provided with the SW carbon writing instructions. The foreign language versions are provided in two forms: on standard stationery, and in reduced printing on water soluble paper. The latter may be given the walk-in for subsequent study at his leisure; however, in no instance should he attempt to return to his country with these instructions.

11. The Attachment "B" instructions are more detailed than the standard WOLOCK forms intended for use primarily in conjunction with actual training by an SW technician. These expanded versions presuppose situations in which the attending case officer can provide little or no instructional assistance to the walk-in. However, it should be clearly understood that while these instructions are as comprehensive as possible their use cannot approach the effectiveness of training by a qualified SW instructor. In most cases where time and circumstances permit, we would prefer that a WOLOCK technician be called in to train the individual. By the some token, Chiefs of Station or Base should avail themselves of the opportunity, when a WOLOCK/CCB technician visits, to have case officers thoroughly trained in the use of the systems provided so that they can compe-

tently perform training if the need arises. As a minimum, all officers who might handle a walk-in should experiment with exemplars provided in Attachment "B". Additional copies for this purpose will be provided on request. All field operations officers should be completely familiar with these basic techniques.

12. Analysis of REDTOP walk-ins in recent years clearly indicates that REDTOP services have *not* been using sophisticated and serious walk-ins as a provocation technique. However, fear of provocation has been more responsible for bad handling of walk-ins than any other cause. We have concluded that we do ourselves a real disservice if we shy away from promising cases because of fear of provocation. We are willing to run any apparently useful case for a reasonable period and can do so in such a way that little or no harm will be done if the case should turn out to be controlled. We are confident that we are capable of determining whether or not a producing agent is supplying bona fide information.

13. A legal matter involving "turn-around" inducement requires special comment. Many walk-ins and defectors appear to be adamant in their insistence on guaranteed resettlement in WODUAL; Stations are not authorized to make such promises on their own; and Headquarters is traditionally reluctant to grant such authority. In fact this problem is more apparent than real. An agent who serves us loyally "inside" for a reasonable period of time (normally several years) will obviously be well taken care of when he wishes to "retire" and competent field operations officers will normally be able to make this clear without specific promise or resettlement in WODUAL. "The West" or "a friendly country" are acceptable. As a last resort, however, Headquarters will consider making a commitment to WODUAL resettlement when a walk-in's value appears to justify it. However, Stations should make every possible effort to turn around all walk-ins without such a commitment.

14. One final problem which has caused some difficulty is the fact that traffic relating to a walk-in is not always received by interested Headquarters elements on a timely basis. To expedite handling, as well as to insure security, cable traffic should be slugged "RYBAT PLAERONAUT" and sent by at least Immediate precedence. Use of a higher precedence may be dictated by time considerations. At least during the initial exchanges, the cable should *not* carry the EIRAS-

DECEPTION

TIME indicator nor should there be any formal involvement with WONICK until approved by Headquarters. The PLAERONAUT slug will usually be used at least until all reasonable hope of turn-around is abandoned.

Robert P. TACEY

Acknowledgments

I owe a deep debt of gratitude to a number of the deception planners and deceptions buffs I met at the conferences described in the text, among them Berel Rodal, Joe Douglass, Jr., Amrom Katz, Roy Godson, Angelo Codevilla, Kenneth de Graffenreid, Herb Romerstein, P. L. Thyraud de Vosjoli, John Sejna, and William R. Harris. I benefited immeasurably from both their ideas and the doors that were opened for me.

I also participated in a half-dozen academic seminars on international deception at MIT, Harvard, and the Hoover Institution. There too I benefited from the ideas of Robert Conquest, Milton Friedman, Arnold Beichman, Edward Banfield, Peter Lupsha, Joe Finder, Steven Rosen, Ithiel de sola Poole, Adam Ulam, Graham Allison, Melvin Krauss, Thomas Sowell, Marty Anderson, Harvey Sapolsky, and Sidney Hook.

I owe appreciation to Rebecca Fraser for her aid in organizing the research, filing Freedom of Information requests, and debriefing Soviet bloc defectors. I am only sorry she returned to London before the book was completed. I would also like to thank Gabriel Schoenfeldt, Abbey Asher, Andrea Stuber, Edmund Levin, and Alexandra Rhodie for their research and assistance. I would particularly like to thank Sir James Goldsmith, Renata Adler, William Harris, and Lou Dobbs for taking time to read the draft manuscript. Their criticisms were of immense value to me. Belinda Loh of Simon and Schuster was enormously helpful in the final stages in keeping this book on track.

Finally, I am indebted to Robert Asahina for his intelligent and thoughtful editing of this manuscript. I deeply appreciate his indefatigable efforts to transform ten years of research into this book.

INDEX

Index

bombs, bombers, 128–29, 130, 134–140, 148
Boyce, Christopher, 160
Branigan, William, 114
Brezhnev, Leonid, 261, 262, 264, 266–268
briefs, 19–20, 29, 44
British Air Intelligence, 131–32
British Secret Service, 33, 41, 71, 131, 145–46
Buckley, William, 219
Bulgaria, 254, 289–90
Bureau of Verification and Analysis, U.S., 162
Burgess, Guy, 37
Burma, 280–81, 285
Bush, George, 270, 271

Canada, 32, 35, 114, 186, 207, 236
Carroll, Joseph P., 175
Carroll Report, 175
Casey, William, 113, 204, 213–14, 219
Ceausescu, Nicolae, 267
Central Intelligence Agency, *see* CIA
Central Intelligence Group, 32
C-4, 283, 284
Chemical-Biological Weapon (CBW) program, 262
chemical surveillance, 203–6
China, People's Republic of:
  intelligence of, 97
  Soviet relations with, 97, 98, 290
Chun Doo Hwan, 280
Church Committee, 47
Churchill, Sir Winston, 136, 256
CIA (Central Intelligence Agency), 11–22, 32–105, 151, 152, 263, 282–84
  as ad hoc group, 186–87
  Angleton in, 13–14, 15, 22, 32–42, 56–58, 64, 65, 69–71, 73–85, 92–101, 103–4, 175–76, 215, 258
  Angleton's firing from, 13–14, 15, 20, 22, 74, 85, 98–101, 104
  Bagley and, 46, 50–64, 74, 75, 77, 79, 94–95, 96
  central computer of, 175–76
  Covert Action unit of, 79
  deception conferences and, 113, 196–99
  denial of deception by, 196–215

Directorate of Plans of, 89–90
document classification systems used by, 86–87
epistemology battle in, 92–100
ex-Nazis used by, 36, 38, 76
FBI relations with, 78, 96
formation of, 15, 32
Golitsyn and, 64–85, 95–98, 199
"Halloween massacre" in, 205
Iranian arms requests and, 218
KGB's closing down of sources of, 201–4
KGB compared with, 189–95
KGB recruitment efforts and, 204, 213
mail-opening program of, 100–101
"marked cards" test of, 77
mind-sets of, 103–4
news stories planted by, 19–20, 100–101, 204
Nosenko and, 12–16, 18–21, 28–30, 43–64, 74–75, 77, 93–95
Office of Policy Coordination of, 33–35, 38, 40, 231
Office of Security of, 62–63, 76–77, 94, 176
prevalence of penetrations in, 186–188
Reports Section of, 184
revisions in (1973), 89–92
Soviet Division of, 32–33, 50, 56–63, 67–71, 73, 76–77, 87, 91, 93–94, 96, 99, 103, 181, 188, 202, 207, 213
Soviet energy estimates of, 241
Soviet missile estimates of, 268–69, 270
telemetry double cross and, 165–166, 168, 169, 171, 175–76
war of the moles and, 177–95
Yurchenko and, 199–216
Clark, Bruce C., 113–14
Clark Air Force Base, 124
Clausewitz, Karl von, 229
Cline, Ray, 114
Codevilla, Angelo, 154, 156, 160, 161
coexistence, 229
Cohen, Stuart, 113–14
Cointellpro (counterintelligence program), 118

326

Index

Index

disinformation (*cont.*)
Nosenko and, 57, 58, 59
telemetry double cross and, 166–69
U.S. public channels and, 191–92
in World War II, 118–25
Yurchenko and, 205
Disinformation Service, 129–30
dispatched agents, 27, 69, 76
dissident movements, 40, 42, 82, 145–148
Glasnost and, 252–53, 258, 260, 261–62, 272, 278
Office of Policy Coordination and, 34–35
techniques of deception and, 116–117
the Trust and, 24–26
Dobrynin, Anatoli, 265–66
"Documents from the U.S. Espionage Den," 86–89, 92
Donovan, William, 32
"doomed spies," 83, 106, 120
Do-17, 134
double agents, 41, 91, 98, 118, 131–132, 140–42, 146–47, 169, 171, 231
CIA denial of deception and, 197–198
Golitsyn and, 70, 72, 78, 79–80, 95
Penkovsky as, 79–80
Yurchenko as, 210–14
Dr. Strangelove (film), 163
drugs, 209–10
Dubberstein, Waldo H., 284
Dulles, Allen Welsh, 40–41, 90, 99
Dunlap, Jack E., 173–75, 177, 187, 188
dust spraying, as surveillance technique, 203, 205–6
Dziak, John, 114
Dzierzhinski, Feliks, 26, 247–48, 250, 251

Eastern Europe, 76, 140, 198, 231, 257, 267
Office of Policy Coordination and, 33–35
see also specific countries
economy:
measures of the output of, 239
of Soviet Union, 23, 24, 25, 237–243, 246–53, 258–60, 262, 266, 273, 276–78
of United States, 239–41
Edemski, Sergei, 172–73
Ekspress-Khronica, 273
Eliot, T. S., 11, 14, 99
Ellis, Charles Howard (Dickie), 146–147
employment, mobility of, 191, 194
energy:
CIA underestimates of, 241
in United States vs. Soviet Union, 240
Enigma, 120
Ermath, Fritz, 113
ESP, 153
Estonia, 23, 40, 230, 250, 257
Euro-Communism, 255

false flags, 11, 27–28, 30, 89, 182–83, 191
FBI (Federal Bureau of Investigation), 12, 13, 32, 37, 41, 76, 116, 169, 173, 200, 203, 206, 220
CIA relations with, 78, 96
deception techniques and, 116, 117–118
Golitsyn thesis and, 95–96
Sullivan and, 46–49
Fedora, 47–50, 60, 74, 95, 96, 169, 170, 171, 197, 198, 220, 262
Felfe, Heinz, 185–86
Finland, 25, 26, 230, 257
fireflies, 29
fishing lures, 101
Fletcher School of Diplomacy, deception conference of, 114–25
Fluency Committee, 72
fluttering, 68
Ford, Gerald, 269, 270
Ford Motor Company, 251
Foreign Ministry, Soviet, 252, 265–66
Foreign Office, British, 257
Fort Meade, 174–75
"Fourth U.S. Army Group" (FUSAG), 119–20
Fox, Thomas D., 172–74
France, 28, 117, 129, 232
counterintelligence in, 38, 41
intelligence service of, *see* SDECE
Nazi deception and, 125, 127–29,

328

Index

Index

Index

Index

Index

Index

Tyura-Tam Missile Test Center, 168

U.S.-Soviet Trade and Economic Council, 276
Ukraine, 35, 40
"Ultra," 121
unexpected intelligence, 88
United Nations, 95, 181, 190, 256, 262
United States:
  economy of, 239–41
  as open society, 189–95
  Soviet relations with, see CIA; Glasnost; KBG; Soviet-American relations
  Soviet Union compared with, 239–243
  see also specific agencies and topics
United States Trade and Economic Council (USTEC), 276–77
Ustinov, Peter, 48–49

"vacuum cleaning," 152–53, 159, 170–171, 174
Venlo Incident, 147–48
Verity, C. William, 276
Versailles Treaty, 127–28, 130, 137
Vietnam War, 97, 268
Vuillemen, Joseph, 132–33

Wallop, Malcolm, 154–55, 161, 205
Wall Street Journal, 238–39, 274
Walters, Vernon, 114
Wannall, Ray, 114
Warren, Earl, 45
Warren Commission, 12–14, 21, 45, 61

Washington Post, 192, 223, 233
Weir, Benjamin, 220–21, 222
Whalen, Henry, 172–73, 182, 187, 188
Whaley, Barton, 115, 122
Whittemore, Reed, 11, 14
Wilson, Edwin, 282–84
Wilson, Harold, 80–82
WIN (Freedom and Independence), 34–42
Winterbotham, Frederick W., 131–32
"wiring diagram," 207
Wisner, Frank, 33, 34, 39, 40
Wohlstetter, Albert, 268–69
Woodward, Bob, 192
World War I, 127–29, 148
World War II, 14–15, 31–32, 255–57
  deception techniques in, 118–25, 158
  as phony war, 144–45

X-2, 15, 32

Yakushev, Aleksandr, 23–27
Yangel Design Bureau, 168
Yevtushenko, Yevgeny, 258
Yurchenko, Vitaliy Sergeyevich, 199–216, 234
  alleged execution of, 214
  background of, 199–200
  CIA doubts about, 205–7
  news conference of, 209, 212
  Nosenko compared with, 207–8
  revelations of, 202–4
  Soviet Embassy and, 208–9, 212

Zuehlke, Arthur, 114
Zurich International Air Meet, 134

335

About the Author

Edward Jay Epstein was born in New York City. He studied government at Cornell and Harvard, where he received a Ph.D. in 1973. Both his master's and doctoral dissertations were published as books. The former, *Inquest,* concerned the Warren Commission; the latter, *News from Nowhere,* the politics of television journalism. He taught political science at Harvard, M.I.T., and U.C.L.A., and since 1975 has investigated and written about subjects of interest to him.